3302536618

CU00832428

To renew this book, phone 0845 1202811 or visit
our website at www.libcat.oxfordshire.gov.uk
You will need your library PIN number
(available from your library)

OXFORDSHIRE
COUNTY COUNCIL
SOCIAL & COMMUNITY SERVICES

www.oxfordshire.gov.uk

John Aubrey &
Stone Circles

He may be regarded as essentially
an *archaeologist*,
and the first person in this country
who fairly deserved the name.

John Britton, *Memoir of John Aubrey. FRS.*, 1845. 3

DEDICATED TO

Russel Lawson, my brother-in-law,
who guided me around John Aubrey's Oxford,
to Trinity, his old university college,
to Merton Street where Anthony à Wood lived,
to St Mary Magdalen church where Aubrey was buried,
and other places in John Aubrey's city.

By my meanes many Antiquities have been rescued and preserved (I
myself inclining to be Ancient) – or else utterly lost and forgotten.

John Aubrey (Clark, I, 18)

John Aubrey &
Stone Circles

Britain's First Archaeologist,
from Avebury to Stonehenge

AUBREY BURL

AMBERLEY

First published 2010

Amberley Publishing
Cirencester Road, Chalford,
Stroud, Gloucestershire, GL6 8PE

www.amberleybooks.com

British Library Cataloguing in Publication Data.
A catalogue record for this book is available from the British Library.

ISBN 978 1 4456 0157 1

Typesetting and origination by FonthillMedia™
Printed in Great Britain

Contents

Acknowledgements

To Professor Richard Atkinson, who, during his time at the Bodleian Library, photocopied John Aubrey's manuscripts of the *Monumenta Britannica*. It contained 'Part I, *Templa Druidum*' (Bodleian: Top. Gen. c.24).

Years later he very kindly gave me those sheets. They have been indispensable but sometimes difficult to decipher. Early technical limitations reversed the original inked handwriting on white parchment into a hard-to-read white writing on a black background.

The problem was overcome by Neil Mortimer, whose expertise enabled those sheets to be restored to a legible black script on white paper.

My thanks are due to the Bodleian Library for providing me with access to Aubrey's original handwritten manuscripts; to the librarian of the Society of Antiquaries of London, who was punctilious in replying to my requests for the loan of otherwise elusive books; to Mr C. Betts, Librarian of Aberdeen University, who generously had photocopies made of James Garden's long letters to John Aubrey; and Dr Lorna Haycock, Librarian of the Wiltshire Archaeological and Natural History Society, who helped me with enquiries about John Aubrey.

The archivist of Merton College, Dr Julia Walworth, and Mrs Clare Hopkins, archivist of Trinity College, provided me with invaluable information about Aubrey's associations with those Oxford colleges.

I am also grateful to the two lady churchwardens at Kington St Michael for kindly reopening the church for me to see the Aubrey/Britton memorial window and plaque there.

No sensible author should fail to acknowledge the considerable encouragement and guidance provided by his publishers. I am very grateful for the meticulous scrutiny provided by Amberley Publishing through Sarah Flight and Jonathan Reeve for tunnelling through the text with such considerable care.

And a very personal statement of gratitude. As always, my wife, Judith, endured the endless months-cum-tedious years of visits to places, churches and, inescapably, stone circles, for the photography and research for a book I had wanted to write for years. Without her patience and encouragement it would never have been done.

Note to the Reader

For those wishing to read Aubrey's own comments about prehistoric stone circles the most accessible source is Volume I of his *Monumenta Britannica*, which was first fully published in 1980. Its editing was a dutiful but demanding labour of love and is commendable for filling a far too long gap. Regrettably, there is a problem.

For the reader's convenience Aubrey's references to a stone circle have often been gathered together in the 1980 book in successive pages even though in the original manuscripts they may have spread over several, well-separated sheets.

There is another difference. John Aubrey wrote on both the left-hand side, *verso*, (a), and right-hand, *recto*, (b), of his foolscap sheets but the *Monumenta Britannica* does not acknowledge this distinction. Regrettably, there are other problems of omission and rearrangement.

As one example, in Chapter 9 of this book there is a section on Scottish stone circles that were mentioned in several of the nine letters that Dr James Garden of Aberdeen wrote to John Aubrey in the 1690s. Aubrey patiently transcribed those letters even though several were very long.

In Letter 2 there were no stone circles, only a long piece about the druids and a seemingly irrelevant very brief paragraph about highland customs on nights of the new moon.

In his manuscript *Templa Druidum*, for Garden's Letter 2 Aubrey copied the remarks about the druids on his pages 123b to 126b but, not understanding the significance of the moon, he made no mention of it.

In the 1980 edition of the *Monumenta Britannica, I*, because there were no stone circles in Garden's second letter, the book jumps from the end of Letter 1 on page 122 to the beginning of Letter 3 on page 123. The moon, even the druids, disappeared. The reader is given no warning of this.

It was for this and other reasons of omission and rearrangement that the present writer withdrew as the intended editor of the *Monumenta Britannica*.

It is an academic explanation. But for the general reader with no access or even desire to see the original work the 1980 and 1982 volumes of the *Monumenta Britannica* are invaluable. The gist of John Aubrey is there. The reproductions of his handwritten pages are very good as are the many printed explanations that accompany them. The writer is delighted to have

them in this study. The reservations are no more than warnings that what
is in the books is not an exact reproduction of John Aubrey's pages.

Many extracts have been shortened, sometimes omitted altogether.
Frequently the vital page number at the top has not been reproduced. That
omission causes confusion. In the *Mon. Brit*, *I*, page 82 is a conflation of
the original manuscript's pages 63b (right-hand side) and 65a (opposite,
two pages later, left) of two quite different sites.

There are also errors. On pages 182-3 there is a reference to the rings
at Templetown (misspelt 'Templeton') at grid reference NO 674 916. In
reality those rings are the Kincardineshire circles of Garrol Wood and
Esslie the Greater and Lesser, *c.* NO 717 916, that are a full three miles to
the east of Templetown.

For this reason two references have been given for each ring. The
Bodleian Library's manuscript *Templa Druidum*, *Temples of the Druids*,
has the reference, MS Top. Gen. c.24 [here shortened to TG, c.24]
followed by its page numbers. This is quoted in the present book. It is
followed by *Mon. Brit I* [MB, I], the 1980 volume and its page-numbers.
The reference for the Wiltshire circle of Clatford is: TG, c.24, 43b-44b;
MB, I, 50-1; and the Somerset ring, Stanton Drew as TG, c.24, 51, a, b,
52a, its three entries crossed through in ink, and 52b-54b; followed by
MB, I, 46-7, 65-9.

For subjects other than stone circles such as events in John Aubrey's
personal life and the historical background to the Stuart Age references are
provided for works more readily available: for John Aubrey, see Barber,
Clark, Dick, Hunter, Powell, and Tylden-Wright. More general books
are listed in the Bibliography and also in the chapter notes for a specific
topic.

For anyone wishing to see Aubrey's original papers, the Bodleian
Library has fifty assorted fine, leather-bound volumes of his manuscripts
and letters. The references are from MS A from A, 1 to A, 26.

Preface

For years the writer has admired the work of John Aubrey. In 1976 my first book, *The Stone Circles of the British Isles*, was dedicated to him:

To The Memory of
JOHN AUBREY
1626 - 1697
Of Easton Pierse, Wiltshire
'The Father of British Archaeology'
Whose work made 'those walke and appeare that
Have layen in their graves may hundreds of yeares:
And to represent as it were to the eie, the places,
Customs and Fashions, that were of old Times'.

and each of its ten chapters was headed by one of his quotations.

With characteristic modesty Aubrey disparaged his collected notes as no more than a ragbag of jottings 'to be interponed as a sheet of waste paper only in the binding of a book'.

That irreplaceable 'ragbag' of loose pages lingered at the edge of extinction for nearly one hundred and fifty years after Aubrey's death in 1697 until, almost casually in 1836, the hundreds of disorganised sheets were deposited in Oxford's Bodleian Library. They were finally published and made available in 1980 and 1982.

In them was the very first list of stone circles in Britain, and the first to prove that they had been erected many years before the Romans. They were prehistoric.

Aubrey's researches were the foundation upon which all future stone circle studies have been built. It is a privilege to write this account of that achievement.

Introduction

John Aubrey could have been a forgotten ghost. He has no marked grave. The small, prehistoric barrow where he wished to be buried was ploughed into oblivion in the 1990s. No gravestone was engraved for him in 1697 in St Mary Magdalen's church, Oxford. Where he lies is uncertain. Both his homes in Wiltshire have been demolished. Where he lived in London was either destroyed in the Great Fire of 1666 or by blitzkrieg bombs and doodlebugs three centuries later. The church of his birthplace in Kington St Michael was vandalised, 'terribly over-restored', grumbled Pevsner, by the ungainly alterations of a mid-Victorian architectural 'improver'.

Only one of Aubrey's many works, and that one the least scholarly, was published in his lifetime. It was two hundred years after his death before his deservedly popular *Brief Lives* was published in Clark's two good but Victorianised volumes of 1898. More recent publishers have been less reluctant to print every tittle-tattle of Aubrey's gossip. The work is now a best-seller.

There is also a strangely sterilised edition, 'ruthlessly edited', by John Collier, who regretted 'Aubrey's wasteful boozing bouts' and was not prepared 'to reverence much his morning hiccups. So these I have cut out'. Modern readers should do the same with Collier if they wish to enjoy *Brief Lives*, with all its entertaining hiccoughs.

Yet, surprisingly, this latter-day puritan, Collier, did include the four-line doggerel about the wife of John Overall, the Dean of St Paul's, 'the greatest Beautie of her time in England':

> The Dean of Paule's did search for his wife,
> And where d'ee thinke he found her?
> Even upon Sir John Selbye's bed
> As flatte as any Flounder.

More predictably, Andrew Clark, the very Victorian editor of an excellent *Brief Lives*, did include that 'Life' but omitted the final 'daring' lines.[1]

Aubrey's *Brief Lives* has been joyfully quoted many times but in various modern biographies his work as a prehistorian has been included almost as an aside although it is his enduring monument.

He knew it was. 'After many years lying dormant, I come abroad like the Ghost of one of those Druids,' he sighed, half-foreseeing how invaluable his insights into the origins and purpose of prehistoric stone circles in Britain would be. Before him there was no more than guesswork. After him there was a foundation. Those researches are his memorial.

Before John Aubrey those circles were mysteries. Over the hills and valleys of western Britain were hundreds of decaying stone circles, stones weathered, leaning, collapsed, rings that no one understood. To Saxons the lintelled uprights of Stonehenge looked like stone gallows; *stanhengen*, 'the hanging stones', it was called and 'Stonehenge' it is to this day. What its first name had been no one knows.

There was other guesswork. Some believed that girls had ring-danced inside the Merry Maidens circle. Witchcraft was suspected at the spacious Long Meg & Her Daughters. A more holy origin was suggested for the tiny Yorkshire Twelve Apostles. The same name was given to another near Dumfries, an enclosure almost thirty times more spacious than the other. Surveyors of 1850 were puzzled that there were only eleven stones rather than twelve. The farmer explained. He had removed one of the disciples to make space for his plough. 'It was,' he said, 'only Judas.'[2]

Much earlier even well-educated clerics of the twelfth century were baffled about the age and purpose of stone circles. There was only guesswork. 'No one has been able to discover by what mechanism such vast masses of stone were erected', and even more frustratingly, 'nor for what purpose they were designed'.[3]

For two hundred years the despair continued. 'But at what time this was done, or by what people, or for what memorial or significance is unknown.'[4]

Even five centuries later in 1893 a Victorian novelist had his heroine ask a companion whether a nearby circle had been an altar, or a grave, or a commemoration of some forgotten battle, or perhaps an observatory for the sun and moon, even a temple devoted to the worship of serpents?

The man 'who knew absolutely nothing at all about the matter, was probably as well qualified as anybody else, to answer the questions'. But he said nothing. The ring, like every other one in Britain, remained an unexplained mystery.[5]

Like most people he was unaware of the answers that Aubrey had provided years earlier. Long before his shoulder-shrugging indifference there had been deductions that would not properly be published until late in the twentieth century. They said:

These Antiquities are so exceeding old, that no Bookes doe reach them. So that there is no way to retrive them but by comparative antiquitie, which I have writt upon the Spott, from the Monuments themselves.[6]

Others had relied on what had already been published, that the Romans had been the builders, or the Danes. That writer disagreed. He did not do no more than sit in his study reading old books and older ideas about the rings. He went out and looked at them. He was a fieldworker.

> Having often been led out of the way, not only by common reports, but by Bookes, and for that I had scarcely seen hitherto any Antiquities, which did not either fall-short of Fame, or exceeded it, I was for relying on my own Eiesight.[7]

And 'I am apt to believe, that in most Counties of England are, or have been, Ruines of these kind of Temples', and he rejected the idea that intruders from overseas had erected the rings.

> Now to wind-up this Discourse. The Romans had no Dominion in Ireland, or (at least not far) in Scotland. Therefore these Temples are not to be supposed to be built by them: nor had the Danes Dominion in Wales: and therefore we cannot presume that the two last mentioned Temples to have been Works of Them. But all these Monuments are of the same fashion, and antique rudenesse; wherefore I Conclude, that they were Works erected by the Britons.[8]

The writer was John Aubrey.

He was born in 1626 in the manor-house of Lower Easton Pierse near Kington St Michael in Wiltshire. He came from a well-born, well-to-do although not rich family and as a young man he lived 'sparkishly', dressing finely, travelling with a servant until, misguidedly involved with a vindictive woman, he was impoverished by premarital lawsuits. He became a penniless man-about-town, maintained by the willing generosity of his aristocratic Cavalier friends.

Yet this seemingly worthless ne'er-do-well compiled one of the most entertaining books in the English language, his anecdotal *Brief Lives* with its often brief but evocative descriptions, such as that of his friend, Sir William Petty, who undertook a survey of the whole of Ireland. Petty was an inventive man of restless mind. For a time he taught anatomy at Oxford

> to the young scholars; anatomy was then but little understood by the university; and I remember, he kept a body that he brought by water from Reading, a good while to study, some way preserved or pickled.

But, being Aubrey, he could not help adding in the same *Life*,

> Sir William Petty had a boy that whistled incomparably well. He after waited on a lady,

a widow, of good fortune. Every night this boy was to whistle his lady asleep. At last she could hold out no longer, but bids her chamber-maid withdraw: bids him to come to bed, sets him to work, and marries him the next day. This is certain true; from himself and Mrs. Grant.

Or there was Aubrey's story of Elizabeth Broughton, who

lost her Mayden-head to a poor young fellow ... Her father at length discovered her inclinations and locked her up in the Turret of the house; but she getts down by a rope; and away she gott to London ... She was a most exquisite beautie, as finely shaped as Nature could frame; had a delicate Witt ... [but] At last she grew common and infamous and gott the Pox, of which she died.[9]

John Aubrey lived in one of the most persistently turbulent periods of history in England: the Royalist versus Roundhead Civil War followed by the puritanical Commonwealth with its fanatical bigots smashing stained-glass windows, and defacing marble memorials of gallant knights and other idolatrous vanities of the loathsome Church of England.

After the Restoration of Charles II in 1660 Aubrey lived through the Great Plague and the Fire of London. He suffered accidents, almost drowning near Holyhead when returning from Ireland. Three times he was dangerously attacked, at home beaten up by burglars who inflicted fifteen wounds to his head, twice threatened in the streets of London, first by a drunken sword-bearing dandy, later, during an election, by an earl.

Yet despite those afflictions he compiled the very first list of prehistoric stone circles in England, Scotland and Wales, even in Ireland, making the first historically intelligent deductions about their age and purpose.

His *Brief Lives* and other books reflecting his widespread interests such as *Education* and the *Wiltshire Collections* have been published in recent centuries, although only one book, his jottings of *Miscellanies* of 1696 about ghosts, dreams and rural superstitions, was printed during his lifetime.

John Aubrey has received three full-length biographies, the first in 1845, a *Memoir* by John Britton, then Anthony Powell's *John Aubrey and his Friends* of 1948, revised in 1963 and updated in 1968. It is the classic book. It was followed by David Tylden-Wright's *John Aubrey. A Life*, 1991.

A few years earlier, in 1985, Michael Hunter had published his scholarly *John Aubrey and the Realm of Learning*, a detailed survey of Aubrey's many diverse interests.

But there had never been a detailed archaeological review of Aubrey's invaluable research into the problems of prehistoric stone circles. It was unique. His was the foundation stone on which the entire structure of stone circle studies has been built.

He discovered Avebury by accident in 1649. He later made the first good plan of Stonehenge. Intrigued by the challenge of understanding silent monuments that had no history he went to ring after ring, riding to site after site. He read descriptions of circles by earlier travellers, John Leland, William Camden, making notes from their descriptions in his spidery handwriting.

He half-jokingly recorded some of his fieldwork as a mini-autobiography, 'to be interponed as a sheet of paper only in the binding of a book', stating,

> My head was always working; never idle and even travelling (which from 1649 till 1670 was never off my horse's back) did glean some observations, of which I have a collection in folio of two quires of paper or more, a dust basket, some whereof are to be valued.[10]

In 1663 he had drawn a plan of Avebury for Charles II. It was completely inaccurate, drawn fourteen years after he had first seen the circles. Shocked, he returned to Avebury and made a proper survey. It was the beginning of thirty years of fieldwork, compiling his own notes and then, unable to go to every part of Britain, he wrote to colleagues and correspondents in England, Scotland, Wales, even Ireland. He called the resulting, disordered manuscript *Templa Druidum*, 'Temples of the Druids', some two hundred quill-written pages of jottings, alterations, additions and copies of replies to his questions.

He recorded details of stone circles as far apart as the Hurlers in Cornwall and the almost unknown Cothiemuir Wood five hundred miles to the north in Scotland. There were others in the Orkneys.

A clergyman in Wales told him that on Anglesey were 'stones pitch'd on end, about twelve in number, whereof three are very considerable', and another, whose Christian name Aubrey forgot, wrote that 'in Ireland, is a monument of Stones like those at Stoneheng', although they, near Kildare, were scattered pillars rather than a stone circle.

All this and much more can be found in the pages of the *Templa Druidum*, the first of two great volumes, his *Monumenta Britannica*, of 1980 and 1982. John Aubrey had completed that work by 1690.

For hundreds of years his unpublished insights were disregarded. Seduced by William Stukeley's eighteenth-century tempting fantasies of a proto-Christian druidical priesthood few scholars were aware of or could be bothered to look at the commonsense deductions about the distant past lingering unread in the archives of the Bodleian Library. Those were lost centuries for the archaeological world. It was not until the late nineteenth century that the untiring researches John Aubrey had made on prehistory's behalf were recognised.

But before then the seventeenth century had been a fortunate period, remarkable for the interlinking of three quite different men and their handwritten records of personal, political and scholarly events. One man made a conventional diary. Another put together a series of recollections, frequently adding to them years later. The third chronicler filled baskets and boxes of jottings with additions and deletions of objects seen and described. The three men were Samuel Pepys, John Evelyn and John Aubrey.

They were an unusual trio. They never met as a group. Pepys and Evelyn were friends who kept up a long correspondence from about 1665 until Pepys' death in 1703. Pepys, although a Fellow of the Royal Society from 1665 and its President from 1684 to 1686, never mentioned another Fellow, Aubrey, either in his *Diary* or anywhere else.

John Evelyn, one of the Society's original Fellows, was a long-standing, close friend of Aubrey's. In February 1676 he praised him for his as-then-unpublished *Antiquities of Surrey*, telling him that 'with incredible satisfaction have I perus'd your Natural History of Surrey & cet, and greatly admire both your Industry in undertaking so profitable a Work, and your Judgement in the several Observations which you have made, it is so useful a Piece, and so obliging that I cannot sufficiently applaud it'.

He termed Aubrey an 'Inquisitive Genius' 'being very Curious to set downe whatsoever he found Remarkable & Extraordinary'.[11]

It is another coincidence that the three manuscripts of Aubrey, Evelyn and Pepys were disregarded, almost forgotten for more than a century after the writers' deaths.

With all his other books Pepys' handwritten, very personal *Diary* was bequeathed to Cambridge University, preferably to his old college, Magdalene. There they were to be kept in a private room in the glazed bookcases that were made at Pepys' orders by naval dockyard joiners.

There the papers lay, neglected, for a hundred and fifty years until interest in them was stirred by the publication of Evelyn's *Diary* in 1818. An impoverished undergraduate, John Smith, had been employed in the task of translating the diary, unaware that an explanatory key to the shorthand lay in the same room. The work took him three laborious years, 1819–22. He converted everything into plain English except for those secretive, very intimate passages that he termed 'obj', 'objectionable'.

To his chagrin he received only £200 for his labours and, even worse, discovered that credit for the translation was being claimed by a higher-placed person in the university.

The *Diary* remained unexpurgated of Pepys' secret activities until the very good, eleven-volume edition of Latham and Matthews of 1976. Even they, perhaps respecting American sensibilities, left many brief entries about Pepys' private assignations unexplained such as the tri-lingual code of 2 June 1668, '*a su cama and there fasero la grand cosa*', that could easily have been clarified for readers as 'to her chamber and her bed where we had long and gratifying sex'.[12]

There were no entries like that in what John Evelyn termed his *Kalendarium, My Journal*. It was not a day-to-day diary. It has been called more of a series of recollections, 'a compendium of memorabilia'.

As well as matters of national importance intermixed with Evelyn's considerable private interests there were snippets of disapproval: Nell Gwynn was impudent, and her attendance at Mass was 'no greate loss to the Church'. The king's mistresses were no more than 'prostitute Creatures'. And Evelyn, like many others, was disgusted at the king's Court at Whitehall with its 'prophanenesse', 'dissolution', and Charles II 'toying' with his concubines. The variety of topics in Evelyn's writing makes vivid reading.

In it there are just a few, very mild 'Pepysian' entries such as that for 9 May 1683. 'Din'd at Sir Gab: Sylvuis, & thence to visit the Duke of Norfolck, & to know whither he would part with any of his Cartoones & other Drawings of Raphael & the greate masters: He answered me, he would part with & sell any thing for mony but his Wife (the Duchesse &c) who stood neere him; and I thought with myselfe, That if I were in his condition, it should be the first thing I would be glad to part with'. It was a humorous comment but it was not a malicious one.

On his death in 1706, three years after Pepys, the mass of papers was left in Evelyn's birthplace at Wotton Hall near Dorchester in Surrey, 'for the benefit of his descendants'. It is rumoured that the huge but disregarded collection was stored for safe-keeping in an old clothes-basket. 'Except for an accident, it might have been cut up for dress-patterns, or served to light fires.'

The 'accident' was William Upcott on a visit to Sir Frederick Evelyn's widow, Lady Mary. Upcott, an assistant librarian at the London Institute, read the papers, made a selection, and it was published in 1818 as *Memoirs of John Evelyn* by a Surrey antiquarian, William Bray.[13]

A prudish version of Pepys' *Diary* was published seven years later.

Aubrey's invaluable archaeological notes had a much less secure history. Despite his continual efforts, that haphazard collection of scribbled sheets of site descriptions and speculations begun in the mid-1640s and moved over the decades from house to lodging to stately home in a luggage of boxes and baskets was not published in his lifetime.

It is a historical irony that three of the most famous of all Stuart personal records should have remained in obscurity for so long, Evelyn's discovered, almost by accident, in 1817. Pepys' undeciphered and uncensored diary rested unnoticed until four years later. Aubrey's indispensable but fragile treasure-house of antiquities was finally deposited in the safety of the Bodleian Library just fifteen years after that 'accident'. There the jumbled sheets rested, almost in oblivion but secure, until their rearranged, sometimes truncated, publication in the two volumes of 1980 and 1982.

That compilation of stone circle notes was irreplaceable. It was not pedantic book-learning. It was the innovation of fieldwork combined with determination and intelligence.

> Twas in that deluge of Historie, the memorie of these British Monuments utterly perished: the Discovery whereof I doe here endeavour (for want of written record) to work-out and restore after a kind of Algebraicall method and so reducing them to a kind of Aequation (being but an ill Orator my selfe) by comparing them that I have seen one with another to make the Stones give Evidence for themselves.[14]

I

1626-48: Childhood & youth

Apparently a sickly child, his parents kept him at home for lessons rather than send him to school, until the age of 12.

Kate Bosley, 1997, 1

It is no surprise that a man who was to become famous for his discoveries at Avebury and Stonehenge should be born in Wiltshire. Yet, strangely, although he had homes there he never lived close to any of Britain's ancient stone circles.

He was born in the uneasy seventeenth century and he lived through years of excess, arguments, quarrels and conflicts over politics and religion, set against a background of rural superstitions and witchcraft. John Aubrey's life would be affected by every one of them.

That background to his life was one of the most unsettled in British history. It had begun with years of struggle between Parliament and a Crown believing in the 'Divine Right of Kings'. Civil War came, then the execution of Charles I followed by the tedious years of the Commonwealth.

The restoration of Charles II in 1660 brought laughter and the ringing of bells but only five years later other bells were ringing to the cries, 'bring out your dead' as a vicious plague killed thousands in London. The next year brought unplanned improvement when much of London was rebuilt haphazardly but sturdier after the Great Fire.

During Aubrey's lifetime there were three naval wars against the Dutch then another struggle against the French. The accumulated cost was so great that the Government had to borrow money and the repayable loans were the beginning of the National Debt in 1693. The Bank of England was formed the next year when Aubrey was sixty-eight.

War and money were not the only concerns. In 1678 a perjurer, Titus Oates, warned of a Popish Plot in which Catholics were intending to massacre Protestants, burn London down, assassinate Charles II and install a king of their own faith. There was panic but these heavy national concerns were accepted with a shrug. Most people, John Aubrey included, went about their daily, humdrum lives.

In 1626 his first home was the impressive manor of Lower Easton Pierse just west of Kington St Michael near Chippenham. A fitting house for a well-to-do family it was only fifteen miles from Avebury but the boy was to know nothing about those stones for more than twenty years. The ring was not a tourist attraction. It was seldom that any stranger visited it, and Aubrey's parents were not adventurous travellers.

Otherwise the nearest stone circle was the almost unknown Gray Hill thirty miles to the west in Monmouthshire. He would be a grown man before he received an unexpected introduction to prehistory and archaeology.

Around 1642 his restless father moved the family miles to the south to Broad Chalke near Salisbury. John Aubrey was still in Wiltshire but, again, there was no neighbouring stone circle. The nearest was Stonehenge and that was ten miles away.

He was born on 11 March 1626, just after sunrise, and was so sickly that he was immediately baptised before morning prayers. Years later his mother told him that he had had a fever almost as soon as he was born. He himself remembered that he seemed to have no real strength until he was eleven or twelve years old.

His mother herself, Deborah, *née* Lyte, had married young, just sixteen and a half years old, and Aubrey was born slightly more than nine months later.

He was fortunate to survive. It was an age when infant mortality was high. Although he had two younger brothers, William and Thomas, two others, both named Isaac, and a sister Anne, all died in their first year. And, almost as though collaborating to extinguish the Aubrey line, not one of the three surviving brothers married. John Aubrey did try but failed expensively.[1]

His early childhood was a lonely one. He remembered that he was

bred up in a kind of Parke, far from Neighbours, and no Child to converse withal: so that I could not speake till late. My father had no one to teach me in the house, and I was pent-up in a Roome by myself melancholy.

Freedom finally came when he went to his first school.

I was like a Bird that was gotten out of his cage amongst the free Citizens of the aire.[2]

The growing boy was to live through seventy years of disrupted history in England. The year before he was born the new king, Charles I, was crowned. Short, elegant, sober, the new monarch was 'careful of majesty, and would be approached with respect and reverence'. He was a firm believer in the divine right of kings to rule and this would bring him into conflict not only with the independently minded members of his parliaments but also with the increasingly active Puritans.

Charles had inherited a kingdom stirring with religious unrest. Puritans with their belief in a religion of rigorous simplicity had been a growing irritation since Tudor times and were becoming a very disruptive threat to the king, his Church and his laws. They were no longer willing to submit to the dictates of Anglican bishops.

Every Puritan, whatever the individual cult, demanded the right for a man to interpret the Bible as he wished, to reject the ritualistic mumbo-jumbo of Communion, to deny the power of bishops to rule by 'divine right', and, above all, the freedom to ignore the idolatry of the High Church. It was the age in which John Aubrey was living.

In turn threatened, persecuted, fined, imprisoned, in 1620 a small group of Puritans, later known as the Pilgrim Fathers, although they were only a small minority of the passengers, emigrated to America, sailing from Plymouth in the *Mayflower*. A family coincidence connected that voyage with John Aubrey.

When his grandfather, also a John Aubrey, died in 1616 his widow, Rachel Aubrey, married Alderman John Whitson of Bristol who was the owner of the pilgrims' *Mayflower*.

That was not Whitson's only distinction. He also unknowingly advanced the knowledge of Britain's early history. At his death his widow inherited the Somerset manor of Burnett that stood only a few miles from the stone circles at Stanton Drew. John Aubrey would see them as a boy.

There were grander events outside his little world. In 1620 when King James I was visiting Wilton near Stonehenge, his favourite, George Villiers, to become the Duke of Buckingham three years later, had a deep pit, 'about the bignesse of two Sawe-pitts', dug near the centre of the circle. Nothing was found but the ugly hole caused irreparable damage to a very sensitive area of the ring. It was also 'the cause of the falling downe or recumbency of the great stone there, twenty one foote long', the formerly leaning sarsen, the great trilithon pillar no. 55.

Not contented with that vandalism Villiers also had labourers plunge into a nearby round barrow unearthing a bugle 'tipt with Silver at Both ends'. Aubrey was told by a local woman, Mrs Mary Trotman, that 'his Grace kept it in his Closet as a great Relique'. The instrument was not prehistoric but the ghosts of the desecrated dead were and it may have been their retribution that caused Villiers to be assassinated in 1628.[3]

Aubrey's ailments continued.

About three or four years old I had a grievous ague. I can remember it. I gott not health till I was 11 or 12 yeares old; but had sickenesse of Vomiting (the Belly-ake: paine in the side) for 12 houres every fortnight for several yeares, then about monethly, then quarterly & at last once in halfe a yeare. About 12 it stopped. This Sickenesss nipt my strength in the bud.

His weakly body developed other ailments. When he was eight years old,

I had an Issue (naturall) in the coronall suture of my head, which continued running till 21. 1634: October: I had a violent Fever that was like to have carried me off. ' Twas the most dangerous sicknesse that ever I had.[4]

During those unsettled years of his boyhood at Easton Pierse he was always reading, a lonely, almost neglected child, solitary but continually curious, one of his great pleasures being talking to all kinds of workmen: joiners, carpenters, coopers, masons, asking questions, learning something of the skills of their trades.

In was in 1633 that he went to his first school, a churchroom at Yatton Keynell, the unusual place-name meaning 'the head of the valley belonging to a thirteenth-century landowner, Henry Caynel'.

The village, a mile or so south-west of Easton Pierse, was only a few minutes' ride on Aubrey's little horse. He came to know and like the rector there, William Stumpe, 'a proper man and a good fellow'.[5]

By that time Aubrey was already developing a serious interest in past times. Before the closing of the monasteries in Henry VIII's reign there had been a nunnery at Kington St Michael. His love of the past caused Aubrey to write a pleasant anecdote about the nuns there. They had learned needlework, confectionary, physics, writing, and drawing. 'Old Jacques could see from his house the nuns come forth into the Nymph-Hay with their books and wheels to spin – this was a fine way of breeding up young women.' Of that nunnery the only surviving part became Priory Farm with its blocked-up doorways and windows.

The past intrigued the young Aubrey and he was continually upset to learn of the destruction of many irreplaceable historic documents in his neighbourhood. He enjoyed the reminiscences of his old grandfather, Isaac Lyte of Kington St Michael, who would endow six fine almshouses there in 1675. Its church still has his fine heraldic tombstone.

Lyte was old enough to remember the destruction of so many antiquities by Tudor 'reformers'.

In my grandfather's dayes the manuscripts flew about like butterflies. All musick bookes, account bookes, copie bookes &c. were covered with old manuscripts ... and the glovers at Malmesbury made great havock of them; and gloves were wrapt up no doubt in many good pieces of antiquity. Before the late warres a world of rare manuscripts perished hereabout; for within half a dozen miles of this place were the abbey of Malmesbury, where it may be presumed the library was as well furnished with choice copies as most libraries of England.[6]

It was not only ancient records that were destroyed. Idolatrous graven images were equally endangered. In the church of St Edmunds in Salisbury there was a delicate stained-glass window showing an image of God as an old man. That, to the Recorder, a man called Shervill, was an affront to the dignity of the ever-eternal deity. In 1631 he began smashing the coloured panes and, unable to reach some of them from the ground, he climbed onto the pews, fell and broke his leg.

Worse followed. For his desecration of a holy place he was so heavily fined by the Star Chamber that he was ruined. It achieved little. The Star Chamber was abolished by a prejudiced Long Parliament in 1640 and the puritanical purging of images continued. John Aubrey grumbled:

> But what Mr. Shervill left undone, the Soldiers since have gone through with, that there is not a piece of glass-painting left … At Croydon in Surrey in the Rebellion, one Bleese was hir'd, for half a Crown per Day, to break the painted Glass-Windows, which were formerly fine [and at Corston] the very barres are taken out of the windowes by the fanatique rage of the late times; here have been two good South windowes, and the doores are gone and the paving, and it serves for any use, viz. Weavers. The Font has gone to make a trough.[7]

By a peculiar coincidence with what Aubrey was to achieve at Avebury, there was a fortunate survival at St James' church there.

In addition to its Anglo-Saxon windows and handsome tower it contained an example of an almost unique beautifully hand-carved and painted medieval rood-loft as a gallery above the chancel-arch. During the iconoclastic destruction of the Reformation it would have been doomed to destruction by anti-Catholic fanatics. Protective villagers neatly dismantled it and hid the sections under lath-and-plastering at the corner of the chancel and nave. It remained hidden and forgotten until there was a restoration of the church in 1810 when it was exposed. Redecorated, it is a rare and delightful survivor of an Elizabethan period of bigotry.[8]

The rector at Yatton Keynell, William Stumpe, was the great-grandson of William Stumpe, a very rich clothier of Malmesbury. In 1539, during Henry VIII's dissolution of the monasteries, the wealthy merchant bought the lands of its abbey for £1,516. He presented the unwanted nave to the parishioners as a replacement for their rundown church.

His descendant, Yatton Keynell's rector, 'had severall manuscripts of the abbey' but, groaned Aubrey, 'when he brewed a barrel of speciall ale, his use was to stop the bung-hole, under the clay, with a sheet of manuscript; he sayd nothing did it so well'. He even told his family how useful the papers were.

Years later in 1647 when Aubrey was preparing to write his *Naturall History of Wiltshire* he went back to the rector in the hope of recovering some of the old papers which he had seen as a boy 'but by that time [they] were lost and disperst. His sons were gunners and souldiers, and scoured their gunnes with them'.[9]

He was innately curious, sometimes almost indiscriminatingly. But that and his considerable intelligence allowed him to transform everyday sights into an imagined future. In his later years he even foresaw manned balloons. 'Fill or force in smoke into a bladder, and try if the bladder will not be carried up in the ayre; if it is, several bladders may draw a man up into the ayre a certain height', a vision anticipating the Montgolfiers' hot air flight of 1783 by more than a century.[10]

A witch-craze, prevalent since medieval times, increased with the rise of Puritanism. With their certainty that man, being born with original sin, could only be saved by rigorously righteous living Puritans obeyed the Biblical injunction of Exodus XXII, 18, 'Thou shalt not suffer a witch to live'.

In England there were accusations, trials, verdicts and executions. There were two examinations in Lancashire. In the first of 1612, twenty were accused, ten were condemned, one died in prison, one was sent to the pillory, nine were hanged, the rest were acquitted. But there was growing scepticism about the evidence. Twenty-one years later, in 1633, on the testimony of a young boy, thirty were accused, and seventeen were convicted. Doubts remained. Justifiably. The boy was found to have lied to benefit his father. No one was executed.[11] But it was the age in which John Aubrey lived.

It was not only the ignorant peasant and the superstitious villager that feared a witch's evil attentions. Even the comfortable inhabitants of London were apprehensive of spells and curses. Aubrey himself was to see how they protected themselves.

'It is a thing very common to nail horse-shoes in the thresholds of doores. Which is to hinder the power of witches that enter the house. Most houses of the West End have the horse-shoe on the threshold. It should be a horse-shoe that one finds', a not uncommon chance with riders and carts a daily sight in the busy streets.

In 1682 a man, fearing that his wife had been cursed by a witch, was told by an apothecary to collect some of her urine, nail-cuttings and hair, boil the mixture and then bury it in a bottle upside-down by the doorstep or the fireplace, anywhere where a witch might enter. His wife would not longer be afflicted.[12]

In 1633, wrote Aubrey, 'at eight years old I had a issue (naturall) in the coronal sutor of my head, which continued running till 21. In October, 1634 I had a violent fevor, it was like to have carried me off; 'twas the most dangerous sickness that ever I had'.[13]

It was also the year when he went to his second school where he was taught Latin grammar by Robert Latimer, the aged rector of Leigh Delamere, a mile's 'fine walk' from Easton Pierse. He was, reminisced Aubrey, an 'easy man, a delicate little person', old-fashioned enough to wear a dagger, knife and long pin at his girdle. He was both gentle and a good teacher.

If a boy asked to be excused, Latimer would give him a Latin word to remember. On his return, the lad had to repeat it. It was an effective method of developing a very good vocabulary. Aubrey learned the conjugation of verbs, tenses, present, future, perfect; declensions of nouns, nominative, dative, ablative, all quietly acquired under the supervision of Latimer, who often encouraged his brightest pupils by keeping them after school, sometimes as late as nine o'clock on summer evenings.[14]

To Aubrey's disappointment and great regret the old man died in November 1634 after educating him for only a brief six months. Aubrey returned to Easton Pierse where, for some years, he was semi-schooled by 'severall ignorant teachers' until he was sent to boarding school in either 1637 or the following year.

Archaeologically those few years between 1634 and 1637 were to be the first sparks of a tinder-box for John Aubrey. For another John, the Puritan John Hampden, they were the prologue to a civil war that would kill him.

The royal treasury had been so wantonly depleted by James I and his frivolous wife, Anne of Denmark, that their son, Charles I in some desperation attempted to restore the funds by imposing a Ship Money tax on inland cities. Hampden, an affluent country gentleman and a member of Parliament, refused to pay. Being a man of importance he was tried by the Court of Exchequer in which seven of the twelve judges found him guilty and he was ordered to pay the twenty shillings tax, several hundred pounds in modern money, that had been imposed on his main estate in Buckinghamshire.

As the orator Edmund Burke observed in a speech about taxes on American colonies a century and a half later, 'Would twenty shillings have ruined Mr. Hampden's fortune? No, but the payment of half twenty shillings would have made him a slave.'

John Hampden paid the tax, but the Court's verdict made him the most popular man in England. He was to be one of the five members of Parliament that Charles I attempted to arrest in 1642.[15]

To an eleven-year-old boy in Wiltshire the affair would have been of little interest, although he probably heard his parents talking about it. Yet it was probably during those historic years, perhaps in 1636, that Aubrey was considered old enough to go on his own to visit Somerset's own 'Stonehenge', the three-stone circles at Stanton Drew.

During the summer holidays, once free from his plodding tutors, a great pleasure was to visit his grandmother, Rachel Whitson, *née* Danvers, at Burnett manor twenty miles away in Somerset. Hers was a fine country house left to her by her late husband. 'Burnet was my grandmother's Joineture, by him; where I was often in my youthhood: and is about fower miles from Stanton Drew.'[16]

Throughout his youth the historic past had intrigued him and the old monuments in Wiltshire encouraged his interest.

> I was inclin'd by my Genius, from my Childhood to the Love of Antiquities: and my Fate dropt me in a Countrey most suitable for such Enquiries. Salisbury-plaines, and Stoneheng I had known from eight years old but I never sawe the country round Marleborough till Christmas 1648: being then invited to Lord Francis Seymour's.[17]

It was years earlier that he had first visited Stanton Drew.

Despite a popular belief, the place-name had nothing to do with druids. It prosaically derived from *stan-ton*, 'the place of stones', that in 1253 stood on the land *Stanton Drogonis*, the Drogon family. By 1291 the name had changed to Standondru, 'Stanton Drew', the property of the Drews.

To a boy not yet in his teens its stones were mysteries. And they were made the more mysterious by being in a ruinous state, stones, standing, leaning, many fallen, some naturally, others toppled because they were in cultivated fields and hindered the plough. Others had been smashed into manageable fragments for doorsteps, lintels, supports for gates. In his rough notes Aubrey was to remember:

> These Stones are 9 or 10 foot high ... it is in ploughed land and so easily worne-out. When I sawe it, the corne being ripe, I could not survey the stones so exactly as I would but this Scheme resembles it.[18]

The chaos told the young Aubrey nothing.

Village gossip offered explanations. Some slabs were so ponderous that no man could have raised them. They were the work of giants. The name of one of them was known, Hackwell. He had been so strong that he had thrown an immensely heavy stone from a distant hill and it landed over a mile away on that ridge on the skyline just above the circles. There were rumours claiming Hackwell was so famous that he was buried in the nearby church at Chew Magna.

Others added a warning. The boy should never try to count the stones. It was almost impossible anyway because of the jumble. But if anyone did reach the right number that person would suffer great misfortune, maybe even death for interfering in what was best left alone.

Another superstition relates how, on the sixth day of the full moon, at midnight, the stones walk down to the river to take a drink. But the best-known whimsy, probably celebrated from Puritan pulpits as justifiable punishment for profaning the Sabbath, was that the stones were the petrified remains of a wedding party that had sinned.

A fiddler and his accompanists had played merry jigs for the dancers until Saturday midnight when, of course, the merry-making had to stop before Sunday began. Defiantly, the young bride refused to abandon her pleasure. She, her husband and all their guests would dance on. Midnight came.

The fiddler vanished. The Devil flashed, flared into the night. Everyone, bride, groom, parson, dancers, musicians, all of them instantly became stones wherever they were. And there they remain.

Superstitiously apprehensive locals told Aubrey that the sinners were still to be seen. Three stones by the church were the solidified bride, groom and parson. In the fields the rings were the rigid remnants of the dancers. The avenues were the tumbled lines of musicians.

The tale-tellers said that the fate of those wicked merrymakers had been observed that dreadful night by horrified bystanders and had been remembered ever since here in this neighbourhood:

> That a Bride goeing to be married, she and the rest of the company were metamorphos'd into these stones: but whether it were true or no they told me they could not tell.

Reminiscing years later John Aubrey mused:

> I know that some will nauseate these old Fables; but I do professe to regard them as the most considerable pieces of ['observable' inserted] of Antiquity' .... After all, was not Lot's wife turned into a pillar of salt?[19]

It would be almost another thirty years before he was experienced enough to see the devilish stones with a more sceptical, archaeological eye. He was living in a superstitious world.

His education continued. When he was twelve years old, on or just before 1638,

> I was transported to Blandford-schoole, in Dorset, to Mr. Wm. Sutton. (In Mr. Wm. Gardner's time it was the most eminent schoole for the education of gentlemen in the West of England.)

Gardner had died only two or three years earlier.[20]

Despite the Head of the school, William Sutton, being an ill-natured pedagogue the boy prospered in his classical studies. His health improved. So did his learning. In both Latin and Greek he was the best of his contemporaries.

A friendly young teacher lent him a copy of Cowper's classical *Dictionary*, and the volume introduced him to exciting authors. He read them: Terence's amusing theatrical comedies for audiences in Rome, Cicero's speeches, Ovid's *Metamorphoses*, his poetical stories of Greek mythology and Roman legends.

The young John Aubrey continued to develop new interests despite not having a good memory. 'My head was always working but not adroit for verse.' On those days when he was free of schoolwork he happily indulged his curiosity about the unusual.

In Blandford he visited the shop and furnaces of an aging craftsman, Harding, one of the few surviving 'country glass-painters' left in England. Puritan abhorrence of statues, icons and depictions of saints in the stained-glass windows of idolatrous churches demanded that God's immaculate houses be cleansed of those blasphemies. It was only a few years earlier that Shervill had smashed such glass-panes in Salisbury.

Aubrey was fascinated by Harding's skill and regretted that he himself did not live in a city like Bristol 'where I might have access to watchmakers, locksmiths etc'. Of those pleasant schooldays he reminisced he had been

> Mild of spirit; mightily susceptible of Fascination. My Idea very cleer; Phansie like a Mirrour, pure chrystal water which the least wind does disorder and unsmooth. Never riotous or prodigall; but (as Sir E. Leech said Sloath and carelessnesse are equivalent to all other vices).[21]

Those were amusements. There were also misfortunes in the life of a young country gentleman. On Monday 15 April 1639, the day after Easter week, Aubrey was thrown dangerously from his uncle's horse. Anthony Browne had lent him a bay nag that the youth had carelessly ridden under the thorny branches of an overhanging brier. Startled, the horse reared and galloped off unsaddling Aubrey, who fell badly but not fatally. '*Deo gratias*'.[22]

But he continued to be ill. 'I had the measills, but that was nothing, I was hardly sick.' Then, in 1642 on 3 May he was entered as a gentleman-commoner at Trinity College, Oxford, his father paying the first of an annual fee of £3.00.

Even in Oxford Aubrey was remote from stone circles. The embanked

Devil's Quoits was ten miles to the west. The Rollright Stones were twice that to the north.

Despite that archaeological lacuna it was a good time for John Aubrey but not for England. The years changed from unsettled to threatening. In 1642 on 22 August the frustrated king, Charles I, raised the royal standard at Nottingham, declaring war on his rebellious Parliamentarians.

In that year when Aubrey was in Oxford carefreely enjoying the newly published *Religio Medici* of Sir Thomas Browne there were military skirmishes like that at Powick Bridge near Worcester in September, and then the first battle of the war at Edghill two months later on 23 October.

> But now Bellona thundered, and as a cleare skie is sometimes overstretch[ed] with a dismall cloud and thunder, so was this serene peace by the civill warres through the factions of those times; vide Homer's Odyssey.
> In August following my father sent for me home, for feare.[23]

It was yet another interruption in his education. Six months later however, in February 1643, he was allowed to return to Oxford where he found that the royal court had been moved and was impressed to see the king. But almost instantly in April there was a dangerous outbreak of plague in the city. He contracted it. Recovering by June weakness forced him back to Broad Chalke and a 'sad life' of more isolation for another three years. He mouldered there companionless.[24]

In 1643 war and witchcraft went together. While battles were being won and lost in the Midlands and in the west of England at Lansdown, a profitable persecution was proceeding in East Anglia. Its leader was the money-lusting Matthew Hopkins, so-called witchfinder-general, of Manningtree in Essex. He was a sadist.

Nearly every village had a lonely old woman who would be suspected by superstitious neighbours whenever there was illness or disease. They denounced her as a witch. Hopkins would examine her body for the 'witch-mark', an extra teat, starve her, leave her without sleep, interrogate, torture, and if no confession came then submit the roped victim to the 'test', thrown into a pond or stream or any deep water. If she sank she was innocent – although perhaps drowned. If she floated she was guilty and hanged, a verdict based on the Christian principle that water, being a sacred substance, would reject anything sinful.

Between 1643 and 1647 there were hundreds of accusations and convictions and for each 'success' Hopkins demanded payment, sometimes a shilling or two, more often as many as twenty, a lucrative pound. But increasing scepticism mixed with resentment at his greed caused his own body to be 'tested'. It is rumoured that it did not sink. Guilty! But, perhaps from the chilled immersion, he died.

It is said he was buried in an unmarked grave in unhallowed ground at the extreme end of Mistley churchyard by the Stour estuary. Perhaps divine anger that such holy land had been desecrated caused the disgraced church to fall into ruin, only its porch surviving, a symbolic relic of its association with 'one of the wickedest men of those bad old days'.[25]

John Aubrey never mentioned Hopkins. He had his own disrupted life to resume. On 6 April 1646 he was back in London, at Mr Birde's house near the Middle Temple, studying to become an unlikely lawyer. Then Oxford surrendered. Many of his Royalist friends returned to the half-safety of the city.

By November he was free to return to Oxford and Trinity and already the tittle-tattle he had absorbed from the indiscretions of bibulous friends were scribbled down, the first of a thousand jottings about people, famous, infamous, hardly known and who would be forgotten had he not written those titbits down as the beginnings of his world-famous *Brief Lives*.[26]

He was living in a world of contrasts. There were Royalists, his friends, and there were Parliamentarians. In religion there were Catholics, High Church Protestants and there were self-denying Puritans and Presbyterians. Superstitiously, there were witches.

Even in appearance there were differences of dress. Cavaliers strode about in fitted jerkins with lace on their cuffs and shirts, wearing long decorated breeches, having pointed beards and full, curly hair under a cocked, feathered hat. Wigs were fashionable later. Ladies favoured high-waisted dresses, the bodices cut daringly low, with much lace and long skirts of elegant folds.

In contrast Puritan men had high-crowned stiff-brimmed hats, usually black, an austerely plain suit and straight, cropped hair. Women wore just as plain clothing, unornamented dark dresses. Both sexes detested jewellery.

The nature of the war changed. Confident royalists were no longer confronted by collections of civilians in armour. They were faced by trained, disciplined soldiers, Oliver Cromwell's New Model Army. It was invincible. A battle was won at Marston Moor in 1644 before the decisive one at Naseby the following year when the king's forces were routed.

Without hope, distrustful of the parliamentary army, the king went northwards and in 1646 gave himself up to the Scottish Covenanters at Southwell. A later attempt to escape failed.

Paradoxes can be ironies. Neither the clean-living Presbyterians nor the abstemious Puritans approved of frivolity or childish games. Yet both were ready, even eager, to abandon such principles and play 'Pass the Parcel' as long as the package was valuable. Charles I was.

In 1647 the Covenanters sold him to the Parliamentary Commissioners for £400,000. The following year the parliamentary army demanded that Charles I, the cause of every disruption, be put on trial. There was a problem. Parliament could not be trusted. A majority of its members were Presbyterians. On 3 December Colonel Pride expelled every one of them in what was nicknamed 'Pride's Purge'. The fifty-three non-Presbyterians that remained formed the notorious 'Rump' parliament that would try the king.

Through those depressing years while John Aubrey idled in London and Oxford his family suffered from the religious upheavals. His father had to pay the fines inflicted on suspected Royalist supporters. For him it was '£33 in sixty fat sheep, and £60 in money accepted for the fine here and Herefordshire' with an extra '£5 already paid ... in North Wilts', although he had long since left Easton Pierse.[27]

John Aubrey, too young to be legally responsible for any property, lived contentedly with his books and friends and also, almost reluctantly, continued with his legal studies between happier visits to Oxford.

But he had been born into a worsening world. Mentally and emotionally it was a paradox. Mentally, there were some who believed implicitly in the literal truth of the Bible. Others, more sceptical, questioned the truth about the Flood and the age of the world. Aubrey did.

Emotionally, many diehards would deny people the simplest of pleasures, humourless spoilsports confident in their righteous insistence in 'clean' living.

In the same years there were poets extolling the glories of living happily and in freedom. In his *Brief Lives* Aubrey wrote pen-portraits of many of them.

Life in merry England became drab. Ascetic living was demanded. Country games were banned. Laughter was permissible as long as it was not raucous. Wherever Puritanism was strong meant misery for freeborn, pleasure-loving commoners. There was to be no bear-baiting nor, depressingly, village folk-dancing around maypoles. All theatres were to be demolished. In an incredibly mean-minded contradiction of Christian charity no merriment or happy religious festivities were permitted at Christmas.

Despite those cheerless edicts England never became a doleful pleasureless land. Some quite un-puritanical joy filtered through that repressive blanket. Great poets sang, extolling the glories of living happily and in freedom. Even amongst them there were differences. There were complex 'metaphysical' poets such as George Herbert, who wrote only deeply religious verse such as 'The Agonie' of sin and love:

Who would know Sinne, let him repair
Unto Mount Oliver; there shall he see

A man so wrung with pains, that all his hair,

His skinne, his garments bloodie be.

He married a second cousin of Aubrey's, Jane Danvers. Aubrey wrote an enigmatic line about him, 'His marriage, I suppose, hastened his death. My kinswoman was a handsome bona roba and ingeniose.'[28] Jane was also distantly related to Aubrey's grandmother, Mrs Rachel [Danvers] Whitson, living near Stanton Drew.

A later 'metaphysical', Henry Vaughan, in his poem, *The World*, wrote some glorious but semi-heretical, almost anti-biblical lines:

I saw Eternity the other night

Like a great Ring of pure and endless light,

All calm, as it was bright,

And round beneath it, Time in hours, days, years

Driv'n by the spheres

Like a vast shadow moved …

He was one of two brothers, and Aubrey did not remember the family with fondness despite its distant kinship with his own. Almost with a scowl rather than a chuckle he wrote, 'Their grandmother was an Aubrey: their father, a coxcombe and none honester than he should be – he cozened me of 50s. once.'

There were also mid-century cavalier poets such as Richard Lovelace and Sir John Suckling. Lovelace on his way to join the war told Lucasta:

I could not love thee (dear) so much,

Lov'd I not honour more.

Aubrey remarked of him: 'He was a most beautiful Gentleman … He was a great lover of pretty girles.'

Suckling, whom Aubrey described unflatteringly as 'reddish fac't and red nose (ill liver) his head not very big, his hayre a kind of sand colour', was less rhapsodical about the ladies, versifying a cynical proverb that 'After three days men grow weary of a wench, a quest, and weather rainy':

Out upon it! I have loved

Three whole days together.

And am like to love three more,

If it prove fair weather.

adding sceptically in another poem,

Know, women's hearts like straw do move ...

There were many other fine poets of Aubrey's lifetime. John Donne had long abandoned verse but John Milton, a supporter of the anti-cavalier Commonwealth, had already presented his lyrical masque, *Comus*, at Ludlow Castle in 1633. Poetry and music also were part of the age in which John Aubrey lived.

It was all in *Brief Lives*, chit-chat, truths, half-truths, rumours and whispered scandals picked from companions in taverns and around the tables of royalist friends, stories about the famous and the hardly known, the capable and the foolish. John Aubrey wrote it down with his hollowed quill of goose feather, constantly wetting its sharpened blade in a pot of ink.

It is a practice half-forgotten in these days of fountain pens, ballpoints, and word processors but the writer is old enough to remember dipping a pen-nib into an inkwell. The school did provide blotting-paper, a facility also enjoyed by Aubrey. As early as the beginning of the sixteenth century praise was given to that unglazed, absorbent material:

Blottynge papyr serveth to drye wette wryttynge lest there be made blottis or blurris.[29]

John Aubrey's *Lives* also included some biographies of unsavoury 'Restoration rakes' of whom John Wilmot, 2nd earl of Rochester, was the epitome, dissolute, hell-heading through sexual perversion into self-destruction. 'He was Raunger of Woodstock-parke, and lived often at the Lodge at the west end ... Here his Lordship had severall lascivious Pictures drawen,' wrote Aubrey. Wilmot wrote:

Love a woman! You're an ass,
'Tis a most insipid passion,
To choose out for your happiness
The idlest part of God's creation!

Then give me Health, Wealth, Mirth and Wine,
And if busy Love entrenches,
There's a sweet, soft page of mine
Does the trick worth forty wenches.

It was typical debauched verse. Rakish, ravaged by every whim and perversity known to the Stuart Age Wilmot died aged thirty-three. He had written, 'See my credentials written in my face.' They were.[30]

Such rakes were not only utterly self-indulgent. They could be dangerous.

Aubrey was nearly murdered by one around 1673. He jotted down:

> Quaere the yeare that I lay at Mris. Neve's (for a short time) for at that time I was in great danger of being killed by a drunkard in the street of Grayes-Inn gate – a gentleman whom I never sawe before but (*Deus Gratias*) one of his companions hindred his thrust.[31]

Some years earlier than that Andrew Marvell, far better poet than Wilmot, member of Parliament but neither a killjoy nor a self-indulgent reprobate, pleaded with his chaste mistress to surrender her maidenhead. At once. Because

> Had we but World enough, and Time,
> This coyness Lady were no crime ...
> But at my back I alwaies hear
> Time's winged Charriot hurrying near:
> ... then Worms shall try
> That long preserv'd Virginity:
> And your quaint Honour turn to dust
> And into ashes all my Lust.
> The Grave's a fine and private place,
> But none I think do there embrace ...
> Now let us sport us while we may ...

Whether he was satisfied or frustrated is unknown and his death was equally uncertain. According to Aubrey, 'some suspect he was poisoned by the Jesuites, but I cannot be positive'.[32]

It was the world that John Aubrey lived in. Both Wilmot and Marvell were his contemporaries in that contradictory period of poetical loveliness, sexual abandon and physical violence of the Restoration in its hedonistic reaction to the repressions of the Commonwealth.

He also had a personal life. On Christmas Eve, 1648, his father became extremely ill and the young man was summoned home, 'to looke after his country affaires and solicite a law-suite'. He was needed. His father was dying, not fifty years old. The superstitious Aubrey believed he had had a premonition of it. 'Three or four Days before my father died, as I was in my Bed about nine o'clock in the morning, perfectly awake, I did hear three distinct knocks on the Bed's head, as if it had been with a Ruler or Ferula.'[33]

None of the male Aubreys was long-lived. John's grandfather had been thirty-eight. And of John Aubrey's four brothers, the two Isaacs died in infancy, Thomas only lived thirty-six years, although William did reach sixty-four. Aubrey himself, despite his sickly childhood, lived longer than any of them.

His father's death had left John Aubrey, his heir, with the responsibility of repaying many outstanding debts. Reluctantly and sporadically he began the unrewarding task.

He discovered Avebury in the following year, 1649. It was to make him an archaeologist.

2

1649-62: Ignorance: giants, the Devil, witchcraft & ignorance

Aubrey had other difficulties to contend with. Were the ancient Britons capable of building such monuments as Stonehenge? As his correspondent William Rogers remarks of conditions in the days of the Druids: 'All was in y^c <u>Woods</u>'.

A.L. Owen, 1962, 106

On Christmas Day in 1648 John Aubrey was invited to stay at the house of his close friend Lord Francis Seymour at Allington Manor not far from Aubrey's old home at Lower Easton Pierse. There, with other friends, there were pleasures to be enjoyed in the Marlborough countryside, riding, hunting, 'the Turfe rich and fragrant with Thyme and Burnet. Nor are the Nut-brown Shepherdesses without their graces'. It was a gift. He wrote as though he were speaking to his reader with a gentle Wiltshire burr. It was customary for people to have local accents in those years. Walter Ralegh, Aubrey said, 'spake broad Devonshire to his dying day'.

And after the shepherdesses and the chase John Aubrey came by accident to the astonishing rings of Avebury, 'so long unregarded'. It was an event that would enrich his life.

On a bitter winter's day he saw Avebury for the first time. It was Sunday 7 January 1649, three weeks before King Charles I was executed. With cavalier friends Aubrey was galloping after greyhounds as they hunted for hares on the Marlborough uplands 'where the Downs looke as if they were sowen with great Stones, very thick, and in a dusky evening, they looke like a flock of Sheep'.

He and the other Royalists rode down the old Saxon *herepath*, 'the army trackway', into the almost unknown village of Avebury where he was 'wonderfully surprized at the sight of those vast stones of wch I had never heard before: and also the mighty Bank and graffe [ditch] about it: I observed in the Inclosures some Segments of rude circles, made with those stones whence I concluded they had been in the old time complete'.

His companions rode off. He lingered, wandered, totally ignorant of what he was looking at. Almost mockingly, the empty rings defied him. Finally, '(cheered by the cry of the Hounds) [he] overtook the companie and went with them to Kynnet, where was a good Hunting dinner provided'.[1]

That was his life. A carefree young man in his early twenties, little spoiled his pleasure. There had been things to distress him. The king had been executed. His own father had died, leaving Aubrey with many responsibilities. But he was well-to-do with wealthy Royalist friends to enjoy laughter and chitchat in taverns. There was gossip about people in high places. Many of his colleagues were part of that social group and the stories they chuckled about were often scribbled down by Aubrey to become part of his *Brief Lives*. Funny, sometimes scandalous, frequently unreliable, the uncensored biographies were a ragbag of anecdotes that would become, as Aubrey remarked of his archaeological findings, 'a collection in folio of two quires of paper or more, a dust basket, some whereof are to be valued'. His was a comfortable, sociable life, visiting friends' comfortable homes, they coming to his. Like himself all of them were handsomely dressed with fine clothes, elegant cloaks, plumed hats. Aubrey had his own manservant to attend to his needs. It was a life of leisure.

He lived sometimes in London near the Inns of Court, sometimes in Oxford at Trinity and between the law and university terms he could do whatever he wished. It is possible that from Oxford he visited the Rollright Stones circle a few miles away. At an unknown date he had drawn the ring, later describing the sketch as 'the draught of them portrayed long since I doe here present to your view'.[2]

His life was not all frivolity. He was widely read, fluent in Latin and Greek, an omnivorous reader of philosophy, the natural sciences, folklore, local history, witchcraft, Classical authors. He had an innate curiosity about the past.

Those dozen casual years of early manhood after the discovery of Avebury were passed against the sombre background of the puritanical Commonwealth.

There was an advent of purgative Christianity with stern Puritans and Presbyterians alike insistently enforcing moral severity. Their Church was against the abhorrence of phallic maypoles, frivolous Morris dancing, the far-from-'innocent' country pleasures. It was the beginning of a sombre decade with its depressing certainty of moral justification.

At its very beginning in 1649 Oliver Cromwell had overseen the merciless massacre of Irish Royalists at Drogheda. In England Prince Charles had raised a Royalist Scottish army but was defeated at Worcester in 1651 and disguised as a grubby woodman sneaked past Parliamentary search parties, hid in an oak tree, counted the uncountable stones at Stonehenge and finally reached the safety of France.

Then there was a trade war with the Dutch. Parliaments were assembled and dismissed. Cromwell was never crowned king but accepted the title of Lord Protector in 1653. Puritanism stifled pleasure. Both bell-ringing and bonfires celebrating the discovery of the Gunpowder Plot and the survival of King James I were forbidden. So was blasphemy. Adultery became a capital offence.

Cromwell died in September 1658, a year that had begun with the worst storms and hurricanes known in southern England for centuries. Two years later on 25 May 1660, Prince Charles returned to England and on the 29th, his thirtieth birthday, entered London. In October a dozen regicides were executed at Charing Cross near the place where Charles I had been beheaded. The bodies of Cromwell and republican cronies were exhumed from Westminster Abbey, hanged publicly at Tyburn and buried at the foot of the gallows.

John Aubrey remembered the almost hysterical celebrations in London when people were told by the Parliamentarian, General Monck, that repression was at an end and that they would have a free Parliament after a drab decade of subordination:

> This about 7, or rather 8, as I remember, at night. Immediately a loud Holla and shout was given, all the Bells in Citie ringing and the whole Citie looked as if it had been in a flame by the Bonfires, which were prodigiously great and ran like a Traine over the Citie, and I saw some Balcones that began to be kindled. They made little Gibbetts and roasted Rumpes of Beefe. Healths to the King, Charles II, were drank in the streets by the Bonfires, even on their Knees, and this humor ran by the next night to Salisbury; where there was like joy: so to Chalke, where they made a great Bonfire on top of the hill; from hence to Blandford and Shaftesbury, and so to Land's End, and perhaps it was so all over England.[3]

'Chalke', of course, had been his home near Salisbury since 1643, and his innate inquisitiveness about the teasingly uninformative stones at Avebury led him to return there over several autumns noting the positions of stones and the shapes of the enormous rings. He could not understand them any more than the many generations before him whether Danes, Saxons or the Romans. One of them, the historian Tacitus, merely shrugged.

> Who the first inhabitants of Britain were, whether natives or immigrants, remains obscure; one must remember we are dealing with savages.

Some six hundred years later Aubrey almost agreed with him.

Aubrey's was a time not long after the Pilgrim Fathers when explorers in North America were encountering Indians whose barbaric habits were compared with the unknown customs of prehistoric people. Aubrey made similar comparisons. 'Let us imagine,' he wrote, 'what kind of countrie this was in the time of the ancient Britons,' and went on to draw parallels between Indian tribal warfare and Caesar's descriptions of British warriors of the Iron Age who were 'almost as salvage as the Beasts, whose Skins were their only rayment. They were 2 or 3 degrees I suppose less salvage than the Americans.' It was an unromanticised view of the past, a hard primitivism that contrasted favourably with some of today's credulous thinking about the life-styles of prehistoric societies.[4]

But it was guesswork. Iron Age communities had ignored the circles. To the invading Romans who had conquered those tribes remote sites like Stonehenge were little more than tourist attractions for casual visits and picnics.

The down-to-earth Saxons ploddingly ploughing and farming completely lacked curiosity about the rings. Stonehenge looked like a mass gallows, *Stan-hengen*, 'the hanging stones'. Other rings provided useful place-names as signposts for someone's land: *Afas burg*, 'Afa's place' for Avebury, *Rollandriht*, 'the land-holding of Rolla' for the Rollright Stones.

The Danes of later centuries were more superstitious, baffled and fearful of the toweringly inhuman works, calling a Cumbrian ring, Elva Plain near Keswick, *Elf-haugr*, 'the hill of the malignant elves'. Men avoided it. It can be visited safely today.

Peasants believed that stone circles and pagan places had fertilising powers. That superstition did not die with the advent of Christianity in England.

The new religion attempted to exist alongside the old, hoping to extinguish it peacefully. In AD 601 the Pope, Gregory, ordered that 'the temples of the idols among that people should on no account be destroyed. The idols are to be destroyed, but the temples themselves are to be aspersed with holy water, altars set up in them, and relics deposited there'. This more probably referred to woodland glades as meeting-places rather than stone circles but it did not matter. True or not, people still went to those unchristian centres.

When paganism persisted there was a papal change of mind. Bishops were to 'suppress the worship of idols, and destroy their shrines'. In AD 658 the Council of Nantes stated, 'As in remote places and in woodlands there stand certain stones which the people often worship, and at which vows are made, and to which oblations are offered – we decree that they all be cast down and concealed' and seven years later the East Saxons 'abandoned or destroyed the temples and altars they had erected, and opened the churches'.[5]

Seven hundred years later in the fourteenth century many stones of Avebury's rings were toppled and buried in pits. The Black Death immediately followed, killing seven-tenths of the villagers. Villagers assumed that to be inevitable, the revenge of an outraged Devil. Perhaps in a premonition of the catastrophe to follow and hoping to diminish its force only the smaller stones had been pushed over.

The Church raged. As late as AD 1560 the Synod of Argyll had a stone circle on Iona destroyed because the islanders persisted in worshipping there.

Everywhere on the Sabbath priests preached obedience to docile congregations. But from Monday to Saturday people still went nocturnally to the fecund stones, indulging in practices that celibate churchmen condemned and, sometimes, covertly, envied. The stones were evil.

Dread and destruction went together for centuries. In Brittany such stones were so blasphemous that early in the twentieth century a fanatical priest, Jacques Cotteux of Louisfert, ordered the eradication of every sign of the Devil in his parish and the ending of indecent practices at the megaliths. Standing stones were demolished. Capstones and slabs from dolmens, burial-cists, dozens of menhirs were dragged to the village by his flock. There, depaganised, they become the base of a platform on which holy statues, crosses and plaques proclaimed the triumph of Christianity.

Débris d'un culte sanguinaire	Wreckage of a bloodthirsty cult
De vieux rochers, gisaient épars	Whose ancient stones lay scattered in
au fond des champs,	the fields,
Nos bras avec amour ont fait	Our faithful arms have made this
ce calvaire,	calvary,
Oeuvre de Bretons bons croyants.	The work of God-fearing Bretons.[6]

Superstition persisted. Just decades before Cotteux and fewer than eighty miles to the west at Carnac in the Morbihan heathenism continued. Barren wives went to the great stone rows whose fertilising gift was attested by generations of mothers.

In Finistère betrothed couples stripped at midnight and rubbed their bellies on the protruding granite bosses of the gigantic Kerloas menhir.

There had been more forbearance of such practices, perhaps wonderment, in the Middle Ages. The twelfth-century monkish historian Henry of Huntingdon considered Stonehenge the Second Wonder of England whose 'stones of extraordinary size are set up as columns with others placed on top like the lintels of enormous doorways ... [but] no one can understand by what means such huge masses of stone were constructed nor for reason they were planned like that'.[7]

A near-contemporary, Geoffrey of Monmouth, was less practical. To him the mysterious monument had been manufactured by a mixture of monsters, magic and Merlin. For several credulous centuries his story was the textbook for understanding un-mortal megalithic rings. Critics were few. (Appendix C.)

One, a scribe whose name is lost, was objective but pessimistic about understanding why stone circles like the Rollright Stones had been built. '*In Oxenefordensi sunt magni lapides* ... In Oxfordshire are great stones, arranged as it were in some connection by the hand of man. But at what time this was done, or by what people, or for what memorial or significance is unknown.'[8]

It was objective but it was useless. In times when almost no one but the learned clergy could read, rural beliefs persisted, providing 'explanations' for the inexplicable. If ordinary human beings had not created those mysterious and enticing places then inhuman, probably sinful, forces had. Either giants or the Devil had set up rings of cumbrous stone that reeked so foully of the fiend that everyone knew that witch covens assembled at the circles in midnight to cast curses and spells on unfortunate villagers.

Such countrywide superstitions were understandable. In the early Middle Ages people could not believe that mortals had moved and erected such monstrous blocks. Only giants could have lifted them. No other explanation was possible and giants were constantly associated with the ponderous megaliths that had been used in prehistoric times for rows, tombs and circles. Giants from Africa were thought to have erected the back-breaking sarsens of Stonehenge.

There had been giants everywhere. In Brittany the three blocks, 'Tri-Men', at St-Gouazec had been hurled by an ogre from the miles-distant Castel-Ruffel at his eloping daughter, who had been seduced by a servant. All missed.

Scotland was filled with giants. Three stones at Tweedmuir church in Peebles marked the burial place of Jack the Giant Killer. In the Shetlands, Norwick churchyard had a stone with a hole through it that locals knew was made by a giant's thumb for tethering his horse. On the island of Hoy in the Orkneys the Dwarfie Stane had been the home of a giant and his wife, although today the shrunken size of the 'chamber' could only accommodate an unmarried elf. The stones of the Callanish circle in the Outer Hebrides were the petrified bodies of giants who had refused to accept Christianity.

Nor in England was there a lack of giants. There is a plethora of their sites in Cornwall, particularly among the 'Quoits' or portal-dolmens of Lanyon, Mulfra, Trethevy, presumably because of the impossible weight of their ponderous capstones.

The credulous medieval acceptance of the long-ago existence of superhumans was encouraged by the publication of a French book in 1366. Its writer stated that he had seen the more-than-men. As far away as

China there had been horrors, men with heads below their shoulders and some thirty-foot-high monstrous cannibals who grabbed sailors from their ships, taking two in each hand and, returning to land, 'eating them going, all raw, and all quick'.

The truth was that the book, *The Voyage and Travels of Sir John Mandeville, knight,* was no more than an ingenious compilation of accounts by genuine explorers. But that anthology of exaggerations was rapidly translated into English and just as quickly accepted as evidence that such man-eating colossi had existed in times long past and forgotten.[9]

Common sense slowly replaced credulity. John Aubrey was not merely sceptical. He was dismissive. In the north-western corner of Wiltshire at Luckington where the Bristol Avon rises is a Neolithic chambered tomb with a false entrance and four blocked side-chambers on its southern side. Aubrey saw them in 1659. 'Here were accidentally discovered since the yeare 1646, certain small Caves about 5, or 6 in number: they were about fower foot in height and 7, or 8 foot long'. The capstones had slipped. Earth had choked most of the small chambers and it was no longer possible for anyone to enter. Aubrey added:

> The curiosity of some ingenious men ... within these 40 yeares, tempted them to dig into it, and make a search for some Antick remains ... but found only a spur and some few things not worth the mentioning.

Aubrey considered the strange tomb to be a burial place of Saxon or Danish 'Heroes (or it may be Romans) slain in some Battle fought not far from the place'. Today the mound is no more than an untidy, overgrown and shapeless heap. One roofless chamber remains visible.

Luckington has another superstitious distinction. Its church has a large Norman font that used to be locked to stop witches infecting infants.

Despite its nickname Luckington had nothing to do with monsters. It is, wrote Aubrey, 'a place called the Caves, and by some the Giants Caves, according to the language of ignorance, fear, and Superstition'. Giants were nothing more than outdated superstitions.[10]

The matter-of-fact John Aubrey would learn much more about those mythical 'giants' when he was confronted by the problem of understanding Stonehenge and the mythical stories linked to it.

Giants could be discounted as the builders of stone circles. The Devil's association with the rings could not. Christians never doubted the existence of that fallen angel. Preachers persistently warned parishioners of the wiles and perils of the demon who was always attempting to inveigle them into sin. The fiend had been expelled from Heaven. He cursed his fate. And he needed their souls.

Only seventy years before Aubrey the Elizabethan playwright Christopher Marlowe, in his tragedy, *Dr Faustus*, had both appalled and terrified his audiences with the groans of Mephistopheles, servant of Lucifer, as he told Faustus who wished to sell his soul:

Why, this is hell nor am I out of it.

Thinkst thou that I, who saw the face of God

And tasted the eternal joys of heaven

Am not tormented with ten thousand hells

In being deprived of everlasting bliss?

Act I, Scene 3, lines 321-4.

Like any seventeenth-century Christian John Aubrey did not doubt the existence of that accursed angel, that resentful and revengeful fiend, the Devil.

He did not doubt him but he did speculate about his appearance. Aubrey quoted a popular belief from Sir Thomas Browne's *Vulgar Errors* that 'the Devil commonly appeareth with a cloven hoof: wherein though it seems excessively ridiculous, there may be something of truth: and the ground at first might be his frequent appearing in the shape of a goat'. The Devil really did have a cloven hoof.[11] John Aubrey went on to lament that earlier invaders had left only superstitious guesswork about stone circles. 'The Saxon Conquerors (being no Searchers into matters of Antiquity) ascribed Works great, and strange, to the Devil – e.g. The Devils ditch, Devills Arrows, Gogmagog-hills & c – or some Giants, and handed down to us only Fables.'[12]

A consolation for the belief in the existence of the Devil was that in stone-throwing contests he always lost. Challenged by a wizard to throw farther than him he flung three boulders but they fell short at Trellech, 'three-stones', near Monmouth. Local people doubted whether that hellishly contaminated windblown row could ever be uprooted by man.

In Yorkshire, angered by Christians at Aldborough, the demon threw five great pillars at their church but they fell a mile short and are now embedded in a field, the Devil's Arrows at Boroughbridge. Only three remain standing today.

The now-vandalised stones of the Devil's Quoits circle-henge at Stanton Harcourt in Oxfordshire stood there because the Devil was rebuked by God's angels for playing quoits on a Sunday. In a tantrum he flung the handful away.

He was persistently associated with stones. Near Avebury there is his chambered tomb, the Devil's Den. There once was a Devil's three-sided cove in the Kennet avenue, and another, three-sided and roofless, is in the circle itself. A huge, heavily pock-marked sarsen, the Devil's Chair, stands at Avebury's south entrance.

Miles to the south, at Stonehenge, the Devil flung a sarsen at a friar who had mocked his attempts to build the stone circle. Hitting the holy man's foot the mark can still be seen on the prostrate Stone 14 in the circle. Later the outlying so-called Friar's Heel Stone was misidentified as the bad-tempered missile.

There are other rings associated with the Devil. At midnight if one walks three times widdershins, anti-clockwise, around the ruinous recumbent stone circle at Innesmill in Moray the Devil will appear. Hence the site's popular name of 'the De'il's Stanes'[13] (see also Appendix B).

In the declining years of the Middle Ages fewer people believed that giants had constructed stone circles. Even the Devil himself changed from a vile-tempered ogre into a seductive goat-like incubus who tempted witches to join him in sexual midnight rites inside the stones. That long-held belief in witchcraft developed into paranoia in the two centuries of the Tudor and Stuart periods.

The Devil would materialise in witch covens as a rough and hairy goat. 'Not only did he assume this shape in elder [ancient] times, but commonly in latter times, especially in the place of his worship, if there be any truth in the confessions of witches.'[14]

Aubrey obtained that information from the 1580 *Demonomanie des Sorciers* of 'Bodinus', Jean Bodin, a sixteenth-century French demonologist of Angers. A Carmelite priest, professor of law, he was a fanatical persecutor of witches whom he sadistically tortured. Perhaps devil-cursed he died of bubonic plague in 1595.[15]

Witches and witch trials were commonplace in Aubrey's time. There was fear. And there was belief. John Aubrey recorded some of those misgivings.

> Tis commonly said in Germany, that the Witches doe meet in the night before the first of May upon a high Mountain, called the Blocks-burg situated in Ascanien where they together with the Devils doe dance and feast. [Local people stuck a thorn on the door of their house] believing the witches can then do them no harm

Similarly in England, Aubrey continued, 'It is a thing very common to nail horse-shoes on the thresholds of doors; which is to hinder the power of witches that enter the house.' People broke the bottoms of eggshells to prevent a witch writing her name there.[16]

It was commonly believed that witches assembled at stone circles for their blasphemies, the rings becoming centres of 'the old religion' practised by witch covens. In 1949 one was observed inside the Rollright Stones. In Aubrey's lifetime witchcraft was widespread. So were their trials. So were their night-time visits to stone circles.

Several rings are associated with witchcraft: the Rollright Stones in Oxfordshire where a witch turned an invading king to stone. Satisfied, she transformed herself into an elder tree. At Long Meg & Her Daughters, Cumberland, the outlying stone of the ring was the petrified witch. The circle consisted of her seventy daughters.

There is also a far less well-known 'witch' circle in Scotland. In 1662, just one year before Aubrey's first proper fieldwork at Avebury, the red-headed Isabel Gowdie freely confessed that for the past fifteen years she 'had been too long in the Devil's service' at Auldearn, 'the fairy dwelling'. She had denied her baptism, put one hand on her head, the other on her foot 'vowing to Satan all that lay between'.

In Nairn, not far from the pleasant town of Auldearn – significantly 'the stream of a pagan goddess' – are the remains of a prehistoric ring-cairn once surrounded by a small circle of four stones. There Gowdie had sexual intercourse with the Devil.

She was one of a coven of thirteen who raised storms, blighted crops and sickened children. In his *Letters on Demonology and Witchcraft* of 1830 Sir Walter Scott speculated that she had 'some peculiar species of lunacy'.

It has been doubted that witches met in covens of thirteen. The Scottish Gowdie contradicted that: 'Jean Mairten is Maiden of owr Coeven. Johne Younge is Officer to owr Coeven – Ther ar threttein persons in ilk Coeven.'

The court ordered her to be stripped and searched for the Devil's Mark, a third teat. It was found and 'despite her repentance and free confession she was condemned to death.'

It may be no more than necromantical coincidence but Auldearn is only a mile or two from Hardmuir, that barren stretch of land where Macbeth and Banquo are said to have encountered the three witches, the 'weird sisters' with their cauldron and its revolting contents, 'like a hell-broth boil and bubble'. Shakespeare wrote the 'Scottish play' just sixty years before Isabel Gowdie's 'confession'.[17]

Giants, the Devil, witches, none of it explained what stone circles were why or when they were built. It was no longer believed that superhuman monsters had set up the stones. The Devil may have infected them with evil but he had not built them. Witches had done no more than use the rings as midnight meeting-places. None of it offered one megalithic step forward for John Aubrey.

As always, Christianity promised solutions. The rings were punishments. They were the petrified bodies of human beings who had offended God. Giants returned. They stood stiffly chilled at Callanish in the Outer Hebrides, flesh into stone, for refusing to become Christians.

At the other end of Britain on Bodmin Moor in Cornwall the Hurlers had been over-enthusiastic men metamorphosed for continuing to play 'hurling', teams clashing brutally, sometimes lethally, against each other with heavy stakes as they tried to knock a wooden ball into a distant goal even though it was the Sabbath day. Across the Channel in Brittany the boulders of the Jardin aux Moines tomb in the legendary, ancient Brocéliande forest of Ille-et-Vilaine were monks and lords punished for their misdeeds.

That was the men. Far worse misdemeanours and more deserving of punishment had been committed by self-indulgent young maidens too intent on indulging their self-centred pleasures. And it explained a puzzle, why the stones stood in a circle. It was a circle because the sinful girls had been ring-dancing hand-in-hand past midnight on a Saturday. It had been sacrilege. They had desecrated the Sabbath. That was why there were so many circles in so many places.

There were the Merry Maidens and the Trippet Stones – the name explained itself – in Cornwall. There was a petrified wedding party at Stanton Drew in Somerset; the Nine Stones at Belstone in Devon, which still dance at noon 'when the conditions are favourable'. Far to the north in the Shetlands at Haltadans, the 'limping dance', girls had danced until the light of dawn petrified them. Across the Irish Sea at Athgreany the stones of the circle were the dancers and the outlying stone had been their musical piper. There had been impious dancing in Brittany. Similarly misguided girls had danced long past the witching hour at Les Demoiselles, Langon, in the Morbihan.

John Aubrey knew something of the fairy-stories, and was intelligently sceptical. He had read about the Cornish Hurlers which were 'fabuled to be men metamorphosed into Stone: but in truth shew a note of some victorie, or els are so set, for Land-marks and Boundaries'. An unobservant visitor saw the stones not as circles but as rows.[18]

Reaching the truth about stone circles, their whereabouts, their age, their purpose, behind all those layers of superstition and guesswork was the archaeological equivalent of being a spectator at Salome's imaginary but tantalizing dance of the seven veils.

With the fall of the first veil the myth of the non-existent giants dropped. Another slow swirling and down fell the stories of the Devil. Then, provocatively suspended for long moments there followed the dismantling of the third opalescent veil and the loss of the deceit of witchcraft and black magic.

It was an intentional suspense. A soft, slow music of blues.

With the fourth went the gauze of petrifaction. Then the fifth and the removal of impiety and the profanation of the holy day of the week. And with that veil gone came a glimpse of the reward of patience.

It would take John Aubrey many years of study between the distraction of his other interests and commitments before he would see the removal of the sixth veil to uncover the disputed age of the rings, Roman, Saxon, Danish or another unsuspected time.

The impatient waiting for the loss of the seventh veil and what followed, the reason for a stone circle, would prove the most tantalizing mystery of all. John Aubrey knew how unreliable the writings of previous scholars had been:

> What uncertaintie doe we find in Histories? They either treading too neer on the heeles of trueth that they dare not speake plaine, or els for want of intelligence (things being antiquated) become too obscure and darke.[19]

Over the years that followed he would clear away much of the obscurity.

There was a double irony in his words about 'Histories'. Realising that he could not reply upon the 'facts' offered even by reliable historians like William Camden, that only his own observations based on fieldwork would take him closer to the 'heeles of trueth' he visited sites, made notes, asked questions of local people, wrote it all down to clear away the darkness. That was his achievement.

The second irony was that those disordered notes also became 'antiquated', almost forgotten for almost three hundred years after his death. Extracts from his *Brief Lives* were frequently quoted in biographies of various celebrities and eventually were published quite substantially in 1813.

Andrew Clark's fine edition, although 'Victorianised', appeared in 1898 and there have been editions by other editors since.

Others of Aubrey's works have been printed from the nineteenth century onwards. There have been biographies, but it was not until 1980 and 1982, long after the others, that his *Monumenta Britannica, I, II*, was published.

The greatest irony of all, however, is that John Aubrey actually anticipated the long delay.

> I have since that occasionally made this following Collection, which perhaps may sometime or other fall into some Antiquary's Hands, to make a handsom Work of it. I am heartily sorry I did not set down the Antiquities of these parts sooner, for since the Time aforesaid many Things are irrecoverably lost.[20]

That was in 1659. Three years later in 1662 Aubrey's maternal grandmother, Israel Lyte, died. In the same year the free-spending Charles II married Catherine of Braganza for her dowry, and sold Dunkirk to the French for £400,000.

1662's third remarkable event was the return to England of a dead man, William Harrison, who had been murdered in 1660. His killers had been hanged. The corpse's reappearance became known as the Camden Wonder.

On 16 August 1660 Harrison, a steward in Chipping Camden, 'being about Seventy Years of Age', disappeared. He had been collecting rents around the village of Charrington for its owner and his employer, Lady Julia Hicks, who was then living with her son, the 3rd Viscount Camden, in Rutland. Those rents probably amounted to a great deal of money. Some £140 had been paid on a market day earlier in the year, a lot of money then and worth a minor fortune in modern times.

Harrison's wife had sent a servant, John Perry to search for her husband but he returned, telling her that he had looked everywhere but found no sign of the missing man.

Next morning, a poor local woman living about a mile and a half from Chipping Camden said she had discovered a hat, a comb and a neckband, slashed and bloodstained, hidden in gorse bushes. It was presumed that Harrison had been waylaid, robbed and killed.

Questioned and telling inconsistent stories Perry was doubted and on 24 May 1661 was arrested on suspicion of murder. He implicated his family, saying that his mother Joan, believed to be a witch, and his brother Richard had murdered Harrison and hidden the body.

The confession, although unsubstantiated, was sufficient to condemn the family. They were tried on 24 August, found guilty, and the three were hanged in chains on the roadside gallows standing on Broadway hill.

A year later Harrison returned.

He told a story almost unbelievable even in those credulous times. He had been waylaid by thieves, robbed and forced aboard a ship. Pirates captured it. Despite his age, Harrison was sold as a slave in the Turkish town of Smyrna.

The Oxford scholar and future friend of John Aubrey, Anthony à Wood, bought a pamphlet about the mystery. He was to meet John Aubrey probably in 1665, a date that Aubrey himself added against Wood's name in the list of his *Amici*.

Wood summarised Harrison's tale: 'Aug. 6, W., Mr. Harrison of ... supposed to be murthered 2 years agoe, came out of Turkie to his home in the country. I have the pamphlet, *A true account of the tryal and execution of Joan Perry and her two sons John and Richard Perry for the supposed murder of William Harrison gent*, published in London in 1676.' Wood added a note about what followed the execution:

John Perry hung in chaines on the same gallowes. Richard and Joane Perry were after execution taken downe and buried under the gallowes. Three dayes after a gentlewoman, pretending to understand witches, hired a man to dig up the grave that shee might search Joan's body (for the witch-mark). Shee being on horseback drew up to the grave when 'twas opened, but the horse starting at the sight of the body ran away under the gallowes and her head hitting against John's feet struck her off the horse into the grave.

   After Harrison's returne, John was taken downe and buried and Harrison's wife soon after (being a snotty, covetous Presbyterian) hung herself in her owne house. Why, the reader is to judge.

The 'Camden Wonder' probably had a mundane explanation. Harrison had absconded with the rents, abandoning his shrewish wife and going far from Chipping Camden, perhaps even to France. Two years later, money spent and penniless, he returned home without fear of arrest. The Act of Indemnity and Oblivion of August 1661 had exempted all wrongdoers, except regicides, from punishment.

He would be believed an innocent man who had been molested, robbed and forced into slavery. It was ridiculous but it could not be disproved. Nor could the three people, guiltless of his death, be resurrected from their graves on Broadway hill.[21]

Mysterious though his story was Harrison's was not the only source of speculation and gossip in 1662. Almost in reaction against the repressive years of the Commonwealth there were aristocratic duels, dissipation and debauchery. Within a year of his coronation the court of Charles II was becoming notorious for its moral laxity.

A few years later that friend of Aubrey's, Anthony à Wood, was disgusted at the behaviour there: 'To give a further character of the court, they, though they were neat and gay in their apparell, yet they were very nasty and beastly, leaving at their departure their excrements in every corner, in chimneys, studies, colehouses, cellars. Rude, rough whoremongers; vaine, empty, carelesse.'[22]

Perhaps unaware of the palace's filthy state Samuel Pepys' wife, Elizabeth, quite unusually cleansed herself for a visit in November 1660. Pepys recorded the exceptional event: 'To bed, leaving wife to wash herself ... against tomorrow to go to Court'. It might have been no more than a rub down with a cloth then a sprinkling of scent, but was more probably a considerably rarer visit to a woman's sweat-house with her servant'. She repeated the novelty five years later in February 1665.

Mrs Pepys did go to Court on 21 November 1660, and met the queen, 'a very little plain old woman', and also the Princess of Orange and Princess Henrietta 'but my wife, standing near her with two or three black patches on and well dressed, did seem to me much handsomer then she'.[23]

It is to be hoped that Pepys' wife was not offended by the uncouth manners of the Court. Even John Aubrey, busily searching for historical curiosities in the English countryside, had heard scandalous rumours about aristocratic behaviour of courtiers, like that of the attempted abduction and seduction of a young heiress by the equally young but already dissolute Henry Wilmot, 2nd Earl of Rochester.

> About 18 he stole his lady, Elizabeth Malet, a daughter and heir, a good fortune, for which I remember I sawe him a Prisoner in the Tower about 1662.

Aubrey was right. The date of that successful abduction and anticipated but frustrated seduction was Friday 26 May 1662.[24]

The teenage Miss Malet, no more than fifteen at the time, Rochester also being a minor of seventeen, was returning with her grandfather from a dinner in London when their coach was intercepted at Charing Cross by armed horsemen. The girl was transferred to another coach in which there were two ladies to reassure her. It galloped off, Rochester, the ringleader, going in another direction.

Pursued, he was caught. But with him there was no coach and no Elizabeth Malet. She was eventually found, unharmed and, perhaps, knowing her later reputation, disappointed.

Rochester was sent to the Tower of London by his former supporter, the king, but was released after a token three weeks. Pepys told his hostess of the affair:

> Then to my Lady Sandwiches, where to my shame I had not been a great while before. Here, upon my telling her a story of my Lord of Rochester's running away on Friday night last with Mrs. Mallet, the great beauty and fortune of the North, who had supped at White-hall with Mrs. Stewart and was going home to her lodgings with her grandfather, my Lord Haly, by coach, and was, at Charing-cross seized on by both horse and foot-men and forcibly taken from him and put into a coach with six horses and two women provided to receive her, and carried away. Upon immediate pursuit, my Lord of Rochester (for whom the King had spoken to the lady often, but with no success) was taken at Uxbridge; but the lady is not yet heard of, and the King mighty angry and the Lord sent to the Tower.

Rochester eventually married the young woman in 1666, and she became Countess of Rochester.[25]

Aubrey added glosses to his brief *Life*, the first about Rochester.

> Mr. Andrew Marvell (who was a good Judge of Witt) was wont to say that he was the best English Satyrist and had the right veine.[26]

Not so agreeably, Aubrey included a comment about the-then-married Elizabeth Malet. In another of his *Lives*, that of Sir John Denham, there was an accusation against Rochester's wife: Denham's 'second lady had no child: was poisoned by the hands of the Countess of Rochester, with Chocolatte'.[27]

3

1663: Charles II & two plans of Avebury

In his crowded curiosity-shop of a brain astronomy and astrology both found a place and were given equal values. When fortune favoured him, however, he could make real additions to knowledge. He was the first English archaeologist.

Lytton Strachey, 1931, 24

At the beginning of 1663 John Aubrey was almost twenty-seven years old. That year was to be a busy year for England, both at home and abroad.

It was the year when the king granted a charter to the Royal African Company, based in Cape Coast Castle, the notorious slave emporium on the Gold Coast, its directors enriching both themselves and merciless native chieftains through the lucrative traffic of transporting slaves to the American plantations. Less than half a century later both Company and the trade would suffer under the audacious plunderings of that most notorious and successful of all pirates, Bartholomew Roberts, 'Black Barty'.

1663 was also the year when the unpopular Turnpike Act was introduced, empowering local magistrates to set up profitable toll-gates, charging travellers so that good roads could be maintained.

In the same year Part One of Samuel Butler's satirical poem *Hudibras* was published. Almost a skit on Cervantes' *Don Quixote*, it had the ludicrous Sir Hudibras, a Presbyterian knight, and his servant, on worn-out horses and with rusty weapons, having ludicrous but extremely anti-puritan misadventures. The poem delighted Charles II.

In 1663 Sir William Davenant had his play, *The Siege of Rhodes*, performed. Grotesquely disfigured after syphilis destroyed his nose he was a successful poet and dramatist. He had been born in a well-run Oxford tavern, the son of a beautiful and wittily companionable mother, Jane.

William Shakespeare had often slept there on his way to and from Stratford and, rumour murmured, in her bed. 'Sir William would sometimes, when he was pleasant over a glass of wine with his most intimate friends ... say that it seemed to him that he wrote with the very spirit that Shakespeare [did], and seemed contented enough to be thought his son'. More probably he was his godson.

In 1663 the Theatre Royal opened in the fashionable Drury Lane, granted a patent by Charles II. Nell Gwynne, or Gwyn or Gwynn according to different contemporaries, lived nearby and before becoming an actress was employed to sell expensive small oranges from China to the theatre's wealthy but rakish audiences of courtiers and gallants.

It was not a ladylike profession. Tom Brown, hack writer, observed, 'Tis as hard a matter for a pretty woman to keep herself honest in a theatre, as 'tis for an apothecary to keep his treacle from the flies in hot weather, for every libertine in the audience will be buzzing about her honey-pot.'

She coped. As another king's mistress, Louise de Keroüalle, mewed, 'Anybody might have known she had been an orange wench by her swearing.'

Easy morals or not, Nell Gwynne was to become an actress the following year. In 1667 the diarist, Samuel Pepys, saw her in a play and afterwards 'I kissed her and so did my wife, and a mighty pretty soul is she', and left the theatre in a very pleasant mood, 'especially kissing of Nell'.

She became the favourite mistress of the king. The notorious rake, John Wilmot, Earl of Rochester, lauded her as 'The mistress of the Cockpit' in his lewd poem, 'Signior Dildo'.

Much more sedately, if not completely soberly, 1663 was also the year when John Aubrey was to begin his apprenticeship as an archaeologist.

It had started, almost accidentally, with other men's interests in Stonehenge.

Early in 1621 in Wiltshire when James I was visiting Wiltshire selling profitable baronetcies to ambitious country gentlemen a plan was made of Stonehenge. The king's royal architect, Inigo Jones, out of curiosity about the design, went to the circle to dig near the bases of the stones, and make a plan of what he thought to be a Roman monument. Thirty years later royalty in the form of James I's grandson intervened again in the history of Stonehenge.

Prince Charles, described by the Parliamentary bounty-hunters seeking him as 'a tall, black man, six foot two inches high', almost by accident became interested in the circle.

Early in October, 1651, he was a refugee. His Royalist army had been decisively defeated at the Battle of Worcester. The fight had been so fierce that Aubrey's friend, Edmund Wyld, told him that 'in the ditches about Worcester, where the great fight was anno 1651 (wherein the bodies of the slaine lye buried) doe grow great thistles'.

After that disaster Charles moved surreptitiously from one Royalist safe house to the next haven, staying for some days at Heale House in south Wiltshire, secreted in a 'priest's hole' concealed in the home of an overawed and over-generous provider of wine, Mrs Amphillis Hyde, a 'worthy and discreet lady'. Next day, Tuesday 7 October 1651, Charles rode out with a friend and 'rid about the downs and viewed Stonehenge and found that the King's Arithmetick gave the lie to that fabulous tale that those stones cannot be told alike twice together'.

Some years later as the king, Charles II told Pepys that 'we stayed looking upon the stones for some time with Colonel Robert Philips, reckoning and re-reckoning the stones'.[1] After more days of dangerous hide-and-seek the fugitive finally reached the safety of France and stayed there in exile for nine more years.

In England Parliaments came and went, the last of them the despised and contemptible 'Rump' of a few time-servers. Cromwell, the Lord Protector, died in September 1658, his last words reported as, 'My desire is to make what haste I may to begone'. His death was the funeral knell of the Commonwealth.

Uncertainty, hesitation, plotting, and counter-plotting followed but on a February evening in 1660 General Monk announced to the public that there was to be a truly free Parliament in England. On 25 May Prince Charles returned to England.

At his coronation on 23 April 1661 there was an ill omen. 'King Charles II was crowned.' recalled Aubrey, 'at the very conjunction of the Sun and Mercury. As the King was at Dinner in Westminster Hall, it Thundered and Lightned extreamly. The Canons and the Thunder played together.'[2]

Despite the dreary decades of the cheerless Commonwealth between 1649 and 1660 those were good years for John Aubrey. He had jovial friends, he also mixed and was welcome amongst the intelligentsia, including the great philosopher Thomas Hobbes whose biography received a long entry in *Brief Lives*. Aubrey knew artists Samuel Cooper, who painted his portrait, Wencelaus Hollar, famous for his panorama of London, David Loggan, who drew some of the earliest, reliable portrayals of Stonehenge. They were good acquaintances. There were also close friends.

In July 1660 Aubrey travelled to Ireland with one, Anthony Ettrick, for a month. Ettrick was such a good friend that in his Will Aubrey left him ten pounds for 'a piece of plate', a sapphire ring, Ralegh's *History*, and the works of Philip Comineus. Ettrick's name was the very first in the list of John Aubrey's fourteen best friends, his *Amici*.

Returning home from Ireland they were almost shipwrecked in St George's Channel off Holyhead. Characteristically, once safely ashore Aubrey took the chance to visit an ancient monument, the megalithic tomb of Trefignath:

In Anglesey, about a mile from *Holyhead* on a hill near the way that leads to Beaumaris are placed certain great rude stones much after yᵉ fashion of this draught here: for want of an Interpreter I could not learne the name of it the cavity is about five foot. I remember a mountain Beast (or two) were at Shade within it [Aug].

Years later, but recollecting his sketch of the burial place, he compared it with another inside Avebury itself. 'One of the Monuments in the Street, [like that above at Holy-head] is converted into a Pigstye, or Cow-house: as is to be seen in the Roade'.

Aubrey's notes about that tomb on the farm of Trefignath are a clear example of his persistent curiosity about such inexplicable monuments. He was not satisfied with his own brief jottings. He wrote to the Revd Robert Wynne of Corwen for further information. Wynne provided it:

a monument ... of great rough stones about 20 in number ... between four and five foot high, at the northern end whereof stand two stones on end about two yards high above ground ... They are called Y-Llêche, llech meaning a flat, thinnish stone.

There is an archaeological irony. Neither Trefignath nor the putative, long-destroyed tomb near the Avebury crossroads was a British form of prehistoric megalithic tomb. Both of them with their heavy, flat capstones and uncovered side-slabs were architecturally related to the *allées-couvertes* of Brittany. There are similar megaliths in the Loire. On his visit to France in 1664 Aubrey saw one at Bagneux and sketched it.

'About a mile from Saumur in the rode to Düay is an ancient Monument neer the high-way, called *Pierre couvert*. The perpendicular stones are, at least fouer foot high from the ground.' Anglesey, Wales, Avebury, England, Brittany and the Loire in France, no one had attempted such a synthesis before John Aubrey. Not yet thirty years of age he was already becoming an archaeologist.[3]

Yet he was living through years of political, religious and civic disturbance with problems over naval wars with the Dutch. They were national matters. Much more interesting to the popular mind were the exploits of highwaymen like the courteous Claude Duval. He became a legend, a robber to the men but a gallant to their ladies.

One story claimed that he and his band held up a coach in Hounslow Heath. A lady, travelling with her husband, instead of shrinking back in fear took out a small flute, a flageolet, and played Duval a tune. Ever the gallant French beau he invited her to perform a *coranto* with him and while one of his companions conveniently provided a musical accompaniment the two linked arms and swirled through that rapid and very lively dance.

Duval was an amusement and a dead hero. Caught drunk in London's Hole in the Wall inn, on 21 January 1670 he was hanged at Tyburn. He was twenty-seven years old.

Ladies pleaded for his reprieve, 'divers great personages of the feminine sex that on their knees made supplication for him'. He was buried in St James Church, Covent Garden. An epitaph on his tomb began:

Here lies Du Vall: Reader, if Male thou art
Look to thy Purse; if female, to thy Heart.

Highway robbery continued for years. In 1693 Samuel Pepys was waylaid on his way to Chelsea in the company of several ladies. He gave the men his valuables, merely asking them to be courteous to his companions.[4]

If John Aubrey had heard about Duval – and a satirical book had been written about the highwayman in 1670 – he made no mention of it. In that year Aubrey had already begun to sell properties to maintain his way of life. He had had happier times.

Eight years earlier in 1662 several momentous events had occurred. It was the year when Aubrey's maternal grandmother, Israel Lyte, died.[5] The second remarkable occurrence that year was the return to England of William Harrison, the man who had been murdered in 1660. 1665 was also the year when on 15 July the Royal Society received the honour of a royal charter from Charles II, an enthusiastic supporter of such intellectual interests.[6]

The Royal Society had had its beginnings as early as 1649 as an informal 'Experimental Philosophy Club' in Oxford, a group of scholars interested in philosophical discussions. The ever-enquiring John Aubrey had been in that 'Invisible College' from its beginning.

Members sometimes met in William Petty's chambers for its early meetings. Later Sir William Petty, he was 'my singular friend', wrote Aubrey, a man full of imaginative ideas such as a design for a double-bottomed boat, another for an ingenious prototype of the modern tank. Petty had been with Thomas Hobbes and other exiles in Paris, once being so impoverished, Aubrey learned, that he had existed for almost a fortnight 'on 2d or 3d of walnuts'. The diarist, John Evelyn, said he never knew 'such another genius'. Aubrey reminisced that 'he can be an excellent droll (if he haz the mind to it.)'

Petty became famous for his assiduous survey of Ireland. 'The kingdome of Ireland he hath surveyed, and that with that exactnesse ... and those that he employed for the Geometricall part were ordinary fellows, some (perhaps) foot-soldiers, that circumambulated with their box and needles, not knowing what they did'. Aubrey and Petty had probably met in 1648 when their Oxford years overlapped.

Both were members of that 'experimental philosophical clubbe', which had been instituted, according to Aubrey, by a new arrival in Oxford, Christopher Wren. Some meetings also took place in his rooms. The mathematician, Seth Ward, later Bishop of Sarum, also in Oxford, was one of the club's thirty members, as they enquired into 'natural philosophy & mixt mathematics ...' So was the remarkable scientist Robert Boyle, who foresaw aeroplanes, ships without sails and electric light.

It was from that casual but intense group of friends and colleagues that the Royal Society was formed, its first meeting taking place in the Middle Temple late in 1660. Its first president was William, 2nd Viscount Brounker, an accomplished mathematician.

Its Fellowship had grown into well over a hundred by 1663 of which hardly a third were scientists: mathematicians, astronomers, physicians and surgeons. The remainder were polymaths like John Aubrey, ever curious, ever enquiring into a multitude of subjects. He was elected a Fellow on 20 May of that year. It was Dr Walter Charleton, 'an old friend', who had recommended it.

Aubrey wrote a brief *Life* of that friend: 'Walter Charleton, M. D. borne at Shepton-Mallet in com. Somerset, 2 Feb, 1619, [actually, 1620] about 6 h. P.M., His mothere then being at supper.'

For years the Royal Society was not academically respected. Samuel Butler, author of the popular *Hudibras*, lampooned its Fellows. In another poem, *Elephant in the Moon*, he mocked their experiments and researches:

Their learned speculations
And all their constant occupations,
To measure wind, and weigh the air,
And turn a circle into a square.

There were also more unpleasant attacks. Although the king had given his royal support to the Royal Society, 'it was for many years bitterly attacked from many quarters for being irreligious, aiming at infringing the prerogatives of the Universities, and competing with or even seeking to supplant such technical foundations as the Royal College of Physicians'. When in 1671 the Society ambitiously proposed to confer degrees the universities were outraged. Anthony à Wood, already an acquaintance of Aubrey's probably for six years, fumed, 'The Universities [Oxford] look upon it as obnoxious – they desire to confer degrees – the Universitie sticke against [this].'[7]

Long before the criticisms and before meeting à Wood John Aubrey had first seen Avebury in a bitter winter, being 'wonderfully surprised at the sight of those vast stones of W^{ch} I had never heard of before'. The entire circle was so vast that to him it outdid the claustrophobic Stonehenge as much as Salisbury Cathedral utterly outmatched the parish church in

Aubrey's own village of Broad Chalke, spacious and handsome though All Saints was.

Walter Charleton of Magdalen College, Oxford, had been one of the first Fellows of the Royal Society. In 1643, fully qualified as a medical doctor, he was appointed an 'honorary' physician to Charles I at Oxford during the Civil War.

The appointment was an act of royal favour. William Harvey, 'Dr. of Physique and Chirurgery, Inventor of the Circulation of the Bloud … always very attentive' was the king's real doctor. He had been present at the Battle of Edgehill at the very beginning of the war in 1642, looking after the two young princes.

During the Commonwealth period and after the king's execution, Charleton became just as equally an 'honorary' doctor, first to the exiled prince and later when Charles became king as his 'Physician in Ordinary'.

Charleton, a man almost obsessively interested in Stonehenge, had also been to Avebury and he was taken aback when Aubrey told him that he considered that circle far more impressive than Stonehenge.

One morning in 1663 in the sprawling court of Whitehall Palace Charles II was discussing Avebury with Lord Brounker, his Navy Commissioner, and Charleton. They all belonged to the newly formed Royal Society.

Earlier that year Charleton had published his *Chorea Gigantum, The Dance of the Giants*, in which he argued that Stonehenge was a Danish monument. The book was prefaced by two extolling poems, one by the poet laureate, John Dryden. Four of its fifty-eight lines read:

Nor is this Work the least: You well may give
To *Men* new vigour, who make *Stones* to live.
Through You, the DANES (their short Dominion lost)
A longer Conquest than the *Saxons* boast.

The book had been dedicated to Charles as early as 27 August 1662 and sent to the printers the following month. The very first copy published was bound in red morocco and presented to the king with a double-crowned 'C' embossed on its sides. It is now in the British Museum.[8]

Aubrey had also dedicated his unfinished *Monumenta Britannica* to the king but Charles died many years before that jumbled mass of notes was ready to be published.

Charleton's book was greatly liked by the antiquarian William Dugdale, but John Aubrey derided Charleton's idea that Danish courtiers had stood on the lintels at Stonehenge while attending their king's coronation, the stones '(being so many foot high) would have been but fickle places for grave electors to stand on; and the wind ought to be very calm'.[9]

The king was astonished to learn from the doctor of Aubrey's opinion.

Aubrey had stated, dogmatically, that Avebury 'did as much excell Stoneheng, as a Cathedral does a Parish church'.

Charles, of course, had already seen Stonehenge when a fugitive after the Battle of Worcester and wondered how Avebury could be so much more impressive. He commanded Aubrey to come to Court. Aubrey remembered the occasion.

> His Matie admired that none of our Chorographers had taken notice of it [Avebury]: and commanded Dr. Charlton [*sic*] to bring me to him the next morning. I brought with me a draught of it donne by memorie only: but well enough resembling it with wch his Matie was pleased: gave me his hand to kisse, and commanded me to waite on him at Marleborough when he went to Bath with the Queen (wch was about a fortnight after) wch I did: and the next day, when the Court were on their Journies, his Matie left the Queen and diverted to Aubury, where I shewed him that stupendious Antiquity.[10]

And Aubrey duly arrived bringing with him a plan 'donne by memorie alone' which, ignorant of its utter inaccuracy, so interested Charles that a fortnight later, while travelling to Bath, he went out of his way to inspect Avebury with Aubrey as his guide.

It is uncertain when exactly John Aubrey was introduced to the king. In his diary Pepys recorded that Charles II returned to London from Royal Tunbridge Wells on Tuesday 11 August 1663, intending to stay for a day or two before going back to fetch the queen who had not enjoyed the cold spa waters recommended to cure her sterility. Then, on 26 August, 'the King and Court going this day out toward the Bath' the wagons and horses of the royal entourage left London in the miserable weather of that summer for the warmer springs of the Somerset spa.[11]

There is a clue that Aubrey was summoned to the king on 13 August. On Wednesday 12 August the Royal Society minutes read, 'The President [Brounker] and his Deputy being both absent this day, there was no meeting of the Society' and it may have been then that Brounker and Charleton had their conversation with the king, Aubrey attending Court next day. This date would fit well with Aubrey's 'about a fortnight after' for meeting the king in Marlborough at the end of August, and then making his plane-table survey of Avebury the following month.[12]

As always, Aubrey was courteous about the king's court, contrasting it favourably with what it had been like before Charles II's accession. The king 'was the patterne of courtesie, and first brought good Manners into Fashion in England. Till this time the Court itself was unpolished and unmannered. King James' Court was so far from being civill to woemen, that the Ladies, nay the Queen herself, could hardly pass by the King's apartment without receiving some affront'.[13]

The reality was very different. Ladies may have been more respectfully treated but behaviour – and sanitation – was worse. The court was very public, 'like a fair all day' wrote an enthusiastic royalist. The manners of the Court were foul and morals loose. Pepys commented on courtly conduct as early as August 1661. A friend had spoken openly about 'the lewdnesse and beggary of the court, which I am sorry to hear and which I am afeared will bring all to ruine again'.

And when apprentices in an outbreak of rare morality began smashing down brothels he added, 'They did ill in contenting themselves in pulling down the little bawdy-houses and did not go and pull down the great bawdy-house at Whitehall.'[14]

It was not puritanical indignation. Others were offended at the moral laxity of Charles II's court. John Evelyn, longtime friend of Aubrey's had dined in a company that included one of the king's mistresses, 'the famous beauty and errant lady, the Duchess of Mazarin (all the world knows her story)', and two royal bastards, one the Duke of Monmouth, who would lead a rebellion against his father.

Later Evelyn was at the Court itself. 'I can never forget the inexpressible luxury and profaneness, gaming, and all dissoluteness, and as it were total forgetfulness of God (it being Sunday evening) which day se'nnight I was witness of, the king sitting and toying with his concubines, Portsmouth, Cleveland, Mazarin etc., a French boy singing love-songs in that glorious gallery.'[15]

Years earlier Anthony à Wood had been outspoken about the literal filth at Whitehall, courtiers relieving themselves everywhere, chimneys, sheds, anywhere.

But the court, whether morally or hygienically, was no fouler than anywhere else in London. There was filth everywhere. And stench. The open, untended sewers down the streets reeked. Timber houses huddled dirtily together. Personal hygiene was irregular. The interiors of even well-to-do homes were no cleaner. In his *Diary* for September 1665, while staying at the lodgings of Mrs Clerke in Greenwich, Pepys wrote:

> ... so to bed, and in the night was mightily troubled with a looseness ... and feeling for a chamber pott, there was none, I having called the mayde up out of her bed, she had forgot I suppose to put one there; so I was forced in this strange house to rise and shit in the chimny twice; and so to bed and was very well again.

No doubt next morning, because of her absent-mindedness, the unfortunate maid had the task of cleansing the filthy hearth. Pepys was to use the same lodgings until the following January.[16]

Stuart England was an age long before any flush toilet. In 1592, during the reign of Elizabeth, Sir John Harington designed a water closet in time for the queen's visit but it was not copied. Almost a century later John Aubrey was to see a similar invention in a stately home at Bedington during his unprofitable *Survey of Surrey*.

> Here I saw a pretty machine to cleanse a House of Office viz. by a small stream no
> bigger than one's finger which ran into an engine made like a bit of a fire shovel which
> hung upon its centre of gravity, so that when it was full a considerable quantity of
> water fell down with some force and washed away the filth.

It would be nearer the end of the seventeenth century before any adequate contraptions were installed in great houses and only in the middle of the eighteenth before improved toilets became widespread.[17]

It is not surprising that 1665 was the year when thousands of Londoners died from another virulent outbreak of plague.

Long before Pepys' unpleasant mishap and just before their visit to the court of Charles II Charleton and Aubrey had already displayed their respective plans of Avebury to the Royal Society. On Wednesday 8 July 1663, 'it raining mighty hard all day and so did every minute of the day after'; the minutes of the Royal Society state only that 'Dr Charleton presented the Company with the Plan of the stone-Antiquity at Avebury neer Marleburgh in Wiltshire suggesting it were worth while, to dig there under a certain Triangular Stone, where he conceived would be found a Monument of some Danish King. Colonel Long and Mr. Awbrey were desired to make further inquiry into the same.'[18] There is no mention of Aubrey's plan but at the top of it, in the same hand as on Charleton's, is written 'By Mr Awbrey, July 8, 1663'. It shows that Charleton's plan was in existence at the time of his conversation with the king, perhaps drawn as early as 1658. A later date is more likely as the Avebury circles are not mentioned in his *Chorea Gigantum* of 1663.

Both Aubrey's and Charleton's plans are grotesquely inaccurate, schematic, misleading and not based on any methodical field-survey. Neither has a scale. Both show the earthwork and the rings as precise circles, Aubrey's showing Avebury as four perfectly symmetrical, concentric rings, one inside each other from the bank inwards, very different from 'this old misshapen Monument' that he was to describe only a few months later, 'not unlike Ariadne's Crowne [a broken ring of stars, the *Corona Borealis*] and no neerer to a perfect circle than is that Constellation'.[19]

Both plans show a pair of portal stones outside each entrance but neither had the Kennet or the Beckhampton avenue even though there was marginal space for at least the first stretch of them on each plan.

Why neither Aubrey's nor Charleton's early plans showed the

Kennet avenue is probably not a mystery. It depends along which road they approached Avebury. If they came directly along the east – west Marlborough to Bath coach road, riding across the downs and descending the Saxon *herepath* they may not have realised that anything existed outside the high, obstructive banks of the earthwork and simply missed the Kennet avenue.

The plans' omission of the ruinous Beckhampton avenue is equally explicable. It was not until 1722 that its few remaining stones were recognised by William Stukeley. 'Two stones lie by the parsonage-gate … Reuben Horsal remembers three stones standing in the pasture.' Others had been broken up in 1702 and 1714. Its remnants were virtually invisible. A stonehole was just visible inside the west entrance. Just outside the western ditch and bank two sarsens lay by the roadside. Beyond the Winterbourne stream were 'more fragments' and there were 'marks yet to be seen in the corn'. It is little wonder that Aubrey and Charleton missed those megalithic wraiths.

Originally the avenue had extended from Avebury's western entrance but by the seventeenth century it was virtually unrecognisable. From medieval times villagers had been toppling its convenient stones for their cottages, gates and walls and only in the countryside, at the Longstones a mile to the west did a few remain erect.

That neither Aubrey nor Charleton recognised the avenues were oversights. There were much more serious, misleading blunders in what they showed the king.

The two plans are incompatibly dissimilar. Aubrey's, apparently hurriedly sketched in pencil, shows four concentric rings of stones, drawn semi-isometrically, half standing, as they might have appeared to someone standing near the centre of the site. The North Circle Cove, marked 'A', is drawn in a similar manner, and there is a second drawing of it in the top left-hand corner. There are pairs of standing stones outside the north-north-west, east-north-east and south-south-east entrances and a pair of stones inside the north-north-west entrance. The two irregular roads that pass through Avebury are drawn as symmetrically as an Easter hot-cross bun.

Charleton's plan, in ink, differs considerably. It was more carefully drafted and obviously not drawn on site but from notes or from later memory. Mistakenly, there are two stones outside all four entrances. Within the great Outer Circle only the southern of the two inner circles is shown with a huge standing stone at its centre.

In the north-east quadrant of the earthwork there is a curious setting of three megaliths standing like the backsights and foresight of a rifle. Two are in line on an east – west axis with a gap between them. Behind that is the third stone also on an east – west axis. What may be a fourth stone lies inside the group, its base against the back stone, its triangular tip in the space between the two at the front. Aubrey had sketched the three standing but not the prostrate fourth. Ironically, research centuries later indicated that Charleton was correct. Architecturally the Cove was a symbolic representation of the entrance to a megalithic tomb, the three erect stones its portals, the stone lying in front of them one that would be erected to block access to the burial place when it was finally closed.

It is very unlikely that either man had remembered what Avebury actually looked like. Although Aubrey had known it since 1649 his reminiscence that with Colonel James Long he was 'wont to spend a week or two every Autumne at Aubury in Hawking ... our Sport was very good' added to his happy recollection of attractive shepherdesses does not suggest any commitment to single-minded fieldwork, although it was presumably because of those autumnal excursions that the Royal Society asked Aubrey and Long to make a further study of Avebury.

In the years before 1663 Aubrey had been collecting historical material but any megalithic research had been more that of a dilettante than a serious researcher. He had planned to visit Italy with friends but was discouraged by his mother.

He was also considering, 'toying with' might be more accurate, marriage. In April 1650, when his mother fell from her horse and broke her arm, he 'was a suitor to Mrs. Jane Codrington', Mrs at that time an abbreviation for 'mistress', an unmarried female. 'Miss' is the modern equivalent.

In another April a year later he had become semi-engaged to the thirteen-year-old 'incomparable good conditioned gentlewoman' Mary Wiseman to whom he gave a diamond ring but she preferred the wealthy John Saintloe, also of Broad Chalke, and married him in 1661. In 1665 and 1666 the optimistic wooer had 'severall love and lawe suites' with no matrimonial outcome. Then John Aubrey found and courted Katherina Ryves but she died in late November, 1657 'to my great losse'.

She had lived in the King's House, now Salisbury Museum, in the Close at Salisbury. She must have cared for Aubrey. In her Will she left him £350.00, and also a mourning ring for Deborah, his mother. Almost ten years later an involvement with another woman, Joan Sumner, brought him to financial ruin.

In between these half-hearted liaisons he began preparing his *Naturall History* of Wiltshire and its old churches and antiquities. He suffered riding accidents, breaking a rib in one. In February 1659 he almost killed himself in Ely Cathedral. To ease any financial problems he sold two Herefordshire properties, Stretford and Burlton, both in a somewhat casual and unbusinesslike manner. Then in 1660 he visited Ireland with Anthony Ettrick, nearly being drowned on the return voyage, and, in between these events, enjoyed himself as a man about town.[20] Time and attitude for fieldwork before 1663 must have been limited. It is apparent in his flawed 'plan' of Stonehenge.

Charleton's credentials were worse. Although between 1650 and 1660 he published ten books his knowledge and archaeological understanding of prehistoric sites were so imperfect and his adherence to traditions about their origins so fixed that he accepted that the Stiperstones, a weathered litter of quartzite boulders on the crags of a Shropshire ridge, 'consisting of great piles of stones ... [were] set up to perpetuate the renown of a fatal defeat given to the Britans by Harald', his source for this geological nonsense being the twelfth-century monkish chronicler, Giraldus Cambrensis (Gerald of Wales).

The two 'plans' of July 1663 by Aubrey and Charleton are combinations of imperfect recollection, casual observation and predetermined ideas about stone circles. With unsuspecting irony Charleton had already expressed the dangers of relying on fallible memories. 'Monuments themselves are subject to Forgetfulness, even while they remain they usually stand rather as dead objects of popular wonder, and occasions of Fables, than as certain records of Antiquity'.[21] Yet, misleading though they were, the plans did archaeology a service because, ironically, of their very blunders.

Until that time any debate about stone circles, especially Stonehenge, had been an arid and verbose exercise based on literary sources with no reference to the monuments themselves, 'a forgotten controversy conducted on forgotten lines of argument', showing 'all too clearly the limitations of the approach – wholly literary, and appealing to written authorities without ever questioning their reliability, or turning again to the monument itself in an empirical return to the original sources'.[22]

September 1663 changed that for John Aubrey. Although Camden and others had preceded him, he was the first to undertake a systematically objective study of circles and other megalithic monuments, realising that fieldwork was the only practical method of understanding their purpose and age. He must have been taken aback to realise how much his plan of Avebury 'donne by memorie' differed from reality, how much he had taken for granted, relying on classical writers rather than on his own observations. Shortly, he began his *Monumenta Britannica*, an invaluable assemblage of field-notes, sketches and plans of ancient structures accumulated between 1665 and the 1690s.

It was the beginning of a great tradition of which he was the forerunner. 'And though this be writt, as I rode, a gallop, yet the novelty of it, and the faithfulness of the delivery, may make some amends for the un-correctness of the Stile.'[23]

That September Aubrey made a plane-table survey of Avebury planning it as the irregular monument that it really was. That survey was entirely different from the travesty that he had shown the king. Despite the obstacles of houses, hedges, roads and trees his plan is a good one, far better for the shape of the bank, the ditch and the northern setting than Stukeley's later more schematic representation.

Following this, 'in obedience to his Majestie's command', Aubrey started to write his *Monumenta Britannica*, a description of ancient remains: stone circles, megalithic tombs, long and round barrows, standing stones and earthworks. The beginning of a manuscript to be compiled over more than thirty years, meant that he was about to become both an archaeologist and, unknowingly, much later, a prehistorian.

4

1663: September 1663
Aubrey's field-work at Avebury

Kenet riseth northe northe west at Selbiri Hille bottom, where by hathe be camps and sepultures of men of warre, as at Aibiri a myle of, and in dyvers placis of the playne.

John Leland, Itinerary, V, Pt. X, c. 1543

In September following I surveyd that old Monument of Aubury with a plain-table, and afterwards tooke a Review of Stoneheng: and then I composed this following Discourse in obedience to his Maties command: and presented it to Him: wch he commanded me to put in print.

When John Aubrey returned to Avebury in September 1663, it was no more than a quiet village, a backwater, yet with 'the greatest, most considerable and ye least ruinated of any of this kind in the British Isle. It is very strange that so [such] eminent an Antiquitie should lie so long unregarded'.[1]

Aubrey was wrong. So far from 'ye least ruinated' it was one of the worst. Three hundred years earlier it had been wrecked by Christianity attempting to eradicate paganism. In the Middle Ages paganism lived in every ancient stone.

The Devil was everywhere around Avebury. His 'Chair' was the enormous sarsen standing at Avebury's south entrance. The three stones that once formed the Kennet cove were the Devil's Quoits. The stones inside the megalithic horseshoe of the north 'circle' were the Devil's Brand-Irons. His 'Den' was the chambered tomb in Clatford Bottom near Marlborough. Silbury Hill was reputed to have been made by the Devil dropping a spadeful of earth.

In the fourteenth century Christians decided to destroy the pagan circle.

It was not a sudden medieval fear. Men had always avoided living amongst the stones. Outside the bank and ditch houses straggled down the slope that led to the erratic waters of the Winterbourne stream. The manor house stood outside the north-west corner of the earthwork. When Saxons built Avebury's first church they chose a place a good walk from the devilish stones. Some of its old windows survive in the nave. The church's Norman font is carved with a mitred bishop using his crozier to impale the winged serpent that had tempted Adam and Eve to stray from God. Avebury was an evil place.

By the early fourteenth century the Church was commanding those sinfully tempting stones to be removed. Avebury's priest appointed himself the overseer of God's work.

Reluctant villagers started destroying the circles. Stones were toppled. Pits were dug in the chalky ground, stones pushed in and covered so tidily with rubble that they were almost undetectable.

Not one stone was smashed. Each was handled almost reverently, buried undamaged, doing God's work without outraging the Devil.

Bits of broken pottery were accidentally buried with the sarsens. None is later than the early fourteenth century. It is probable that the destruction began some years after 1300. When a stonehole in the Kennet avenue was excavated in the twentieth century a badly worn Short Cross silver penny, minted between 1222 and 1237, was found in the hole, perhaps already sixty or seventy years old.[2]

It is unlikely that the circles were attacked to make room for ploughing. If space were needed it would have been more sensible to drag the stones into the ditch. Nor need they have been so neatly concealed.

Christianity is more persuasive. It is easy to visualise the villagers, perhaps at the time of the yearly fair, apprehensively overthrowing the monstrous stones, encouraged by their priests, Thomas Mayn who died in 1319 and then John de Hoby, then Robert Durelyng de Faireford.

Yearly the 'purification' continued. Stones were tumbled. The thick centre stone of the south circle, the fancifully, much – later-nicknamed 'Obelisk', was pushed over. Of the hundred stones of the outer circle long segments were buried. So were many avenue stones. It was the smaller ones that were chosen first. Whether giants like those at the north and south entrances could have been manhandled safely is questionable.

One can imagine those superstitious peasants, small dark men, muttering that it was ill fortune to disturb the stones. Retribution could be expected.

With such dreads it is less surprising that the stone-felling ceased than that it had ever begun. And after the appalling visitation of the Black Death in the winter of 1349 when nearly half the population of England was infected and died agonisingly of the plague there were too few people left in Avebury. Even Avebury's priest, Robert Durelyng de Faireford, may have succumbed. For two hundred years the village slept.

The remaining stones were left. Village life returned to drudgery: herding cattle, digging cess-pits inside the circles, quarrying marl for cottage walls. The former place-names, *Aveberig* and *Avesenesbur'*, became *Abury*.

Aubrey joked about the name. 'As to the Etymologie of the *word*

Aubury it is vulgarly called *Abury*: and is writt of late times by ignorant Scribes *Auebury*; (the 'e' quiescent being interposed after yᵉ old Fashion) .... I see some Reader smile to himselfe, thinking how I have strained this Towne (Place) to be of my owne Name: not heeding that there is a letter's difference, which quite alters the Signification of the words. For Aubery [*Alberis*] is a Christian name'.[3]

A tower was added to the church. *Aibyri* or *Aubury*, the village's optional names, remained in use until as late as 1689 when 'Avebury' replaced them.[4] A memorial brass there with a half-figure of a priest, once in Berwick Bassett church, records: 'William Bayly lies here, so it pleases the Lord. He left 100 shillings to the Church for ever. He died 9 November, 1427.' In contrast to that devout generosity one of his descendants profitably shattered stones at Avebury three centuries later. A sarsen in the cross-street, 'containing 20 loads', built the dining-room of the inn.[5]

It was not until the mid-sixteenth century that Avebury was recognised as an antiquity. John Leland, Henry VIII's chaplain and librarian, on his famous tour of England searching for monastic documents, rode through Wiltshire around 1541 and came to the Avebury district, riding from Marlborough westwards past the headwaters of the River Kennet. 'Kenet risethe Northe Northe West at *Selberi* Hille Botom, where by hathe be Camps and Sepultures of Men of Warre, as at Aibyri a Myle of, and in divers placis of the Playne. This *Selbiri* Hille is about a 5. Miles from *Marlberi*.' Although this referred only to the earthwork Avebury had become an ancient monument.[6]

Near Marlborough in 1634 Sir John Harington, son of the hygienic 'water closet' Harington, saw 'great stones of unmeasurable bignesse and number that lie scattered about the place', a description which probably was of the sarsens on the Marlborough Downs rather than Avebury itself.[7]

Yet no one thought Avebury's stones important. William Camden, that perceptive Elizabethan antiquarian who published the first general guide to Britain's antiquities in his Latin *Britannia,* did not mention Avebury in the first edition of 1586. Even the first English translation, *Britain,* of 1610 said only:

Within one mile of *Selburie* is *Aiburie*, an up-landish village, built in an old Campe, as it seemeth, but of no large compasse, for it is environed with a faire trench, and hath foure gappes as gates, in two of the which stand huge Stones as jambes, but so rude, that they seeme rather naturall than artificiall, of which sort, there are some other in the said village.

To the south around Silbury 'a round hill' and a burial place, added

Camden, there were '*Burrowes* they call them and *Barrowes*, raised happily in memorial of Souldiers there slaine. For bones are found in them ... and Silbury was raised if not by the Romans, then certainly the Saxons'.

 Camden also mentioned the great man-made hillock of the Marlborough Mound without naming it or realising that it was a semi-miniature imitation of Silbury Hill. Camden did ridicule the superstition that the name 'Marlborough' was a derivation of 'the burial mound of Merlin'.[8]

It was not until 1695 when another edition of his *Britannia*, again in English, was published that a description of Avebury's stone circles were first put into print.

> About half a mile from Silbury, is Aubury, a monument more considerable in it self, than known to the world ... It is environ'd with an extraordinary Vallum or Rampart, as great and as high as that at Winchester, and within it is a graff [ditch] of a depth and breadth proportionate. For a village of the same name being built within the circumference of it, and (by the by) out of it's stones too; [the first reference to destruction for material for houses] what by gardens, orchards, inclosures, and such like, the prospect is so interrupted, that 'tis very hard to discover the form of it.

The deep ditch was inside the bank 'from which Mr. Aubrey infers that it could not be design'd for a fortification, because then the Graff would have been on the outside. The graff has been surrounded all along the edge of it, with large stones pitch'd on end, most of which are now taken away; but some marks remaining give one the liberty to guess they stood quite round.'[9]

The marginal note to this entry explains who the author was, this archaeological observer of stoneholes, the discoverer of the circles: '*Aubury*. Aubr. Monument. Britan. MS.' The description had been taken from a manuscript, the *Monumenta Britannica* of John Aubrey which itself was not to be published until 1980-82 almost three centuries later than that edition of the *Britannia*.

Today Aubrey is best remembered as the writer of a compilation of often-witty biographies, his *Brief Lives*. 'William Sanderson dyd at Whitehall ... went out like a spent candle.' Or of Archbishop George Abbot, 'Old Nightingale, his servant, weepes when he talkes of him. Everyone that knew, loved him'. And sometimes Aubrey knew a little and needed more as appeared in his note about Francis Anthony, 'He had a sonne who wrote something, I think (*quaere* Mt. Littlebury); and a daughter married to ... Montague.'

Aubrey also had the gift of summarising a lifetime in a short sentence,

'Madam Curtin, a good fortune of *3000li.* [£], daughter to Sir William Curtin, the great merchant, lately married her footman, who, not long after marriage, beates her, gets her money, and ran away.'[10]

But Aubrey was not merely an idle gossip. He was inquisitive about almost everything and that curiosity he extended magnificently to the study of antiquities. He was, without question, the first great English fieldworker and archaeologist. That invaluable scholarly career began, quite by accident, at Avebury.

It had been in a cold January that Aubrey first saw the stones. Fourteen years later Charles II became so interested by Aubrey's enthusiasm for the great circle that a fortnight later, while travelling to Bath, he went out of his way to inspect Avebury with Aubrey as his guide.

The monument's north 'circle' and its Cove at that time stood behind the long-since-demolished Catherine Wheel Inn, and the king rode through its yard to see the ring, so exciting the villagers that their descendants told the antiquary, William Stukeley, about it sixty years later during his detailed survey of Avebury.

It was because of that royal visit of 1663 and of his own realisation of how poor his 'plan' had been that in September Aubrey made a plane-table survey of 'this old ill-shapen Monument'. The result was completely different from the travesty he had shown the king.

Despite the obstacles of houses, hedges and trees his plan is good, far better for the shape of the bank, the ditch and the northern setting than Stukeley's later more schematic representation.

Following that second, more conscientious survey that September, 'in obedience to his Majestie's command', Aubrey started to write his *Monumenta Britannica*, that disordered compilation of ancient remains, stone circles, megalithic tombs, long and round barrows, and earthworks.

Although much of his own physical fieldwork was completed by 1670 he added to his own records by writing to correspondents as far away as Aberdeen until the 1690s.

For Avebury itself there were informants living nearby: John Brinsden and Walter Sloper. There was also the visitor to Avebury, Dr Robert Toope, searching for medicinal elixirs for his patients in Bath.

Brinsden was a reliable helper. 'Parson Brunsdon' was the vicar of Winterbourne Monkton, a village of long-thatched houses a mile north of Avebury. Aubrey remembered that the clergyman possessed a 'Thigh-bone and two pieces of Urnes' dug out of a Ridgeway round barrow on the land of Walter Sloper. Brinsden was one of the first to watch the destruction by fire of Avebury's sarsens.

Villagers were already smashing circle stones.

I have *verbum sacerdotis*, for it, that these mighty stones, (as hard as marble), may be broken in what part of them you please without any great trouble: sc, Make a fire on that line of the stone, where you would have it crack; and after the Stone is well heated, draw over a line with cold water, & immediately give a knock with a Smyth's sledge, and it will break like the Collets at the Glass house.

Twenty years earlier in 1644 the cavalier Richard Symonds had noticed people on Fyfield Down breaking the 'grey pibble stone of great bignes' for building material.

In Brinsden's parish were the sites of the chambered tombs of the Shelving Stones and Mill Barrow. 'In the same vicinity [were] over 30 other skeletons ... all or mostly in circular cists covered with sarsen slabs ... 3 of the men's skulls were cleft prob. before death.' In such sepulchral ground it is fitting that Brinsden himself chose to be buried under a sarsen at the east end of his church. Even more fittingly the slab was a megalith from the ruinous Mill Barrow upon which a windmill had stood. The stone is still there.[11]

Another of Aubrey's informants, Walter Sloper, was an attorney of St Clement's Inn. Like Brinsden he lived at Winterbourne Monkton. Sloper told him of the fall of a great sarsen outside Avebury's southern entrance.

He was related to John Sloper, vicar of Broad Chalke where Aubrey had a farm. In 1649, a month after he chanced upon Avebury, Aubrey was godfather to John Sloper's son. Of Sloper's other child, Abigail, he wrote a succinct note which he considerately omitted from his *Brief Lives*, 'Pride; Lechery; ungratefull to her father; maried; runne distracted; recovered.'[12]

It was near the autumnal equinox when Aubrey began his second, much more methodical survey at Avebury, a time of the year when from dawn to dusk he would have had twelve hours of daylight to make his plan.

'In September following I surveyd that old Monument of *Aubury* with a plain-table,' he wrote as though that had been an uncomplicated matter. It had not. In itself the task would demand three or four days' work.

For the work he needed a plane-table, a square, flat board set on a detachable tripod. It had to be levelled perfectly with a spirit level to ensure that any planned angle was correct. For that a reliable magnetic compass was needed and also an alidade, a sighting-device for Aubrey to peer through a narrow slit and, with compass and ruler, measure the angle to his target. He needed sturdy sheets of paper, quills, pencil, and a flask of ink.

Distances had to be measured. Several linked lengths, chains of sixty-six feet in length, were required with helpful and no doubt well-remunerated villagers extending them across uneven ground in lines pulled as straight as possible from the surveying-table outwards. (For readers more arithmetically comfortable with the artificial metric system the metric equivalent of a chain is 20.1 m. There were ten chains, 201 m, to a furlong, the traditional length of a furrow in fields of the medieval Three-Field System).

For his planning Aubrey needed a servant to take care of the equipment and supervise the local assistants. And, very important and also very difficult, a place had to be chosen as near to the centre of the site as possible to avoid constant changes of position. East – west was easy because the road through the village passed directly across the site towards the eastern entrance where the *here-path* had led upwards to the Marlborough Downs.

North – south was more demanding. There were two right-angle bends in the highway from Swindon to Devizes. Because large stones stood obstructively in each direction the choice of positioning the plane-table was limited. Somewhere at a corner where the roads crossed was preferable, very dangerous today with cars, vans and lorries streaming around the bends but easier centuries ago with only an occasional rider and slow farm-cart to interrupt the survey.

There was, as always, a further problem. During the years since the superstitious Middle Ages people had become less fearful of building inside Avebury. Now there were houses, barns, byres and sheds. Aubrey described the handicaps.

> By reason of the crosse-streetes, Houses, Gardens, orchards and severall small Closes; and the Fractures made in this Antiquity for the building of those Houses; it was no very easy Taske for me to to trace the Vestigia [remains], and so to make this Survey. Wherefore I have distempestred and un-projected [omitted from] the Scheme of the Enclosure, and Houses &c: w[ch] are altogether foreigne to this antiquity, and would have clouded and darkned the reall Designe. The crosse-street within that Monument, was made in process of time for the convenience of the Rodes.

He added, 'The Houses are built of the Frustrum's of those huge Stones, which they invade with great Sledges, for hereabout are no other stones to be found (except Flints).'[13]

Stimulated by his work at Avebury and always interested in other old places Aubrey also visited nearby monuments like the West Kennet chambered tomb to the south and other megalithic burial places, some later uprooted, like the Shelving Stones and the nearby imposing Mill Barrow.[14]

Aubrey was a pioneer and many of his plans and descriptions were made before avaricious stone-breakers obliterated wide sections of Avebury, not to build their own homes but to jerry-build others for profit. Aubrey's plans show stones in the circles that had gone fifty years later, thirteen out of thirty-one in the outer circle.

Avebury was being systematically dismantled and the demolition continued for years after Aubrey's fieldwork there. In 1694 what would now be termed a 'cowboy' builder, Walter Stretch, smashed a stone the outer ring of the north setting, standing in the main street. Already many stones had been taken from the south circle. In 1663 Aubrey had noted about twenty stones standing there whereas Stukeley in 1724 found only five.

By the beginning of the eighteenth century most of the stones at the south-east of the outer circle and other sarsens were uprooted from the south circle. By 1706 all the pillars of the north setting had fallen. One at the crossroads became a market-day fish-stall. By 1710 many of the stones of the south circle had been destroyed. The north-east arc of the outer circle was taken away and other stones to the west had been 'broke off to the stumps'. By 1719 when William Stukeley first saw Avebury it was a wreck.

Had it not been for his researches and Aubrey's earlier it would be impossible now to write confidently about Avebury. Aubrey discovered it. Stukeley wrote its chronicles. He heard of Avebury almost by chance. The father of his friend Roger Gale had copied parts of Aubrey's still unpublished *Monumenta Britannica* and from them Stukeley made his own transcription in December 1718. Years later in his journal he lied: 'In 1718 Mr. Roger and Sam. Gale and I took a journey, through my eager desire, to view Avebury, an antiquity altogether unknown.'

The deception took all credit away from Aubrey even though Stukeley only visited Avebury because of Aubrey's unpublished description. But it was consistent with the ungenerous attitude he had towards Aubrey. He even gave the wrong date for his journey, quite deliberately, to enhance his 'discovery'. His first visit was not until 1719, months after he had entered Aubrey's account in his own 'Commonplace Book'.

Between 1719 and 1724 he went to Avebury six times, sometimes staying for two or three weeks at the Catherine Wheel Inn, plane-tabling, taking magnetic bearings, making good plans of the circles.

Years before William Stukeley, archaeologist and fantasist, John Aubrey, hindered though he was by the clutter inside the earthwork, had planned the bank and ditch and the outer circle including a run of stones at the south which were soon dismantled for building material.

The base of the bank and the width of the internal ditch, he recorded, were of the same length, 'fower perches or 66'. The ditch had originally been narrower. Centuries of weathering had eroded the chalk both of the bank and the ditch. The bank's top had been worn away by rain and frost.

The lips of the ditch had collapsed, widening its breadth but reducing its depth.

Similar disruptions, added to by human interference, had affected the enormous ring that stood inside the ditch's inner edge.

Round about the Graffe [ditch] (sc. on the edge or border of it,) are pitcht on end huge Stones, as big, or rather bigger that those at Stoneheng; but rude, and unhewen as they are drawn out of the earth: whereas those at Stoneheng are roughly-hewen. Most of the stones thus pitched on end, are gone, (taken away); only here and there doe still remain some curvilinear Segments; but by those one may boldly guesse (conclude), that heretofore they stood quite round about, like a Corona (Crowne).[15]

Aubrey's improved plan showed two inner settings north and south of each other, the southern three-quarters of a true circle lacking its northern arc. The northern is more equivocal. He recorded it in the shape of a horseshoe rather than a regular ring. Three centuries later it appeared that he was correct.

When William Stukeley, planned the disrupted setting, he presumed that a long gap in its southern arc had formerly been occupied by a run of stones, and it became an accepted truth that that segment of Avebury with its great inner Cove had been a circle.

Doubts were expressed only when a geo-physical survey of the late 1980s detected grassed-over stoneholes seemingly forming a shape similar to an open-mouthed horseshoe rather than a complete ring.

The report of 1991 stated:

The N 'circle' was not necessarily geometrically exact and may have had a centre significantly W of that usually proposed. It is therefore at least possible that Aubrey's plan 'A' version of this area [that printed in the *Monumenta Britannica, I* of 1980] may yet turn out to be the most accurate of all – conceptually, if not in detail!

It was grudging and conditional but it was revealing.[16]

Megalithic 'horseshoes' are rare in Britain and Ireland but common in prehistoric Brittany with its megalithic *fers-à-cheval*; the one at Avebury hints at a version of Breton architecture, a suggestion strengthened by Aubrey's own sketch of what resembles a Breton *allée-couverte* standing just south of the Catherine Wheel Inn. That monument had been dismantled and broken up fifty years later. Stukeley never saw it. Today the controversial 'tomb' has gone.[17]

Neither the *fer-à-cheval* nor the *allée-couverte* demands a belief in a violent invasion from Brittany nor even a peaceful settlement of friendly foreigners. Cross-channel influences provide a simpler explanation.

Although Aubrey's diameters of both the internal south and the north settings differ too much as did his dimensions for the interior of Avebury which was rather too small, he did include an irreplaceable sketch of the three stones called the Cove inside the north setting. It had resembled an unroofed sentry-box. Not long afterwards one of the stones fell and was split up. There had been other isolated Coves, one to the west where the Beckhampton avenue stretched, and another to the south against the Kennet avenue.

Coves, possibly representing the stone side-chambers of tombs, may have been architectural intermediaries between the abandonment of those tombs and the development of unroofed circles.

In his first, hurried plan, the one that he had shown to the king, Aubrey had drawn the Cove inside Avebury as three stones apparently standing alongside each other. Later, following his survey, he showed the same three stones but rearranged with one in front of the others.

Charleton's plan, however, was possibly more accurate, depicting a back-slab with two others in front of it and a fourth stone lying between them. His appended Notes described them.

> G. The three high stones standing in ye North-east quadrant of the greater Circle, in a Triangle.
>
> J. a Triangular stone, of vast magnitude, lying flat on ye ground, but, (probably) at first impos'd on ye heads of ye other three, in manner of an Architrave.[18]

If his plan is correct then what he had seen was an imitation of a chambered tomb's prostrate blocking stone, laid there until ready for erection when the tomb finally closed.

The Cove may have been Avebury's earliest megalithic feature standing isolated on the site before first the south circle was set up, followed by the horseshoe, then the outer ring, the bank and ditch and, finally, the two avenues, one extending towards the River Kennet and up Overton Hill, the other leading eastwards towards the Cove known as Adam & Eve beyond to what remains an unknown terminus.

The process that created today's Avebury may have taken a thousand years.

Aubrey made a schematic plan of the Kennet avenue. Rain prevented him from measuring it. But, riding between the stones in his lace and ruffles, he thought it had been for processions going to the stone circle on Overton Hill. Slight though his records are, sometimes imprecise, they show an awareness of the importance of ordinary things unusual in antiquarians before him.

He wrote quite a long description of that avenue.

> The great Stone at Aubury's southern [?] end, where this Walke begins, fell down in

Autumne 1684, and broke in two, or three pieces: it stood but two foot deep in the earth. From Mr. Walt. Sloper of Mounckton, Attorney.

From the south entrance [ ] runnes a Solemne Walke, sc. with (of) Stones pitched on end about fower foot high - + , wch goes as far as Kynet [wch is (at least) a measured mile from Aubury] and from Kynet is turned with a right angle eastward crossing the River, and ascends up the hill to another Monument of the same kind [but less] as in Plate II.

That anonymous ring was to be pseudo-romantically called 'the Sanctuary' by William Stukeley.

The distance of the stones in this Walk, and the breadth of it, is much about the distance of a noble Walk of Trees of that length: and very probable this Walke was made for Processions.

Perhaps at this angular Turning, might be the Celle [or Convent] of the Priests belonging to these Temples: to be sure they did not dwell far from them: and Kynet their Habitations might happily be the occasion of the rise of this Village.[19]

Aubrey left some puzzles. He made no mention of the Beckhampton avenue, and when he referred to what has since been presumed to be the Beckhampton Cove on the avenue 'three huge upright stones ... called the Devill's Coytes', Aubrey unambiguously placed them to the south not the east of Avebury, the third of Avebury's Coves, that in the Kennet avenue. Presumably he was unaware of the remnants of an avenue and distant Cove at Beckhampton.

Aubrey's method of investigating the past, his comparisons, his collection of seemingly trivial data were important. Misleading though they were, the plans did archaeology a service because, ironically, of their very blunders. Until that time any debate about stone circles, especially Stonehenge, had been valueless, verbose exercises based on literary sources with no reference to what could be seen.

September 1663 changed that for John Aubrey. Although Camden and others had preceded him, he was the first to undertake a systematic study of circles and other megalithic monuments, realising that fieldwork was the only practical method of understanding their purpose and age.

The stones were there and could be plotted but there was no information coming from them. They could not tell him how long ago men had raised them, or who those men were, or what the various settings meant. Aubrey planned them but he knew nothing about them and no earlier historian or traveller had anything to say. The stones stayed as they had been, in a long silence with only folk tales of ogres, battles, Holy Grails and witchcraft to explain them. Aubrey sighed at the lack of any reliable history.

> The Saxon Conquerors (being no Searchers into matter of Antiquitie) ascribed Works great, and strange, to the Devil, or some giants, and handed down to us only Fables.[20]

He must have been taken aback to realise how much his plan of Avebury 'donne by memorie' differed from reality, how much he had taken for granted, relying on classical writers rather than on his own observations. Shortly, he began his *Monumenta Britannica*, that invaluable assemblage of field-notes, sketches and plans, gathered between 1665 and the 1690s.

> These Antiquities, [wrote Aubrey], are so old that no Bookes doe reach them. These Remaynes are *tamquam tabulata naufragii* (like fragments of a Shipwreck) that after the Revolution of so many yeares and governments have escaped the teeth of Time and [which are more dangerous] the hands of mistaken zeale, so that the retrieving of these forgotten things from oblivion in some sort resembles the Art of a Conjurer who makes those walke and appeare that have layen in their graves many hundreds of yeares: and represents to the eie, the places, Customs and Fashions that were of old Time.[21]

That 'retreiving' often needed the assistance of others. A third person to help Aubrey was Dr Robert Toope who had a medical practice in Bath. In 1678 he was pharmaceutically plundering the ground around the Overton Hill circle searching for human bones that he could pulverise into potions for his patients.

Aubrey transcribed Toope's letter of heavily looped writing of 1 December 1685. Its information was invaluable when Aubrey began examining the circle on Overton Hill, one of the ancient monuments in the neighbourhood of Avebury.[22]

5

1664: Local megalithic tombs & standing stones

This tradition of field archaeology is one which has been built up over the centuries. It began with exact observers and painstaking travellers to the past like John Aubrey …

Glyn Daniel, *The Idea of Prehistory*, 1962, 72

To John Aubrey it had been a struggle. The past is not just a foreign country, it is an Eldorado, a city of gold that can never be rediscovered. But Aubrey, like thousands before him, and after, persisted.

Lewis Carroll observed that if people did not know where they were going then any road would take them there. Aubrey wondered and wandered along forgotten lanes with no sign-posts except for his curiosity and persistence.

His fieldwork at Avebury lured him to look for other nearby monuments: burial places; standing stones; little-known circles. In the years around 1664 he had to search for them. No one had ever made even the briefest of lists about those uninteresting relics of an unknown past.

Also in 1664, even four long years after the Restoration, there was still unrest in England over the differing religious beliefs. It was an uneasy time. In May that year the Conventicle Act banned all unauthorised religious meetings of more than five people. In August Jews in England were assured of royal protection as long as they did 'demean themselves peaceably and quietly'.

With the whimsies of a rakish royal Court periwigs became fashionable, short artificially woven pads of human hair to cover baldness or to be fashionable. Samuel Pepys had had one made a year earlier and wore one continually from 1665 onwards. Such small head-pieces were to develop into the shoulder-length full-bottomed wigs of the reign of Queen Anne.

The mid-seventeenth century had also been a remarkable period for the interlinking of three well-known men: John Aubrey, John Evelyn and Samuel Pepys.

For the three men the year 1664 linked them through two deaths and a near-lethal accident. It was the year when Pepys' brother Tom died on 15 March. Eleven days later Evelyn's son, Richard, also died unexpectedly, a baby just one month old. 'We suspected,' wrote Evelyn sadly, 'the nurse had over-laid him.' In the same year, on the Monday after Christmas, John Aubrey 'was in danger to be spoiled by my horse, and the same day received *laesio in testiculo*', an agonising injury to his testicles, 'which was like to have been fatall. *Quaere* R. Wiseman *quando* – when? I believe 1664.'[1]

Wiseman was a new servant who would be employed by Aubrey on his return from a sadly spoiled visit to France in October.

France was a strange choice to be the first country to explore in Europe. Aubrey himself later agreed with that having read Richard Lassels' book of 1670, *The Voyage of Italy: or a Compleat Iourney through Italy*. For young gentlemen going abroad, Lassels advised, 'tis the best way to begin with Holland and Germany or Switzerland and return by Italy and France, for the frippery of France, especially Paris, would too much allure them to vanity, and make them disrelish their more serious and useful studies.' Aubrey added 'Mr. Lassalls [sic] has writ the best directions for European travel', probably recalling his own somewhat disappointing experiences in France some time earlier.[2]

Six years earlier, and unusually for such a gregarious person, Aubrey went abroad for the first time entirely on his own, going to Calais, then on to Paris where he lodged in the Sorbonne. Thomas Hobbes, his longtime friend since the years when Aubrey had been a small boy, wrote him a letter addressed to 'Monsieur Aubray, Gentilhomme Onglais, Ches Monsieur de Houlle dans le Cloistre de St. Julien le pouvre au Riche d'or devant la Fontaine de Severine pres du Chattelet'.[3]

Despite the rabid mid-nineteenth century architectural depredations of Baron George-Eugène Haussman, who 'sanitised' much of the medieval Sorbonne in southern Paris and elsewhere in the city by displacing 25,000 people and demolishing ninety streets, St Julien's cramped church is still there in glimpsing distance of Notre-Dame on the Île-de-la-Cité in the Seine.

In 1462, almost exactly two hundred years before John Aubrey's visit and only a few minutes from the church, François Villon, petty thief and poetical genius, had been an innocent onlooker at a scuffle when a drunken associate, jeering at scribes copying manuscripts, had wounded the indignant proprietor. No property was damaged, nothing was stolen but Villon's criminal past condemned him to death. He was reprieved, exiled and vanished from history.

From Aubrey's lodging the affray had occurred less than a quarter of a mile away, down the short and narrow rue des Parcheminières, onto the now 'modernised' rue de la Harpe and then just a few steps to the scrivener's opposite the Mule tavern. It has all gone. The 'tourist' Restaurant Villon on the nearby boulevard St Germain is one of the very few architectural indications that François Villon ever lived in Paris.[4]

From Paris Aubrey went on to Tours and then Orléans. His friend John Evelyn disapproved of that city. He spoke well of its architecture and elegant statuary but considered it a city of very strong wine much frequented by Germans 'which causes the English to make no long sojourn here, except such as can drink and debauch'.[5]

How Aubrey reached that city and how long it took him is unknown. No details of his excursion exist. From mid-June to mid-October would have occupied some eighteen weeks and an assumed fortnight's stay in each of the three cities would have taken six of them.

A round journey from Calais to Paris, Tours, Orléans and back to Calais was a distance of more than seven hundred miles. For travel in a foreign country horses could be hired from inn to inn, taking riders some ten to twenty miles a day depending on the weather and the state of the poorly maintained roads. Fifty days may have been spent on horseback, another forty in the three cities leaving some thirty more for diversions.

Probably Aubrey had time to satisfy his curiosity about the mysterious distant past by digressing to some ancient monuments in France that he had heard of, one of them being the megalithic tomb of Bagneux near Saumur that on his return from Ireland he had likened to Trefignath on Anglesey.

It can still be visited in the centre of the village. One enters the bar-tabac, either buys a bière-pression, a coffee or pays a small fee and goes to the tomb through a side-door. The stones are enormous.

Aubrey then rode to see another a few miles to the south, the Pierre Folle in the woods of the Bois de Chalmont seven miles north of Loudun. He described it in his *Monumenta Britannica* with a small sketch on the same page as Bagneux 'for the neer resemblance they have to one another'. It was very similar to Bagneux 'but more demolished, and not altogether so big: it is called Pierre levé. I have arranged these Monuments together, for the neer resemblance they have to one another.'[6] It is still there – without charge.

Aubrey may have seen both after leaving Paris and travelling along the road to Le Mans then southwards on the way to Tours and Orléans miles to the east.

Sadly, in Orléans his persistently frail health failed him once more and in August he fell unpleasantly ill from a 'terrible fit of the spleen and piles'. Recovering in hospital 'I sawe in the Hospitall there a young fellow in cure whose left Cheeke was eaten (he sayd by this *Garloup* [a werewolf]) for sayd he had it been a woolfe he would have killed me outright and eaten me up'. Aubrey observed, 'This the *Lycanthropos*; the French call it *Garloup*: and doe believe that some wicked cruel men can transforme themselves into Woolves and bite, and worry people and doe mischief to mankinde,' quoting both Ovid and Virgil to support his statement.[7]

By 13 October he was back in England with his new servant, Robert Wiseman, whom he nicknamed 'Robinet' and 'Prudhome' because the man had the great advantage of speaking fluent French and Italian. Two months later Aubrey suffered his near-catastrophic *laesio in testiculo*. Finally recovering from that alarm he began his fieldwork in Wiltshire.

He had already planned Avebury and wandered around Stanton Drew. He had visited some megalithic tombs in England and Brittany but knew little more about them than their size and the stones from which they were built. Nothing more. There was no guidance, only guesswork and superstition.

In Brittany folk tales said that fairies had constructed megalithic tombs to be well-protected homes. They had lived in Finistère's vast mound of Barnenez. They baked bread for a farmer living near their tomb at Tressé in Ille-et-Vilaine. They could be helpful. At Pleslin they carried heavy slabs to build the long stone rows of the Champs des Roches.

But they could be aggressive if threatened. At the passage-grave of Ty-ar-Boudiquet, in Breton 'Ti ar Boudiked', the 'home of the little ones', they were constantly at war with the giants of the allée-couverte of Mougau-Bihan six miles to the west. Legendary conflicts between 'tiny ones' and 'monsters' were widespread on the Crozon peninsula.[8]

In Britain popular gullibility preferred ogres to elves. Belief in giants was widespread. Fairies were too effeminate for Saxon and Scandinavian tastes. It would be left to John Aubrey to expose the whimsies.

When he began enquiring about megalithic tombs he repeatedly heard from locals that he was looking at giants' beds because of the length of the mounds. Such places could only have been erected to cover some enormous being. 'It is only natural that long barrows and cairns, usually of considerable size, should be popularly named after or embody traditions of giants.'[9]

The stretches were too exaggerated for the six-foot-long graves of mortal men. Even the shortest were ten times longer. The average exceeded a hundred feet or more. The greatest like West Kennet near Avebury could take as long as four minutes to stroll around. Even a very brisk walk would have taken two!

The belief in 'giants' beds' was widespread in Britain from the farthest south in the Scilly Isles to the far north in the Shetlands where there was a Giant's Grave at both Northmaven and Sandsting.

They were as far west as Anglesey with Barclodiad y Gawres, the 'giantess's apronful'. Across Britain in non-megalithic Lincolnshire was yet another Giant's Grave at Ludford and two Giants' Hills at Skendleby. Giants had existed everywhere even in regions where there were no megalithic tombs, only earthen long barrows and stone circles. Stonehenge on the stone-free Salisbury Plain was known as the Giants' Dance. Robert Gay, rector of Nettlecombe on Exmoor, identified them as Somerset giants.

Even when optimistic treasure-hunters dug into the excessive mounds in search of riches but finding only human bones the explanation was that those were the remains of a giant's cannibalistic feast.

Megalithic tombs were mysteries because like stone circles there was nothing to date them. Aubrey visited several in Wiltshire including Lanhill, Lugbury, Millbarrow and the Shelving Stones.

One he missed, south of Avebury, overlooking the Vale of Pewsey, was a tomb that showed how superstition itself could change. Danes knew it as *Wodnes beorge*, 'the home of the god Odin'. Christianity destroyed the paganism, renaming it 'Adam's Grave'. Nothing was known of its history.

Aubrey looked at four long mounds quite close to his first home at Lower Easton Pierse. By the mid-seventeenth century the denuded Shelving Stones a mile or so north of Avebury was no more than two isolated, upright entrance stones with the capstone propped on them, 'a long picked stone seaven foot and more; it leaneth eastward upon two stones as in the figure: it is called Shelving-stones'.

Whoever demolished the long mound had been careful to leave three stones behind. The same happened at Lugbury just a few miles away. It was a religio-superstitious safeguard. Stones might be removed to make doorsteps, window sills, gateposts but three should be left as a Trinity to satisfy God. At Fortingall in Scotland three remained erect in each of the two adjacent eight-stone rings, the rest deeply buried to make room for the plough. Fortingall also happened to be the legendary birthplace of Pontius Pilate. Christianity was everywhere, even in megalithic monuments.

The Shelving Stones were no more than the remains of a skeleton when John Aubrey saw it. Nearby, Millbarrow was almost intact although the chamber's sideslabs and capstone had been exposed because 'Some yeares since a Windmill stood on it: from whence its denomination'. The tomb was wrecked in the late eighteenth century. The man who levelled it told an excavator that inside was 'a sort of room built up wi' big sarsens put together like, as well as a mason could set them; in the room was a sight of black stuff, and it did smill nation bad'.[10]

Not far to the west was Lugbury, 'a great Table-stone of bastard freestone leaning on two picked perpendicular stones', behind which, Aubrey surmised, had been two more 'like the legges of a Table', forming a false entrance.

The tomb had no passage. Rather, there were five side-chambers. Like many long barrows; Lugbury had been a family vault. Two nineteenth-century excavations discovered the bones of twenty-six skeletons, including those of ten children. None of this could be known to John Aubrey. He still had no answer to the antiquity of such monuments. Even whose bones they were, if no longer those of giants, was unclear.

At Lanhill, the 'long hill', they were thought to be Danish.[11] There was nothing else. Recent chronicles informed him of Vikings and Danes who had invaded England eight centuries earlier, and of Angles, Saxons and Jutes who came before them. Classical historians had described the Roman conquest and added snippets about native tribes in Britain before the time of Julius Caesar. They were no more than whispers on the wind that never mentioned the long-lost memories of the barrows that Aubrey investigated. What 'history' there was about Lanhill reveals how little was known, how much there was to discover.

Lanhill, two miles from Lower Eastern Pierse, was a tomb of three side-chambers and a false entrance. Its physically similar skeletons suggested it had been a family vault, used for generations. Remains of two females aged about twenty and fifty were found in the dummy entrance, the bodies put there just before Lanhill was blocked.

In Aubrey's time 'Barrowe-hill' was almost intact except for some pits in the mound dug by a tenant for laying earth on his lane. Sir Charles Snell told Aubrey in 1646 or 1647 that the 'hill' was called Hubba's Low but, as Aubrey discovered, Caxton's *Chronicle* wrote that Hubba had been buried in Devon, 'which I presume is an errour'.

The past is an Eldorado. Like all his contemporaries Aubrey had not only to peer into the blackness of prehistory but, first, remove the thick screen of misinformation in front of it, a tapestry of threads of facts, skeins of fiction, coarse strands of forgetfulness and filaments of inaccurate recording.

A reminiscence several centuries later than John Aubrey illustrates the difficulties confronting any enquirer into the secrets of antiquity.

When the present writer began researching the problems of prehistoric stone circles forty years ago, not the distant four hundred of John Aubrey, it was generally agreed that the hundred or so rings known at that time in Britain were Bronze Age in date and had been casually laid out with neither careful design nor precise measurements; 'rough stone monuments' Peet called them. There was no thought of the sites being aligned upon the sun, moon or star.

In his *Bronze Age* of 1930 the prestigious prehistorian Gordon Childe derided the idea. 'It is fantastic,' he wrote, 'that the ill-clad inhabitants of these boreal isles should shiver night-long in rain and gale, peering through the driving mists to note eclipses and planetary movements in our oft-veiled skies.'

Everything about those 'facts' was wrong, the number of circles, their date, the regional designs, the absence of yardsticks, the climate, the astronomy and the prehistoric societies that erected those elaborate monuments. But that is today. Four hundred years ago none of that was either known or considered.

The inquisitive John Aubrey wondering about Lanhill's history had only the mound, the emptied chambers and legends of giants, hobgoblins, rape and murderous Vikings to help him.

In the 1670s he wrote to Anthony à Wood asking him to find whether the true name was Hubba's Low or Barrowe-hill. Folk tales said that invading Danish chieftains, Hinguar and Hubba, had fought against Alfred the Great. Hubba was killed, 'and when Danes found Hubba's body lying, they did inter it and made upon it a great logge [mound] and let call it Hubbeslow and so it is called to this day'.[12]

John Milton's *History of England* of 1670 elaborated on Lanhill's nickname of Hubba's Low. 'Bruern a Nobleman whose wife King Osbert had ravisht, called-in Hinguar and Hubba [Danes] to revenge him', and in Aubrey's own *Wiltshire Antiquities*, almost finished in 1671 but not published until 1862, he himself repeated the tale. 'In the reign of King Ethelred, Hinguar and Hubba, two brothers, Danes, Leaders, who had gott footing amongst the E. Angles. These pagans, Asserius saith, came from Danubias. Bruern a nobleman whose wife King Osbert had ravished, called in Hinguar and Hubba to revenge him'.[13]

That statement was an accumulation of four sources: the *Anglo-Saxon Chronicle*; the late ninth-century records of the Welsh monk and historian Asser; the early twelfth-century *Historia Anglorum* of Henry of Huntingdon; and the contemporary *Flores Historiarum* of the Benedictine monk Roger of Wendover. Each added more details about Hubba. All were wrong.

Roger of Wendover embellished the accumulated misinformation, recording that invasion of 'Ynguar' and Hubba. Having raided, raped and ransacked profitably, the two Danes then invaded Wessex. At 'Anglefield', modern Englefield, west of Reading, the Danish and Saxon armies 'fought fiercely on both sides, until one of the chiefs of the pagans being slain, with the greater part of his forces, the rest took to flight'. That 'chief' was unnamed. He was not Hubba.[14]

Englefield is fifty miles east of Lanhill and Hubba's supposed burial place but fragmentary history and inventive story-telling ignored the geography, typifying the fact-cum-fiction that confronted John Aubrey as he puzzled over 'Hubba's Low'.

He wondered whether that fateful battle had been fought at the significantly named Slaughterford village on its steep hill two miles west of Lanhill. 'Hereabout countryfolk say groweth great plenty of a good vulnerary herb, called Dane's Blood. They doe believe it sprang from the blood of the Danes shed in battle.' In his *Natural History of Wiltshire* he added, 'There was heretofore (*vide* J. Milton) a great fight with the Danes, which made the inhabitants give it that name.'[15]

In reality there had been not one but two separate battles fought by two different sets of Danes. One had been the fight at Englefield. The Danish leaders were Bagsecg and Halfden.

Hinguar and Hubba had not been with them. They had crossed to South Wales and western England in search of lands to conquer. There is a vague story that Hubba was killed at Cynuit, somewhere near the western coast of Devon close to Bideford. The error came from the *Decem Scriptores*, unpublished until 1652 and possibly compiled by John Brompton, abbot of Jervaulx in Yorkshire in 1436. William Camden copied it in his *Chronicle*. Of that battle John Thurnam sardonically remarked, 'In such ways, do we find what may be called spurious traditions arising, even in the present day; which are much more difficult to deal with, and contain generally less truth than the genuine traditions of the vulgar.'[16]

The Danes were reported as going from Exeter to Chippenham pursued by Alfred, who killed 'Hubba, Inguar and Bruen Bocard'. It completed the accretions of centuries of misstatements about Lanhill that confused John Aubrey. Chippenham was conveniently close to Lanhill. The story had taken eight centuries to accumulate and embroider from the year AD 867 in the *Anglo-Saxon Chronicle* to AD 1652, the *Decem Scriptores* and the fictitious burial of Hubba in Wiltshire.

Everything about Lanhill except for the mound and its burials was completely wrong and historically misleading. Even that 'scene of carnage', Slaughterford, had never known a brutal conflict. It did not mean the spilling of blood.

Early versions of the village's name were the eleventh-century *Slachtoneford* and *Sclachtesford*, from Old English *Sl h- orn*, meaning 'the ford by the sloe-bush'. That bush's nastily scratching thorns may often have drawn blood from people picking its sour berries but never from the body of a non-existent, murderous Danish invader.

But Aubrey did regret how badly the village's pretty church had been desecrated by Puritans for the contradictory reasons of religious iconoclasm and personal greed; 'the most miserably that ever I saw, the very barres are taken from the windows; here have been two good South windowes, and the doors are gone and the paving, and, it seems, for any use, viz weavers. The font gone to make a trough'.

Luckily there were still excellent trout in the gravelly Box brook.[17]

The church at Slaughterford had been fortunate at such slight damage. Many elsewhere in England had been far more systematically ravaged.

On the far side of the country in Suffolk lived the most zealous of all the fanatical iconoclasts, William Dowsing of Laxfield, literally 'the hammer of the Puritans'. It had probably been a sledgehammer that he had enthusiastically wielded.

In 1644 that destructive demolisher of the Devil smashed and shattered his way through no fewer than one hundred and fifty churches in seven weeks, fragmenting stained-glass windows, splintering carvings of 'seven Fryars hugging a Nunn', breaking oak figures of the Twelve Apostles. 'He went about the county like a Bedlam', breaking even undecorated windows, great organs, altar-rails, hurling stone images of saints down from the roof.

Yet that predecessor of modern vandals in Europe was momentarily awed at a glimpse of the medieval beauty around him. At the village of Ufford he noticed the wooden cover of the font and 'was held spellbound at the font and stopped to admire this glorious cover, like a pope's triple crown, and gilded over with gold'.

It was perhaps because of that brief aesthetic awareness of the loveliness around him and of the devoted hands that had created it that God, always merciful, allowed Dowsing to live sixty more years. He died an unpunished centenarian.[18] The fate of his sacrilegious colleagues in Wiltshire is unknown, even the trough-makers of Slaughterford.

Although there had been no battle at Slaughterford Aubrey did know of places where there had been historical fights in Wiltshire.

On his way to Avebury or galloping across the countryside hunting hares with his friends he must often have jumped over the challengingly weathered Wansdyke bank and ditch, that long stretch of British defence against the intrusive Saxons that extended from a prehistoric round barrow cemetery near Devizes to the Savernake hunting forest to the east.

'The walk along the twelve miles or so of Wansdyke between Morgan's Hill and Savernake Forest provides one of the most spectacular experiences in British field archaeology' was the enthusiastic opinion of that splendid field archaeologist Leslie Grinsell.[19]

The defensive bank and ditch had been known as *Ealden Dic*, 'Old Dyke', as late as AD 825, evidence of its antiquity. It had older names. 'If the name *Wodnes dic* means that the Saxons believed Wansdyke to be a supernatural work, it would seem to follow that they cannot have become acquainted with this post-Roman earthwork until the circumstances of its making had been forgotten.'[20]

The likelihood is that Wansdyke had been dug as the eastern extension of a protective, linear earthwork, the western being even longer in Somerset, as a defensive barrier separating the British kingdom of Wessex from the growing power of Saxon Mercia to the north.

By the time John Aubrey found it the age and significance of the bank and ditch had already been argued about. William Camden thought it 'divided overthwart from East to West, with a Dike of wonderfull worke, cast up for many miles together in length: the people dwelling there about, call it *Wansdyke*, which upon an errour generall received, they talke, and tell it to have been made by the devil upon a Wednesday'.[21]

Dismissing this comical folk tale Aubrey later included an extract from the *England Described* of 1569 by Edward Leigh. That Member of Parliament for Stafford had been a Civil War colonel with the Parliamentary army. In 1642 he had published a book, *Critica Sacra*, on primitive Hebrew words in the Old Testament.

About the significance of Wansdyke that unreliable historian had perceptively observed, 'The Saxons made Wansdyke a limit to divide the two Kingdomes of the Mercians and the West Saxons asunder: for this was the very place of the Battle between them, which each strove one with another to enlarge his Dominions.'[22]

It had been twenty years earlier than Leigh's book that Aubrey had first seen Wansdyke on that memorable day in January 1649, when he also chanced upon Avebury. 'I happened to see *Wensditch*, and an old Camp: & two or three Sepulchres', perhaps an earthwork and the lines of round barrows on the North Downs.

On the same page as his transcription of Camden and opposite the later addition from Edward Leigh he added what he had observed about the bank and ditch, riding its length, sketching, making notes of its irregular course, debating its date and purpose.

> I have retrived this Ditch westwards, into Spye-park: it runnes through Hedington grounds, on Saint Anns-hill and before: and I have then traced it eastward as far as Milton; wch is at the foot of St. Anns-hill [*vulgo* Tann-hill] they say it runnes into Savernake-forest. Memdm. at Wensditch, the Rampire is to the Southward the Graffe is to the Northward; both Rampire and Graffe are of a prodigious greatnesse.

Revealing how observant and painstaking a fieldworker he was becoming, he added a visual aid: 'It runneth not all along straight, but sometimes makes elbows, thus.' And at the bottom of the page he drew a jagged line to show the sudden bends and corners where section had been added to section.[23]

It was, literally, down-to-earth archaeology that conflicted with established superstitions and legends. And as scepticism gradually replaced credulity in his mind John Aubrey recognised identical misinformation everywhere in his search for truth, whether in a megalithic tomb, a stone circle, even in a single standing stone. He saw several in Wiltshire.

One was in the River Avon. 'As I remember. There is a great stone that lies in the water at Figheldean (wch Dr W. Charleton shew^d me) as left by the way to Stonehenge: another is somewhere on the Downs which rests there on three low stones as in order to be carried away.' He was assuming that these were sarsens intended for Stonehenge and as Figheldean is only three miles from that circle it did not have to be a whimsy.[24]

There was another stone, this one erect, and it is evident from Aubrey's description that he was developing the eye of a field-worker. His account was not that of a thoughtless onlooker seeing nothing more than a slab of stone. In the grass around the stone Aubrey noticed overgrown patches where other stones had once stood.

He wrote, 'At *Brome* near Swindon in Wiltshire in the middle of a pasture ground called *Long-stone* is a great stone ten foot (or better) standing upright; which I take to be the Remainder of those kind of Temples; in the ground below are many others o o o o o o o o o o o o o o in a right line. This ground is y[e] Inheritance of the right Hon[le] Charles Lord Seymour', his friend.[25]

It was excellent observation. The combined Broome circle and row was one of several locally. There had been similar lines, perhaps avenues, in the vicinity, one at Day House Lane, Coate, the stones taken in the nineteenth century for footpaths in Swindon, and another at Langdean Bottom.[26]

It is rather surprising, therefore, that John Aubrey did not realise that another standing stone was an important feature in itself not just a component of a much larger complex. To be fair, that is what the Heel Stone at Stonehenge did become. Originally it had been an isolated standing stone on Salisbury Plain long before the ring was set up, one of a series of widely spaced landmarks to guide travellers along prehistoric tracks that were to link into the medieval Harroway across southern England.[27]

Aubrey was unaware of that. And, to be fair to him in another way, he was the first to mention the pillar. It was ignored. From the early twelfth century reference to Stonehenge by Henry of Huntingdon to as late as Inigo Jones' *Stone-Heng* book of 1655 not one writer mentioned that detached stone. John Aubrey did.

Referring to various features in his plan of the circle he wrote:

the two great stones marked *a* and *w*, one whereof (sc. *w*) [the Heel Stone] lieth a good way off, north-east-ward from the circularish bank, of which there hath not been any notice taken: but I doe guess it to be materiall: and to be the remaines of the avenue, or Entrance to this Temple; which will appear very probable, by comparing it with the Temples of *Aubury*, Kynet, and y[e] Wedding at Stanton Drew, one of the stones hath a marke or scratch how far/deep it should be sett in the earth.[28]

It was excellent field-observation. No one had ever considered the former existence of an avenue at Stonehenge. Its stones had been removed by nearby farmers and masons years before Aubrey. Yet they had existed.

His archaeological successor William Stukeley sixty years later noticed the traces where they had stood. 'There is not one stone left therof, yet a curious eye without difficulty will discern a mark of the holes whence they were taken tho' the ground ... is so much trod upon', adding that there had been fifty stones on each side.[29]

By 1664 John Aubrey was twenty-eight years old. To satisfy his constant curiosity about the forgotten past he had gone to many old places, stones, tombs, medieval manors, visited churches for memorials, recorded country customs, looked for antiquities of all kinds, scribbled pages of notes for years. But he had done nothing with them. They existed as insubstantial as shadows. Aubrey knew it.

He wondered what use those explorations had been in his life? '*Quod digni feci hîc process. viam?*' 'What have I done?', 'truly nothing, only umbrages'.[30]

Worse, having indulged his whims but giving little attention to the estate and properties that he had inherited, including his father's substantial debts, those debts and other financial commitments were to accumulate, neglected and unpaid, for fifteen years. In desperation properties were mortgaged, some were sold, until, finally, he was completely ruined by 1670.

Before that disastrous time came the year 1665. During that twelve-month period John Aubrey's archaeological searches prospered. Conversely, both his private life and the lives of London's citizens changed for the worse, his because of a woman, theirs from the most murderous plague since the Black Death three hundred years earlier.

But there had also been an archaeological advance. Shortly after he had first met Anthony à Wood in 1665 Aubrey wrote to his new friend about a further visit he had made to Stanton Drew in 1664 whose stones he had first seen as a boy years earlier.

At that time he had been unable to see them in their entirety. His youth, growing crops, private land, an unusual feature out of sight behind the church, all these disadvantages had permitted him only a limited inspection of a monument that was to became as intriguing as Avebury. And an impressionable boy had been just as interested in the folk-story of a petrified wedding party as the meaning of the stones themselves. As he informed à Wood it was only years later that he went to Stanton Drew with a more dispassionate eye.

Mr. Anth. Wood: Twas a strange chance that I should come to know this old Monument, wch lies so very obscure in a place far from any great Roade. But it came to pass that Rachel Danvers the relict of my Grandfather Jo. Aubrey married to John Whitson /his fourth wife / [who was my Godfather] wch was a great Benefactor to the city of Bristow; having no child living he gave the Mannours of Dundery and

Burnet and severall houses in Bristow in the county of Somerset ... Burnet was my Grandmothers Jointure by him; where I was often in my youth hood: and it is about fower miles from Stanton Drew.[31]

Today there is a central stone circle and its two smaller rings and avenues at Stanton Drew. Today, so many stones are fallen or missing that the site seems unpromising, offering few insights into the nature of the societies that raised and used the complex.

But there, below Wales, a dozen miles from the Severn Estuary is the largest stone circle in Western Europe after the outer ring at Avebury. Two much smaller rings flank it to the north-east and south-south-west. The circles stand in a 366 m [1,200 feet] long but angled line, the central an enormous 114.6 m [376 feet] in diameter. They lie just south of the River Chew in a valley, Broadfield Down, rising steeply to the west with the Mendip Hills to the south.

With the rings are the remains of two avenues, a Cove and an outlying stone, Hauteville's Quoit. The group has similarities to Avebury but was almost barricaded in prehistoric times from that monstrous earthwork and its megalithic rings by bewildering miles of forest and uncertain trails through marshes.

The name of Stanton Drew is a composite one. In the Anglo-Saxon Charters and in *Domesday Book* the hamlet was known only as *Stantune*, 'the homestead by the stones'. The 'Drew' was added in the thirteenth century when the Drogo or Dreux family became the landowners.[32]

Nor had Stanton Drew anything to do with druids. Despite Aubrey's conjecture that 'it is very probable that the village hath its name of Drew from the Druids' he was cautious enough to add, 'Drew is the name of an ancient Family in the Westerne parts: so I will not adventure to straine the etymologie of this place too much, to my own Hypothesis. but leave it as a Quaere.'[33]

The first recognition that the stones were of importance came with the building of the Norman, perhaps Saxon, church of St Mary's, deliberately erected between the Great Circle and the Cove presumably to discourage pagan practices at the stones.[34]

Then, for centuries, the circles, so far from large towns, were disregarded by outsiders and maltreated by their rural owners. The remoteness of the circles hindered research. Just as Avebury was not noticed until 1649, and even then only by accident, the even more isolated Stanton Drew had to wait until 1697 before it was described in a printed book, William Camden's *Britannia*.

Stanton-Drew, where is to be seen a monument of stones like those of *Stone-henge* in Wiltshire; but these being not altogether so big as the *Stone-henge* ones, nor standing in so clear a plain, the hedges and trees mix'd among them have made them less taken notice of.[35]

But that was in 1695 many years after Aubrey had mentioned the rings to Anthony à Wood.

In the chapter about Somerset in his earlier edition of *Britain* of 1637, Camden recorded distorted rumours of giants known as Cangis who had been defeated by the Romans during the reign of the emperor Claudius. But of Stanton Drew he wrote nothing in the county's twenty-one detailed pages.[36] It is one more irony of prehistoric archaeology that John Aubrey had already seen the circles a year or two earlier than that book.

There had been a disadvantage. Whenever he had visited the rings, whether as a credulous boy or later as a more critical adult, he had been unable to determine how many rings there were or their layout because of agricultural cultivation and rural destruction. But on his subsequent visits he revised his earlier notes about the heights of the stones, reducing them by several feet from his original nine or ten.

> They are 5. or 6. high and as hard as Marble., of a dirty reddish, and take a good polishe. they seeme to be of the very same sort wth S[t] Vincent's rocks neer Bristowe [Bristol]: about 6 miles hence.
>
> They are of severall Tunnes: in some is Iron-ore: as likewise appears at S[t] Vincent's rock.
>
> As hard as these stones are, they make a Shift to break them with Sledges, because they so incumber the good land, and they told me [1664] they are much diminished these within these fewe yeares.
>
> This monument is [much *deleted*] bigger than Stoneheng: the Diameter is ninety paces. I could not percieve any Trench about it as at Stoneheng. it is in ploughed land and consequently easily worne out. When I sawe this, it was in Harvest time, and the Barley being then ripe I could not come to survey the Stones so exactly as I would otherwise would have donne But this Scheme (as it is) resembles it.[37]

It did not. Because of the dense crops he was never able to wander amongst the rings whose stones, upright, fallen, were half-hidden in an enclosure known as Stony Close. It was surrounded by a hedge. At its farthest corner towards the River Chew he was able to peer at the nearest ring, the north-eastern. Not far beyond them were the lower pillars of the great central ring.

As Dymond was to remark it had been an unfortunate time to examine the site. 'But as it is, he got an utterly confused idea of its form; imagining that he saw here (as he believed he had seen in several other cases) a concentric arrangement of the principal group.'[38]

Aubrey continued,

The Stones a a a a seeme to be the remainder of the Avenue, as at Kynet, and Aubury, the length of the Avenue is about halfe a quarter of a mile: and the stones d d d might be a leading to another Temple; as from West Kynet to the Temple at the top On the top of the Hill. See the Scheme.

I doe presume, that the like Approaches (or Avenues) were at Stoneheng, and at Roll-rich, as are here, though now deranged by time.[39]

The only avenue that he could see clearly was the one from the first ring. He never noticed the other extending from the central circle. Nor did he ever see the three pillars of the Cove on the far side of the church. Instead he seems to have identified them as the fallen petrified figures of the legendary bride, groom and parson on the other side of the hedge from that ring. 'But to returne again to these Stones: [β] they call the Bride. [γ] the Parson's stone [δ] the Cookes stone.' Aubrey was careless. As Dymond noticed, 'These letters are not on the plan.' And the luckless groom had vanished.[40]

Also missing from Aubrey's description was the south-west circle. It was understandable. That tumbled ring lay on higher ground behind a hedge a quarter of a mile from the others. Worse, what few stones did stand were concealed by the hedge and an adjacent wall.[41]

Aubrey did, however, see a fallen pillar on a rise a quarter of a mile from the circles.

Northeastward from Stonheng is a stone a good distance off, which seemes (to me) to be the remaine of it: and the stone called the Kings-stone at Rollrich seemes to be so there. See the Schemes of both Temples Places.

About a quarter of a mile from this Monument of the Wedding is a stone called Hakewell's Coyte ... [Aubrey deleted the next section. It reads] which may be what only remaines of the like Monument. In these parts lived anciently one Hakewell a person of great Estate, and great Strength of body. He lies interred in Chew-church where he hath a monument.[42]

There is a wooden effigy dressed in armour in the south aisle of the church but it is not of Sir John de Hauteville, who lived during the thirteenth century when noblemen wore chain mail in battle.

The man could have been a descendant, 'possibly Sir William Cheney of Norton Malreward', but more probably the figure was John Wych, another local landowner, who died in 1346 almost eighty years later than de Hauteville.

In its recess Wych's leaning figure is dressed in plate-mail fashionable at the time of the battles of Agincourt and Poitiers.[43]

John Aubrey's description of Stanton Drew was the least successful of his long reports on individual stone circles. Despite several visits and revisions of his original notes he offered few insights into the site's layout, circles or its other features. There was nothing about its age or significance.

Handicapped by the crops he never realised that there was a third circle and mistook the north-eastern and central rings to be the remnants of a single concentric circle. His sketched plan was of no value.

He was wrong about Hauteville's Quoit. That stone had probably been a prehistoric marker on an ancient trackway. He was wrong about other outlying stones at Stonehenge and the Rollright Stones, believing them to be the survivors of demolished avenues. They were not.

He was wrong about Sir John de Hauteville, simply reporting a local belief in the prowess of an exceptionally strong man who could hurl a heavy stone across a long stretch of countryside.

Yet, despite these defects, there had been progress. He never suggested that de Hauteville or giants had set up the stones of Stanton Drew. He was realistic about the place-name. And although he faithfully recorded the puritanical fairy-story of a sacrilegious wedding party punished for their transgression of the Sabbath he gave it no credence.

Instead, he provided clear-headed notes of what he had been able to see. They were the forerunners to his later good fieldwork at Avebury and Stonehenge.

6

1666: Local stone circles & a 'Sumner' of discontent

As the amiable and slightly eccentric author of *Brief Lives*, Aubrey is now well known. But his reputation as a biographer has almost eclipsed his wider achievement as a writer, and few are aware either of the sheer range of his works, or of the originality of the most notable of them.

Michael Hunter, 1975, 13

By January 1665, John Aubrey was more than halfway through his life, a well-to-do, sociable bachelor, popular wherever he went. But the fateful year of 1665 was to change his life. It also ended the lives of many Londoners who died in the worst outbreak of plague that the city had ever known.

Aubrey had had a variety of lodgings in London since 1651. By 1665 he was using a room or rooms over a Fleet Street stationer's, 'at the sign of the Rainbow' near Temple Bar. By the end of the following year the house had endured the plague only to be burnt down in the Great Fire of London because it stood 'just on the wrong side of Temple Bar'. Except for some minor personal possessions Aubrey would have been little concerned about that conflagration, being far from the capital, enjoying the pleasures of society, antiquities and discoveries in his native Wiltshire.[1]

By the beginning of spring he would have left the crowded, dirty streets of London for the open air of Wiltshire and its intriguingly secretive ancient monuments. Less enjoyably, and regrettably, he became involved with a twenty-nine-year-old woman, Joan Sumner, of Seend a few miles from Easton Pierse.

But being so far from London he was many miles from the worst outbreak of plague that overcrowded city had ever experienced. For a present-day escapist Stuart London was not the ideal place to visit. It was crowded, dangerous and it was filthy.

The city, especially its suburbs, stank. Fewer than seventy years earlier in 1598 the London tailor-turned-surveyor, John Stow, had given that specific reason for the stench, the city's ditch.

> On the other side of that street lieth the ditch without the walls of the city, which of old time was used to be open, always from time to time cleansed from filth and mud, as need required; of great breadth, and so deep, that divers, watering horses, where they thought it shallowest, were drowned, both horse and man. But now of later time the ditch is inclosed with gardens, carpenters' yards, buildings, and the ditch filled up, a small channel left, and that very shallow.[2]

It became a dumping-ground for rubbish, refuse and decaying matter. It reeked.

And there were horses, teams of horses drawing coaches, handsomely apparelled steeds for upper-class riders, workhorses harnessed to carts, drayhorses dragging laden wagons. Their dung fouled every street and any alley wide enough to be ridden through. It could be smelled everywhere, even in the inner boroughs where people dwelt in comfort.

There were other animals. Pigs, sheep and cattle were driven into the city and killed in licensed slaughterhouses and butchers' backyards. The skins were sold to tanners and treated with dog-dirt and urine; the animal fat to soap-makers who also used urine. Bones went profitably to glue-makers and boiled. John Evelyn listed some of the polluting trades that contributed to the pervasive foul odours: brewers, chandlers making candles, fishmongers, dyers and many others. Not surprisingly, London stank.

The well-to-do living in well-built houses in the City had their own problem, human excrement. There were no flush toilets. Everything dropped into the cellar. One night Pepys went to his basement and 'I put my foot into a great heap of turds, by which I find that Mr. Turner's house of office is full and comes into my cellar.'[3]

Such cess-pits were emptied only once every other year after dark by men with lanterns, the aptly named 'rakers', whose scrapings left such an intolerable stench that every door and window of neighbouring houses had to be kept tightly shut. London stank.

Even personal cleanliness was variable. Washing properly was so rare that Pepys made a special reference it. 'I had washed myself, it having been the hottest day that hath been this year.'

Bathrooms were uncommon, almost unknown, even in stately homes. Pepys envied Mr Povey's 'bath at the top of his house'. In 1697 Celia Fiennes saw a very elaborate one in Chatsworth House near Matlock, 'a batheing roome ... the bath is one entire marble all white finely veined with blew ... it was as deep as ones middle on the outside and you went down steps into the bath big enough for two people'. It had cold and hot taps'. Oddly, she did not mention the toilets that had been installed there a few years earlier.[4]

The city was an unwashed host whose door was always open for disease, the house dirty, crowded, unprotected by adequate medical practice. Stuart London was a mixture of wealth and poverty, with the poor nudging grubby shoulder to dirtier shoulder, inhabiting squalid lean-to tenements. Those filthy conditions and fouled sewers and drains made London in any warm summer a breeding-ground for disease. Conditions in 1665 were perfect for plague.

According to the official Great Bill of mid-December 1665, almost 70,000 people, men, women, children and infants died of it that year. The likelihood is probably twice that number. There had been almost a quarter of a million Londoners crammed into one and a half square miles, the majority of them squashed into the outer suburbs of grubby, narrow streets.[5]

Rats were everywhere. So were their fleas. Those parasites infected human bodies causing swellings, 'buboes', that were lethal evidence of approaching death.

The bubonic plague began almost unnoticed at the end of 1664 with one or two deaths and 1665 began without alarm with a very cold winter that lasted two or three months.

John Aubrey would have been in his lodgings indulging his curiosity about a miscellany of interests, all of them to be included in the only book to be published in his lifetime, his *Miscellanies*: a jumble of omens, dreams, apparitions, invisible blows, magic, second sight, even 'transportation by an invisible power'. That accumulated hotchpotch of facts and fantasies displayed his inquisitive but credulous mind.

By the beginning of spring when the increasing number of London deaths was alarming authorities Aubrey was far away in the untainted countryside of Wiltshire.

In April a sudden increase of some four hundred victims had died of the plague in the city. The symptoms were well known: fever, headaches, agonising swellings known as 'buboes' in the groin and armpits that erupted into scarlet-red blotches under the skin where blood was haemorrhaging. Sardonically the fatal signs became known as the 'spotted death'.

Sixty years earlier in his *Antony and Cleopatra* William Shakespeare had described it:

> ... the token'd pestilence
> When death is sure.

The play may have been written in 1605 in the middle of nine successive years of plague from 1603 to 1609. Elizabethans had experienced its physical horrors. A contemporary of Shakespeare's, the writer Thomas Nashe, wrote an elegiac poem of which the lines of the third of its six verses were some of the loveliest ever written about that horror.

> Beauty is but a flower
> Which wrinkles will devour;
> Brightness falls from the air,
> Queens have died young and fair,
> Dust hath closed Helen's eye.
> I am sick, I must die.
> Lord, have mercy on us! [6]

After 1609 there had been a lull in the attacks, then another outbreak in 1625 and, finally, the catastrophe of 1665 with the return of the 'token'd pestilence' through which only few survived.

The doomed became delirious, days away from death. A few, a very few, maybe one in four, did recover if the swellings burst outwards. Everyone else died. And for London worse was to follow. May, June, July, August and September gave England the driest, hottest summer that men could remember. People in the country loved it. Thousands of Londoners did not live through it.

In Wiltshire John Aubrey carefreely sketched stone circles including the nameless, isolated ring on Overton Hill.

In London two thousand people may have died of the plague in June. Ignorant of the cause of the outbreak there were desperately ignorant attempts at prevention. Dogs and cats were killed. Fires were lit. Charlatans sold quack nostrums. Walls were plastered with advertisements for infallible pestilential pills, the only true, curative plague water, the purchase of the elixir of the Balm of Gilead, tablets to be hung around the neck, a hundred 'cures'. In Cheapside the Green Dragon tavern sold 'an Excellent Electuary' beer, a medicinal paste of powder and honey or treacle, at an outrageous price of sixpence a pint. Desperate people drank it. Desperate people died. The royal Court moved to Hampton Court. [7]

On 7 June, wrote Samuel Pepys, 'This day, much against my Will, I did in Drury-lane see two or three houses marked with a red cross upon the doors, and "Lord have mercy upon us" writ there.'[8] By law the crosses had to be at least a foot high and the houses were to be bordered up and left shuttered for forty days.

Pepys bought some chewing tobacco for its protective properties. It was widely, optimistically believed that the smell of tobacco smoke, like the fragrance of flowers, kept the air sweet and warded off the plague's poisonous odours. Everyone knew that 'no tobacconist in London died of the Great Plague'. People smoked. 'Men, women and even children lit pipes night and morning, or chewed quids of strong black leaf, spitting out the bitter dark juice on to the floor.' Floral and herbal nosegays were just as popular. So was vinegar. Grocers rapidly sold out.

By July thousands had died in London. Every graveyard had been filled with dead parishioners. Ugly, enormous plague-pits were dug for putrefying corpses. The royal Court moved to Salisbury.

The stifling heat made August the worst of the months. Plague killed more than seventeen thousand.

There were plague deaths in Salisbury and the royal court moved to Oxford.

In London dead were collected at night. 'All the Musick in the night was the sad sound, "Bring Out Your Dead!" which, like dung, were thrown into a cart and tumbled into a Pit without numbring.' 'The day was always summoning to our Grave with Knells and tolling of Bells.'[9]

On the eighth, Samuel Pepys physically enjoyed his licentious 'heart's wish' with the compliant Mrs Bagwell, '*a corason a hazer con ella*', and then went out and was shocked by what he saw: 'The streets mighty empty all the way now, even in London [the City], which is a sad sight.' He remembered Will Griffith who had served him with ale in Old Palace Yard, 'his wife and three children dead, all I think in a day'.[10]

The plague was undemocratic. There were five times as many deaths in the outer suburbs as in the City proper.

In the same month of August John Aubrey went to Oxford where he met a man who for years was to be an on-and-off friend and colleague, Anthony à Wood.

September was the worst plague month in London. In the persistent heat-wave the death-rate increased. Twenty thousand was an estimate. At the beginning of the month, Sunday, the third, Pepys dressed foppishly. 'Up and put on my coloured silk suit, very fine, and my new periwig, bought a good while since, but durst not wear it because the plague was in Westminster when I bought it. And it is a wonder what will be the fashion after the plague is done as to periwigs, for nobody will dare buy any haire for fear of the infection – that it had been cut off the heads of people dead of the plague.'[11]

London was a desolation. Four days after Pepys John Evelyn grieved at the silent emptiness. Walking about was 'a dismal passage and dangerous, to see so many Cofines exposed in the streets, & the streets thin of people, the shops shut up, and all in mournfull silence, not knowing whose turn might be next'.[12]

But there was gradual relief. There were fewer deaths in October. That slight decline continued into November and the colder weather hastened the recovery. Ironically, it was in November that John Aubrey's poor judgement caused him to propose marriage to Mistress Joan Sumner.

By December the worst of the epidemic was over and in January 1666 Charles II and his court were returning to London. There was deep snow at the end of the month.

A hundred miles from that long-drawn-out macabre tragedy, at some time in 1665 on his Wiltshire explorations John Aubrey was looking at stone circles, mysterious rings that increasingly interested him. Already he had deduced that there had been an avenue of standing stones leading to Stonehenge. There had also been several other single rows and double avenues to stone circles in Wiltshire. Aubrey had already noticed them a Day House Lane and Broome.

It was possibly in 1665 that he looked for others nearer Avebury. He never saw the large concentric ring of Winterbourne Bassett probably because it was more than three miles to the north and then a further mile off the Swindon road. It was a big double ring, its stones small but with a central high pillar. Just west was an isolated high stone. Today everything has gone.

Nor did Aubrey notice the inconspicuous 'Falkner's' ring near Avebury, its twelve stones down the slope below the Kennet avenue but concealed by hedges. Just one stone survives the intensive farming of the nineteenth and twentieth centuries.

But on the road to Marlborough Aubrey did see the 'Broadstones' at Clatford Bottom near the River Kennet, its poetical place-name being derived from the Old English 'Clāto', the 'ford where water lilies grow'.

Aubrey described the ring. 'In a Lane from Kynet toward Marleborough, doe lie, fall'n-down, eight huge stones in a Circle, as described in the figure.'[13] Halfway between Avebury and Marlborough the tiny site was finally destroyed in the 1880s, everything gone by 1890.

The circle was only half a mile south of the Devil's Den chambered tomb but being well away from the main road and with no worthwhile lane leading to it that monument was never mentioned by Aubrey.

Nor was it visited by superstitious locals who believed that it was guarded by a huge white dog with eyes like burning coals just as the West Kennet long barrow was protected by a white, fairylike, red-eared dog. These were not places for courting lovers.[14]

Legends could be dismissed but the meaning of the circles, their age, their origin, none of this was known in Stuart times. John Aubrey had only guesswork as he rode, perplexed, from ring to ring.

He would have had other concerns. Aware of his increasing debts and declining income he may once again have looked for a well-to-do spinster whose dowry might solve those problems. Joan Sumner lived in Seend, conveniently close to the mortgaged Easton Pierse ten miles away and the megalithic enticements around Avebury the same distance to the east.[15]

She was the daughter of a wealthy clothier, John Sumner, whose luxurious house with his escutcheon on its façade still stands in the village. He was financially so well provided that he had a second house at Kington St Michael and a third at Sutton Benger. To a merchant the prospect of acquiring a son-in-law who was a member of the landed gentry was a social elevation. During the summer of 1665 John Aubrey often stayed in Seend at Sumner's home.

Since the fifteenth century clothiers and weavers from Flanders had been living there. They became rich. One, John Stokys, had a splendid north aisle added to Seend's Holy Cross church. In the moulding of its west window is Stokys' emblem, a pair of sheep-shears. In the aisle is a small brass memorial of 1498 to Alys, his wife, and Stokys himself in his long, fur-lined robe. Some of the weavers' cottages still stand, men who provided Stokys with the cloth necessary for his trade.

Despite the profitable work not everything was right in the village. The water of Sumner's house was undrinkable. Aubrey described it.

> The water in Jo. Sumner's well was so bad for household use that they could not brew nor boyle with it, and used it only to wash the house &c., so that they were necessitated to sinke a well in the common, which is walled, about a bow shott or more from his dwelling house, where is fresh and wholesome water.[16]

If John Aubrey had already begun tentatively courting Joan Sumner he must have been taken aback when on 10 July a marriage licence was applied for between her and Samuel Gayford, yeoman, of twenty-seven years, she herself two years older. But nine months later another marriage licence was applied for, this one between her and John Aubrey, perhaps considering him a better social catch. It was odd.

> There remains on Joan Sumner's part a suspicious appearance of shuffling with the bonds, as if deliberately trying to bring off a more or less dishonest stroke ... To have remained, in spite of her dowry, single until the age of twenty-nine or thirty in the seventeenth century suggests that some unusual impediment must have stood consistently in the way of her marriage; while the fact that she was prepared to break her engagement to Gayford to accept Aubrey's ostensibly better offer implies that her heart was not much involved in either case, especially in view of her subsequent treatment of Aubrey.[17]

During that unsettled time Aubrey, following his custom of looking for local health-giving springs, chanced upon some medicinal waters not far from the village. It was early May 1665. His discovery of the deposits occurred during the annual village festival, the 'Seend Revell'.

That celebration 'was traditionally held on a Sunday early in May, being linked with a patronal festival of the Church on 3 May. There was a church service and a sort of fair, with stalls in the lanes near the 'Bell'.[18]

By long tradition a tall pole was brought to villages from the local woods for May Day, where it was lavishly decorated. Originally it had been a phallic symbol at the ancient festival of Beltane from prehistoric times, bringing in Nature's new life, its fecundity, trees in leaf, emerging crops, and to celebrate local people gathered flowers and hawthorn branches and decorated the erect pole with flowers, branches, garlands and flags. By custom the prettiest girl was made Queen of May.

Such seemingly pagan, enjoyable pastimes were condemned during the Commonwealth. In 1644 every maypole was banned, that 'stinking idol', and all Christmas celebrations were exterminated. That day was not for human happiness.

With the Restoration everything was restored. Maypoles were brought back. People laughed and danced. It was a time of gaiety.[19]

Aubrey had seen the poles elsewhere. 'I doe not remember that ever I sawe a May-pole in France. *quaere* if there are any there. In Holland they have their *Maybooms*, which are straight young Trees set-up: and at Woodstock in Oxon, they every May-eve goe into the Parke, and fetch away a number of Haw-thorne-trees, which they set before their Dores: 'tis pity that they make such destruction of so fine a tree.'[20] The hawthorn, popularly nicknamed 'may', was never brought into the house. Its blooms smelled of rotting flesh and corpses.

Not everything about local Mayday festivities was innocent. 'Needless to say, the activities on 1 May also involved much amorous and raucous behaviour among both young and old: the gathering of flowers and branches was not the only thing that went on in the woods that day.'

In his *Anatomie of Abuses* the Puritan, Philip Stubbes, grumbled.

All the men and maides, olde men and wives, run gadding overnight to the woods, groves, hills and mountains, where they spend all night in pleasant pastimes; and in the morning, they return, bringing with them birch and branches of trees, to deck their assemblies withal … I have heard it creditably reported [and that vive voce] by men of great gravitie and reputation, that of fortie, threescore, or a hundred maides, going to the wood over night, there have scarcely the thirde parte of them return home againe undefiled.

An even more censorious but probably statistically unsound killjoy added that 'I have heard of ten maidens which went to fetch May, and nine of them with child'.[21]

Little of this mattered to John Aubrey. He was more excited by his discovery of the richly black, odorous iron ore in the woods close to Seend. It was its close existence to the village that had so coloured the strong-smelling waters there.

The brackish flavour of those medicinal waters intrigued him. 'Whereupon I sent my servant [Wiseman] to the Davizes for some galles. to try the waters, and made my first experiment at Mr. Jo. Sumner's (where I lay).'

Galls were the ironically named 'oak-apples', tiny brown balls in clusters on oak twigs. They were caused by wasps puncturing the bark and laying eggs. When powdered they provide a powerful astringent excellent for dysentery and diarrhoea.

Aubrey experimented with them from the waters of the spring. After heavy rain had washed the overlying sand, exposing a bedrock of iron ore he discovered that the chalybeate waters were impregnated with the mineral.

> I sent some bottles to the R.[oyal] S.[ociety] in June 1667, which were tried with galles before a great assembly there. It turns so black that you might write legibly with it, and did there, after so long a carriage, turn as deepe as a deep claret. The physitians were wonderfully surprised at it, and spake to me to recommend it to the D[rs] of the Bath (from whence it is but about 10 miles).[22]
>
> This advertisement I desired Dr. Rich. Blackburne to word. He is one of the College of Physicians, and practiseth yearly at Tunbridge Wells. It was printed in an almanack of Hen. Coley about 1681, but it tooke no effect. It was about 1688 before they became to be frequented. – Advertisement. At Seen (near the Devizes, in Wiltshire), are springs, discovered to be of the nature and virtue of those at Tunbridge, and altogether as good. They are approved by severall of the physitians of the college in London, and have donne great cures, viz. particularly in the spleen, the reines, and bladder, affected with heat, stone or gravel, or restoring hectic persons to health and strength, and wonderfully conducing in all cases of obstruction. There are good howses and accomodation at reasonable rates.
>
> And towards the latter end of summer there came so much company that the village could not containe them, and they are now preparing for building of houses against the next summer. Jo. Sumner sayth (whose well is the best) that it will be worth to him 200 lib. p[r] ann.[23]

Later John Aubrey was rebuked by the Earl of Abingdon, because the publicity was attracting visitors who disturbed his closely protected game-birds.

The year 1665 had not been a good one for Aubrey. He made new acquaintances. Joan Sumner was to cause him great trouble. Anthony à Wood, with his unpleasantly argumentative, self-satisfied nature, was no better. A glimpse of insecurity is shown in his name.

He was born plain Anthony Wood. He added the 'à' to distinguish himself from the many other ordinary Woods.

Wood had been born in Oxford in the street facing Merton College where he was to be educated and gain a degree. When his father died in 1643 his son inherited an adequate private income. Until 1669 he lived with his brother but after an inevitable disagreement he returned to his birthplace and lived there until his death in 1695.

On 14 July 1673, he wrote, 'The society of Merton would not let me live in the college for fear I should pluck it downe to search after antiquities: and that I was so great a love of antiquities that I loved to live in an old cottleloft rather than a spacious chamber.' It was a half-truth. 'At this time A. W. being resolv'd to set himself to the study of antiquities and do something in them; in the house where he was borne, he set up a chimney in the upper roome looking east; and in the next room joining he put out a window next to the street, and made it a study, in which he composed for the most part those things which he afterwards published.'[24]

In that garret he planned to write a history of Oxford and its university and over the years he used, and misused, much information that the congenial John Aubrey provided.

In Wood's later notes he wrote that the two men met in 1667 but the probability is that it was two years earlier on Saturday 31 August 1665 when Aubrey visited Oxford with his manservant, Wiseman. Years later Wood wrote a bitterly bad-tempered account of the occasion.

... John Aubrey of Easton Piers in the parish of Kington S. Michael in Wiltsh. Was in Oxon with Edward Forrest, a book-seller living against All Souls Coll., to buy books. He then saw lying on the stall *Notitia Acadamiae Oxoniensis*, and asking who the author of that book was, he answer'd the report as that one Mr. Anthony Wood of Merton Coll. was the author, but was not [the true author was William Fulman]. Whereupon Mr. Aubrey, a pretender to antiquities, having been contemporary to A. Wood's elder brother in Trin. Coll. and well acquainted with him, he thought he might be as well acquainted with A. W. himself. Whereupon repairing to his lodgings [Wood's brother's], and telling him who he was, he got his acquaintance, talk'd to him about his studies, and offer'd what assistance he could make, in order to the completion of the work that he [Wood] was in hand with. Mr. Aubrey was then in sparkish mood, came to towne with his man and two horses, spent high, and flung out A. W. at all expenses [paid for everything]. But his estate of 700li per annum being afterwards sold, and he reserving nothing of it for himself, liv'd afterward in a very sorry condition, and at length made shift to rub out by hanging on Edmund Wyld esq. living in Blomesbury neare London, on James bertie earle of Abendon whose first wife was related to him, and on Sir John Aubrey, his kinsman, living sometime in Glamorganshire, and sometime at Borstall near Brill in Bucks. He was a shiftless person, roving and magotie-headed, and sometimes little better than crased. And being exceeding credulous, would stuff his many letters sent to A. W. with fooleries, and misinformation, which sometimes would guide him into paths or errour.

It was as late as 1694 after the two had had an enormous quarrel that Wood, embittered, alone, unwell and near to death, wrote that venomously distorted account.

On the day some thirty years earlier, when he first met Aubrey Wood had had his hair cut just before enjoying a midday meal with John Aubrey. The two dined together at the Mermaid Tavern, the bill for three shillings and eightpence, paid for by Aubrey, who repeated his offer to help Wood with his researches.[25]

It was a fair price for the food. In February of the same year Samuel Pepys took colleagues to a tavern and was given a bill for seven shilling and sixpence 'which was too much', although in June he paid only £1 14s, one pound fourteen shillings for himself and nine others.[26]

Meals were not quick. Dinner was the main meal of the day, eaten at midday and going on for some hours. It consisted of many dishes, all laid out in front of the diners, platters of a leg of mutton, a loin of veal, assorted meats, plates of tender poultry, prawns, anchovies, a big tart, choices of fine English cheeses. Everything was on the table to be taken at choice.

There were wines from France, Germany, Spain, Italy, but there were not yet reliable vintages. Selection was a lottery. One did not sip. The glass or flagon was drained, waiting to be refilled. Insobriety was a custom. One temperate host lavished wines on his mayoral guests and

> so plied them – sitting, standing and walking – that they spent the night in ditches homeward bound, while he himself retired "like a wounded deer to a shady moist place" and there lay down and "evaporated four or five hours".[27]

John Aubrey had enjoyed many convivial meals with his friend Edmund Wyld. It is doubtful whether the industrious and melancholy Anthony à Wood provided such company.

Wood had been working on his Oxford book since 1661 and in October 1669 it was accepted by the University Press at the personal recommendation of Dr Fell, Dean of Christ Church College. Fell suggested that Wood should include some short lives of Oxford's literary and ecclesiastical celebrities and the outcome was Wood's compilation of *Athenae Oxoniensis*, 'an exact history of all the writers and bishops that have had their education in Oxford since 1500'.

Fell, a tall, rigorous man, was a firm royalist who with three others, had ignored puritanical disapproval and maintained Church of England services throughout the morose years of the Commonwealth. Later, when Dean of Christ Church he lived opposite Merton College near Anthony à Wood's house.

Fell had been rigorous in improving university standards, demanding the wearing of academic dress, attendance at lectures, insisting on good discipline, and, for ensuring their education, frequently visited students' rooms, questioning the scholars about their studies.

In 1669 he began the restoration of Christ Church collegiate buildings that had been ruined during the long Commonwealth years. He developed the neglected University Press. In 1676 he became Bishop of Oxford.[28]

Firm, almost fanatical in his reformation of university standards Fell still found time to help poor scholars, employing two to translate Wood's book into Latin.

Stern, aloof, scholarly but humourless, righteous, dogmatic, the dean was a natural target for satirists like the young Christ Church scholar, Tom Brown, who became a student there around 1670. Brown was an idle, unenthusiastic student whom Fell, his college principal, threatened with expulsion for the youth's unsatisfactory attitude to university studies.

Fell, almost uncharacteristically, forgave him on his promise to improve. But Brown resented the criticism and took advantage of Fell's name to mock him with a witty quatrain.

> I do not like thee, Dr. Fell,
> The reason why I cannot tell,
> But this I know and know full well
> I do not like thee, Dr. Fell.

In those days of widespread classical scholarship the result was doubly witty for Brown's contemporaries would hilariously have recognised it as a paraphrase of the Roman poet Martial's epigram 32 in Book One of his *Epigrammata*.

> *Non amo te, Sabidi, nec possum*   I do not love thee, Sabidius, I can't
> *dicere quare;*   say why;
> *Hoc tantum possum dicere, non amo te.*   All I can say is, I do not love thee.

Brown's contemporaries were probably mistaken. That unscholarly, lazy undergraduate was unlikely to know Martial's poem. More feasibly he had simply revamped an English translation of that epigram published in 1661 by Thomas Forde in his *Virtua Rediviva*.

Forde had written:

> I love thee not, Nell,
> But why I can't tell.

Brown would not resist taking advantage of such a convenient rhyme as Nell with 'Fell'.

Despite his brief fame as the composer of Fell's witty quatrain in later life Brown achieved little more than a mediocre reputation as a wit and writer.[29]

It was that rigidly correct but helpful Fell who proposed that Wood should write his proposed lives of Oxford worthies for the University Press.

For that book Aubrey generously offered to send Wood the mini-biographies that he was assembling for his *Brief Lives*. Some of those reports were not what either Wood or Fell had anticipated. His account of the lawyer, historian and antiquary John Selden was an example. Wood used some but not everything in it.

Selden had been an MP during the Civil War but did not agree with many of the extreme measures of that time and soon retired from public engagements. In his home life he was studious and, having inherited a comfortable private income, was something of a dilettante, indulging himself by writing on arcane subjects such as the ancient gods of Syria. He seldom used his status as a barrister.

Aubrey added that in food and drink he was very temperate. That observation was included in Wood's detailed biography.[30]

When Selden died in 1654 it was remarked at his funeral that 'when a learned man dies a great deale of learning dies with him'. Wood used that appraisal as well.

John Selden's best-known work was his posthumous *Table-Talk*. John Aubrey was uncharacteristically dismissive; 'Mr. J. Selden writt a 4to. Booke called *Table-Talke*; which will not endure the Test of the Press.' He misjudged it. Unpublished in Selden's lifetime the book was printed posthumously in 1689 and was Selden's most popular work, written in a lucidly crisp style, and was widely sold and read.

Aubrey provided more dubious details of Selden's enthusiasms. He had slept with the Countess of Kent who 'being an ingeniose woman and loving men, would let him lye with her, and her husband knew it'. There were also lascivious rumours about 'my Lady's She-Blackamoor'. Selden also went to bed with Mris Williamson, 'a lusty bouncing woman'.

Aubrey added, 'I remember my Sadler (who wrought many years to the family) told me that Mr. Selden had got more by his Prick than he had done by his practise. He was no eminent practiser at Barre.'

Predictably, Wood omitted that unacademical, intimate observation. Had he accepted it then the censorious Dr Fell would certainly have deleted such an un-Oxonian vulgarity. Far away from Oxford prudery John Aubrey cheerfully smiled at his wittily alliterative 'prick' and 'practice'.[31]

It was probably at some time during 1665 that Aubrey undertook his survey of the now-destroyed Sanctuary stone circle on Overton Hill near Avebury.

Today it is an unimpressive collection of rings of drab concrete cylinders and slabs overwhelmed by the noise of hill-climbing lorries on the main road but once a lovely stone circle. The site is almost a chronicle of the history of megalithic rings in Wiltshire, their origins, their modifications, their destruction and their quiet mysteries.

The 'remodelled' Sanctuary does not excite the casual visitor. The road roars past it. Concrete blocks and cylinders show the positions of former posts and stones but do little for the imagination.

Long before that architectural travesty John Aubrey saw it early in 1649, its sarsens quite big but 'most of them (now) are fallen downe'. He gave no name for it, simply calling it a 'British Trophie'.

The Sanctuary was not mentioned in William Camden's earlier editions of the *Britain*. The site may first, have been described by Robert Gay, rector of Nettlecombe in Somerset at some time in the mid-seventeenth century. He wrote one of the several mad books about Stonehenge in that time, his nonsense stating that the ring had been built by 'Cangick giants' from his own county.

A glimpse of his political inclinations occurred in 1643 when he led a mob to burn down the Tudor home of George Trevelyan, a Royalist. Gay was imprisoned.

Twenty years later he mentioned some stone circles in Wiltshire, one being the tiny ring at Clatford, 'a pettie *Stonage* there, of eight huge Stones, now called the *broad stones*, antiently standing, but now lying circularly in London way, testified to be a British Trophie, by the fragments of mens bones found in the Burrowes in the fields adjoyning'. There was also the Sanctuary.

On *Sevenburrowes* hill, 4 Miles West of Marleburrow near London way are 40 great Stones, sometimes standing, but now lying in a large Circle, inclosing an inner circle of 16 great Stones, now lying also, testified to be an old British Trophie by the Anglo-British name thereof (viz) *Seaven Burrowes*, and by those 7 huge Burrowes very near it with fragments of mens bones.[32]

In 1663, Sir Robert Moray, a founder member of the Royal Society, noted the same fifty or sixty stones, 'many whole, some broken, some removed' in two circles but confused the radii with the diameters, reducing the rings to half their true size.

Aubrey had already seen the stones 'on the Brow of the hill above Kynet'. It was a concentric circle of stones 'fower or five feet high' although 'most of them (now) are fallen downe'. 'Tis likely that here might in the old time have been the Celle or Convent for the Priest belonging to these Temples.'[33]

Of his Royal Society acquaintances John Evelyn never saw Avebury. In

June 1654 he and his wife left London, stayed in Reading, then dined in Marlborough but went on to Newbury leaving Avebury unseen behind them. Years later, on 15 June 1668, his friend Samuel Pepys did visit the ring, paying a local man a shilling for guiding him.

Then by coach he went on to the Sanctuary, describing it as 'one place with great high stones pitch't round which I believe was some particular fine building like that in some measure like that of Stonag. But about a mile on it was prodigious to see how full the *downes* are of great stones'. It made him think less of Stonehenge whose sarsens must have come from those downs, just 'as well as those at *Abebery*'.[34]

At the circle a helpful local witness for Aubrey was the physician Dr Robert Toope who told him the 'name of the place is Millfield'. Aubrey transcribed Toope's letter of 1 December 1685.

The physician had been digging near the ring for bones to grind 'into a noble medicine that relieved many of my distressed neighbours'. He had found dozens of skeletons round Sanctuary, 'soe close one by another that scul toucheth scul … I really believe the whole plaine, on that even ground, is full of dead bodies … the bones large and almost rotten, but the Teeth extreme, & wonderfully white hard and sound. (No Tobaco taken in those daies)', an indication that the teeth were probably prehistoric.[35]

Looking for another place where there had been a comparable collection of human bones John Aubrey found an apparently similar site described in the 1686 *Philosophical Transactions, 185*, the burial place of Cocherel near the river Eure in north-west France.

Discovered in 1685 it was a megalithic tomb with a deep stone-lined crypt, containing a group of tidily arranged skeletons. Outside it were two standing stones. Hundreds of scattered bones around the grave suggested a likeness to what Toope had unearthed near the Sanctuary.

> This antiquity found at Cocherel in France, having a little resemblance to ye Temple fig.
> 1 [Sanctuary] I thought it not improper to insert it, here after that.[36]

It was an ironical observation by Aubrey. Although he could never have realised its significance the entombed skeletons and the disarranged bones in the neighbourhood of Cocherel were a wordless indication of what the English stone circle had been.

In its beginning the Sanctuary had held bodies of the elite of Late Neolithic society. Outside lay the buried remains of commoners, those found by Toope. Aubrey was puzzled because he knew only about the stones, unaware that they had been much later replacements for an earlier wooden structure. It would not be until a twentieth-century excavation that the sequence and the reason for the building was understood.[37]

Centuries later that claustrophobic place was converted into an unroofed concentric stone circle as an open-air replica of the earlier building. Open to the sun it was eventually linked to Avebury by the serpentine Kennet stone avenue.

It had been a 'mortuary', a charnel house, for privileged members of society, a society that changed over the generations from the entire members of leading families to only the one male clan chieftain.

On page 226 of the *Philosophical Transactions* Aubrey read a stimulating question about the Cocherel bodies. 'There remains now to guess, by these Stones and what antiquities we have left in History, who these *Barbarians* should be, and at what time this Sepulcher might be made.' They had had no metal, neither iron nor bronze, just flint and stone.[38] It was one more clue about dating for John Aubrey.

His fieldwork was gradually providing him with some insights about the possible age and meaning of stone circles, their differing sizes, avenues, nearness to water. Their whereabouts outside southern England was as yet unknown to him.

His private life was becoming ever more difficult involving him into a matrimonial fiasco-cum-disaster. '1665: 1 November; 1665, 'I made my first addresse (in an ill howre) to Joane Sumner.' Worse was to follow.

7

1666: Aubrey's field-work at Stonehenge

For that famous circle John Aubrey had copied "the following extract from *England Described* by Edward Leigh, Esq. 1659: 'About six miles from Salisbury in the plaines before named (they are but rarely inhabited, and had in late times a bad name for Robberies there committed) is to be seen a huge and monstrous piece of worke Stonehenge'".

William Long, 1876, 31

Stonehenge is an enigma. The monument mutates with every arrival of new people. To the superstitious incomers who succeeded its builders it was a place to be avoided. To the Romans it was a tourist attraction, somewhere to have picnics, the visitors unaware of the bones of women and children buried in the surrounding ditch.

To Saxons the lintelled circle looked like a mass-gallows and *stan-hengen* they called it, 'the hanging-stones', and the name has persisted, little changed, for more than a thousand years.

Then Stonehenge became famous. Shortly after the Norman Conquest it was the subject of the most widely read story in Western Europe, a fantastic mélange of monsters, Africa, and a sacred ring called the 'Giant's Dance' in Ireland that Merlin magically uprooted to re-erect on Salisbury Plain. The literate population, mostly monks and prelates, loved the *Historia Regum Britanniae* by Geoffrey of Monmouth, his fictitious Latin *History of the King of Britain*, and it remained popular, the accepted truth about Stonehenge, for almost four hundred uncritical years. It was not until the final years of the fifteenth century that the few medieval murmurs of scepticism developed into clearly spoken Tudor doubts.[1]

All this was known in 1663 when John Aubrey attended Charles II at the court of Whitehall. With him he had taken a plan of Avebury 'donne from memorie alone'. Contrasting it with the one displayed to the king by his own colleague, Walter Charleton, Aubrey was embarrassed to realise how inaccurate his own was and, the following month, 'I surveyed the old Monument of Aubury with a plaine-table and afterwards took a Review of Stoneheng', a site he 'had knowne since eight yeares old'.

That review came three years after Avebury, 'The Ichonographie of Stoneheng as it remaines this present yeare 1666'. Unlike Avebury's inaccurate draft it was far better than anything done by others before him, including that drawn by Inigo Jones, James I's royal architect, drawn some twenty years earlier in the 1640s.

But before Aubrey could begin considering when Stonehenge had been built and for what reason, even as late as Stuart times much archaeological nonsense about the ring existed.

There had been occasional medieval critics of Geoffrey's story of African giants in Ireland, Merlin and Stonehenge and by the sixteenth century those doubts had been succeeded by complete scepticism. Unfortunately, those sceptics provided a different but equally persistent foolishness.

Having rejected Geoffrey of Monmouth's Merlin's transportation of the monstrous boulders of Stonehenge no one could imagine how those sarsens had been moved. Speculative history was replaced by speculative geology. The circle was a mineralogical contradiction. That impossible structure of colossal stones stood on Salisbury Plain, a bleak landscape of sterile chalk and flint entirely lacking stones whether large or small. The logical conclusion was that the sarsens were not natural but artificial, ingeniously created by man.

Following Dr George Hakewell's 1627 suggestion of the stones being artificial a London printer and lawyer, John Rastell, in *The Pastyme of People* of 1630, decided that the stones were 'so hard that no yryn tole wyll cut them without great bysynes ... not Natural, or had their first growth here, but were Artificially cemented into that hard and durable Substance from some large Congeries of Sand, and other unctuous matter mixt together'.[2]

Seven years later the antiquarian and traveller William Camden, whose pioneering survey of Great Britain, *Britannia*, was published in Latin in 1586 and in English in 1610, cautiously agreed. 'Yet some there are, that thinke them to bee no naturall stones hewne out of the rocke ... stuck together by some glewie and matter knit and incorporate together'. He found some classical support for that belief from Pliny's report of man-made stone at Puteoli in Roman Italy.[3]

John Aubrey despaired at such gullibility. Some people believed that stones even of churches and cathedrals could be 'cast, forsooth, as chandlers make candles ... and not onely the vulgar swallow down the tradition gleb, but severall learned and otherwise understanding persons will not be perswaded to the contrary, and that the art is lost ... and the like errour runnes from generation to generation concerning Stoneheng, that the stones there are artificiall'.[4]

The petrological fact was that the sarsens were natural and came from the Marlborough Downs near Avebury. Aubrey had seen them and common sense and local knowledge supported him.

Enormous blocks of sarsen covered the upper slopes of the Marlborough Downs. Hundreds had been used for the erection of their great circles and avenues and for nearby chambered tombs.

Formed by the natural cementing of a bed of quartzite in a prehistoric sea from clays, sands and loams millions of years ago, a thick layer of sacharoidal sandstone concreted on the chalk of the sea-bed. When the sea retreated forests grew on the surface, their roots penetrating the sand. The holes can still be seen in stones at Avebury and Stonehenge.

The freezing Ice Ages broke the bed of sarsen into gargantuan slabs ideal for the building of a stone circle. Sometimes called druid-stones, bridestones and grey-wethers from their similarity to grazing sheep, the stones are best known as sarsens, perhaps because they are 'saracens' or 'foreigners' in their chalk landscape. There are other explanations, one of them local and convincing.

John Aubrey, writing about northern Wiltshire, noted, 'They are also (far from the rode) commonly called Sarsdens, or Sarsdon stones.' In Anglo-Saxon the word was the hybrid *sar-stan* or 'troublesome stone'. *Sar* had the meaning of 'grievous' as in several Saxon elegiac poems such as 'The Wanderer'. 'Grievous stones' was poetically apt for the reactions of early farmers as they struggled to extract and drag unwieldy, half-buried sarsens from intended fields. *Sar-stan*, 'sarsen', is just as alliterative and far more expressive than today's 'Bloody boulder!'[5]

The stones were excellent for a megalithic ring. 'Those that lie in the weather are so hard that no toole can touch them,' wrote Aubrey, 'They take a good polish.'[6]

William Lambarde, historian and Keeper of the Records in the Tower of London, agreed and provided more details. In an unpublished manuscript of 1580 he decried Merlin and Ireland as 'mere vanities', and observed that the sarsens of Stonehenge were local because 'theare is within the same Shyre great Stoare of Stone of the same Kinde, namely above *Marlborow*, from whence I thinke they weare chosen by the Greatness, for other Difference eyther in Matter or Fashion I see none'. It was commonsense. There were hundreds of them scattered over the Marlborough Downs twenty miles north of Salisbury Plain.

Lambarde ridiculed Geoffrey of Monmouth. The sarsens had not been brought by Merlin from Ireland. 'They are of the very kind of Stone with the Grey-weathers about fourteen miles off: that tract of ground near Marleborough.' Nor were the stones artificial and carried by magic to Salisbury Plain. Commonsense told him that they had been dragged on 'Rowlers' from near Avebury. He did not, however, speculate on the origin of the bluestones, perhaps did not notice that they were different in appearance and texture from the sarsens.[7]

Such occasional flickers of common sense against the traditionally accepted medieval bewilderment of fairies and hobgoblins encouraged John Aubrey to begin a lifetime's search for the truth about Stonehenge and other prehistoric stone circles of Britain.

The earlier antiquarian Willliam Camden did not speculate about origins. 'For mine owne part, about these points I ... lament with much griefe that the Authors of so notable a monument are thus buried in oblivion'. 'I feare me greatly that no man is able to fetch out the truth, so deeply plunged within the winding revolutions of so many ages ... they lie so hidden in the utmost nooke and secretest closet of Antiquitie, as it were in a most thicke wood, where no pathwaies are to be seene ... oblivion hath so long removed out of sight of our ancestours.'[8] That reluctant acceptance that the present was helplessly ignorant of the prehistoric past was to endure throughout the seventeenth and eighteenth centuries and well into the nineteenth.

Some of Camden's contemporaries believed that the circle had been a memorial. A Swiss student, Herman Folkerzheimer, visiting Stonehenge in 1562 decided that the stones were set up as trophies to the Romans, because the actual positioning of the stones resembles a yoke, 'the yoke symbolising the enslaving of the Britons'. Camden disagreed. '*Ambrosius Aurelianus*, or his brother *Vther* did reare them by the art of *Merlin* that great *Mathematician.*'[9]

Decades later Edmund Bolton deduced that Stonehenge had been Boudica's burial place and shrine. Having taken poison after her defeat by the Romans, 'the BRITANNS entered [interred] her pompously, or with much magnificence, cannot be better verified than by assigning these orderly irregular, and formlesse uniform heaps of massive marble to her everlasting remembrance.'[10]

Unsurprisingly, no evidence for that burial was unearthed when the Duke of Buckingham had a hugely optimistic treasure-pit dug at the centre of Stonehenge in 1620 when he had accompanied King James I to Wilton near the circle.

Forty-six years after 1620 when James I had visited Wiltshire to sell lucrative £30 knighthoods, John Aubrey saw that near the centre of Stonehenge 'is a Pitt, which the Duke of Buckingham ordered to be digged ... at which time, and by wch meanes, the Stone [55] twenty one foote long (now out of the ground) reclined by being under-digged ... it is about the bignesse of two sawe-pitts', big enough for two men to stand sawing through a log lying above them across the top of the hole. Archaeological retribution followed. The iconoclastic Duke of Buckingham was assassinated eight years later.[11]

Aubrey added that some time later Inigo Jones discovered 'a Thuribulum or some such like vase lyeing three foot within the ground. I think it was in the Pitt', apparently Buckingham's. Possibly it had been an Early Bronze Age incense cup.[12]

Aubrey was misled about Buckingham and the toppling of Stone 55. The Stonehenge sketch of 1574 showed that the sarsen had already fallen with its partner, the tall 56, tilting forward. By Aubrey's time around 1660 it was leaning at an angle of 75° and the inclination increased steadily over the centuries.

The Duke also had several barrows opened but by Aubrey's time any finds had been lost. Except one, a silver-tipped bugle that 'Mrs Trotman told me his Grace kept in his Closet [as] a great Relique'. Otherwise, dissatisfied by his profitless efforts the nobleman decided to purchase the ring and 'offered Mr. Newdick (then Owner of this place) any rate for it but he would not accept it.

Aubrey was given the information about Buckingham by Mrs Mary Trotman of West Amesbury Farm, wife of Anthony, a tenant of the then owner of Stonehenge, Lawrence Washington. Aubrey recognised where Buckingham's outrage had been and marked the oval spot just off-centre of the circle some paces north of the broken 55's tip.[13]

It is a cameo of Stuart social life: the king's proud favourite, intelligent, charming, arrogantly assuming that no one could oppose him, the independent gentleman and landowner providing that opposition, and the ever-inquisitive John Aubrey nosily asking questions at local farms about things that had happened almost half a century earlier, and the gossipy farmer's wife telling how exciting those years had been. No wonder Aubrey had so often, half-contentedly, murmured to himself:

How these curiosities would be quite forgot, did not such idle fellowes as I am putt them down.

In 1620 when James I had visited the Earl of Pembroke at Wilton seven miles south of the circle some of the royal party rode out to the ring and, not content with looking, dug into various parts, finding skulls of bulls, oxen 'or other beasts'. A prominent member of those primitive archaeologists was Dr William Harvey, discoverer of the circulation of the blood.

Curious about Stonehenge the king had asked the earl what the circle was and, knowing nothing about the ring, Pembroke wrote to Inigo Jones, the royal architect, 'and requested him to dispel the fogs of ignorance and antiquity for the benefit of the inquisitive monarch'.

Jones, who five years earlier had been appointed prestigious Surveyor of the King's Works', remembered that he had been commanded by the king, 'out of mine own experience in *Architecture*, and experience in *Antiquities* abroad, what possibly I could discover concerning this *Stoneheng*'. The

1. John Aubrey. Portrait by William Faithorne, 1666. (*Ashmolean Museum, Oxford*)

Above: 2. Kington St Michael's church. (*Author's collection*)

Below: 3. Anthony à Wood's house, Merton Street, Oxford. A plaque to him can be seen on the wall to the right. (*Author's collection*)

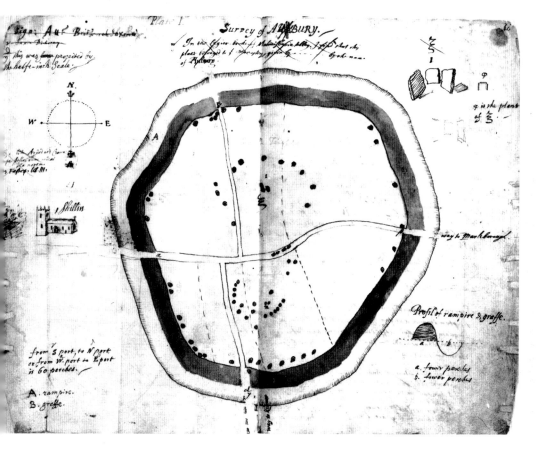

6. Aubrey's plan of Avebury. (*Bodleian Library, Oxford*)

Opposite top: 4. Avebury. Stones in the south-eastern arc of the great circle. (*Author's collection*)

Opposite bottom: 5. The outlying stone and circle of Long Meg & Her Daughters, Cumbria. (*Author's collection*)

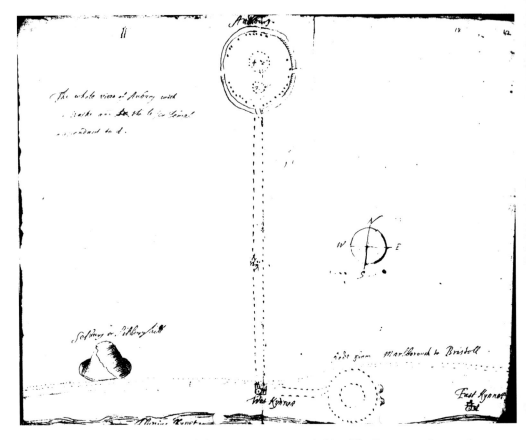

7. Aubrey's plan of Avebury and the Kennet avenue, Wiltshire. The Sanctuary ring can be seen at the end of the avenue. (*Bodleian Library, Oxford*)

Opposite: 8. Stonehenge. Inigo Jones' plan and Aubrey's sketched criticisms. (*Bodleian Library, Oxford*)

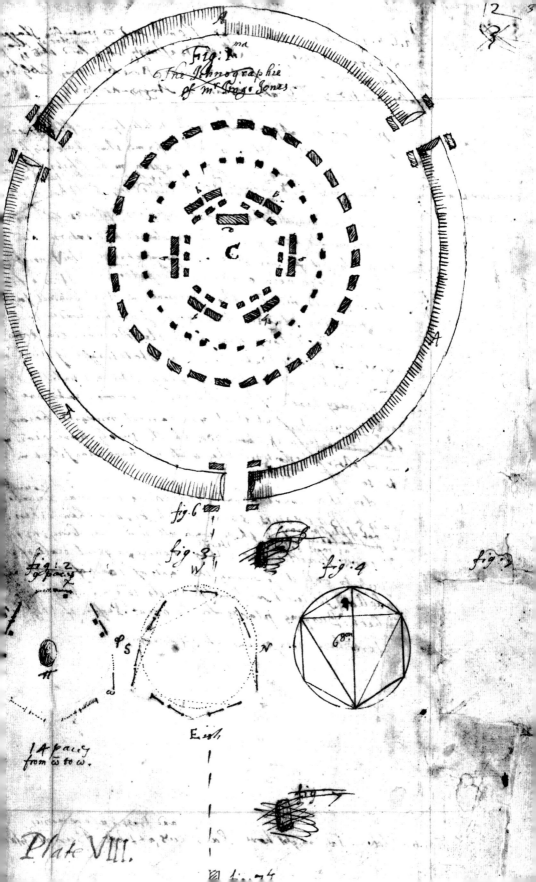

Fig: ma
The Ichnographie
of Mr Inigo Jones

C

fig. 6

fig. 8

W

fig. 2
fig. spacy

ϕ S

ω

fig. 4

6 80m

fig. 3

E

14 spacy
from ω to ω.

Plate VIII.

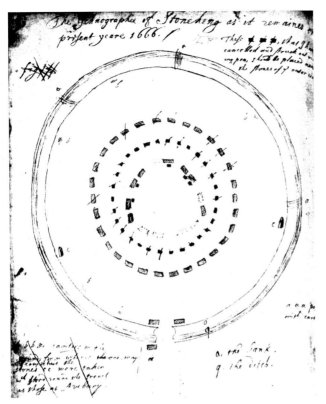

9. Aubrey's corrected
field-plan of Stonehenge,
Wiltshire, in 1666.
(*Bodleian Library,
Oxford*)

10. The Rollright Stones circle, Oxfordshire. A sketch in William Camden's *Britannia*.
(*Author's collection*)

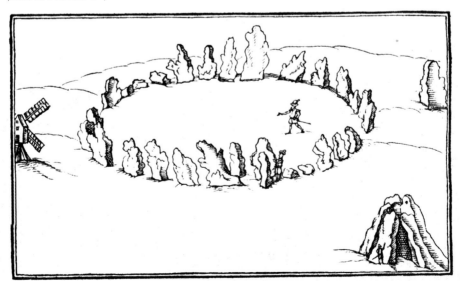

Above: 11. Chalk rings marking the places of some Aubrey Holes, Stonehenge. (*Author's collection*)

Below: 12. St Mary Magdalen church, Oxford. John Aubrey was buried there in 1697. His grave is not known. (*Author's collection*)

outcome was to be the first book entirely devoted to the circle and, more importantly, was based on fieldwork instead of the established custom of relying on earlier unreliable guesswork.[14]

Having pitched a tent near the ring Jones cleared the ground of bushes and began his investigations. A meticulous architect, Jones was not content to measure diameters and record the heights of stones. He excavated and discovered how deeply they were set in the chalk. He 'digged throughout all the Foundations'. He checked that there had been no stones between the circle and the surrounding earthwork, proving that 'there could never be found, by whatever digging, though no Cost or Pains was spared, the Footsteps or Fragments of any Courses of Stone between those of the Trench, and the outward Circle'.

The result was the first plan of the circle, 'The Groundplot of the work as it now stands', some stones already missing, a trilithon 57-58, lacking its lintel, leaning, to fall two centuries later, many lintels missing from the outer circle.[15]

From faulty reasoning Jones deduced there had been three gaps through the bank placed geometrically at the corners of an equilateral triangle, a wide one at the north-east, a narrower at the south, and a mistaken one at the north-west, each with four portal stones to dignify the entrances.

Forty years later John Aubrey called this trio 'absolutely false' and the plan he made for Charles II showed only the earthwork's north-east entrance with two stones inside the bank and one more outside the ditch. Jones' nephew, John Webb, using his uncle's posthumous and 'indigested' notes, corroborated this. 'He hath described in his Draught two Stones ... these were the two parallel stones that stood upon the inside of the Trench, at the Entrance from the North-East.'[16]

Presumably written nine forgetful years after 1620 when Jones was staying at Wilton in 1649 he was also wrong about those portals, 'at each of which was raised, on the Outside of the Trench aforesaid, two huge Stones gatewise, parallel where unto on the Inside two others of less Proportion'. He had mistakenly confused the inner with the outer pair. It was the external pillars that were smaller and smashed. He described them as 'four foot broad, and three foot thick; but they lie so broken, and ruined by time, that their proportion in height cannot be distinguisht, much less exactly measured'. The inner pair, the Slaughter Stone and the now-lost 'E' still stood, 'seven foot broad, three foot thick, and twenty foot high'.[17]

Jones' strength was his wide knowledge of classical architecture. From his plan he decided that Stonehenge was Roman, of the Tuscan order, 'rude, plain, simple'. 'The *Order* is not only *Roman*, but the *Scheam* also (consisting of 'four [intersecting] equilaterall triangles, inscribed within the circumference of a Circle) by which this work *Stoneheng* formed, was an *Architectonicall Scheam* used by the Romans.' It followed that Stonehenge was a Roman work. It could never have been a British monument.[18]

'As for their manner of living, the Britans were then a savage and barbarous people, knowing no use at all of garments ... Now, if destitute of the knowledge, even to clothe themselves, much lesse any knowledge had they to erect stately structures, or such remarkable works as *Stoneheng*'.[19] The great circle could only have been designed by cultured Romans.

Although Aubrey rejected Jones' explanation for his 'greater Hexagon' he did wonder, 'Why might not be then, the seaven-sided figure in the foregoing scheme be made in relation to the seaven Planets, & seaven daies of the Weeke? I cannot determine. I only suggest.'[20] It was speculation without foundation. In early prehistoric Britain there were no weeks, only daytime and night, the waxing and waning of the moon and the slow changing of the seasons.

Nor, in the early seventeenth century, were there seven genuine planets. Uranus, 1781, Neptune, 1846, and Pluto, 1930, were to be discovered. Aubrey's seven were Mercury, Venus, Mars, Jupiter and Saturn plus, astronomically incorrect, the earth and the moon.

As late as 1771 John Smith used an almost identical combination when labelling the trilithons on his plan. 'I call them the seven planets, which at present give names to the seven days of the week.'[21]

As Horace Walpole much later acidulously observed, 'It is remarkable that whoever has treated of the monument has bestowed on it whatever class of antiquity he was particularly fond of'. It was true of Jones and it was to be true of Charleton half a century later.[22]

Jones decided that there must have been a sixth trilithon to complete 'the greater Hexagon' most of whose stones 'after so long a contest with the violence of time, and injury of weather, are for the most part standing at this day'. But integrity made him omit the speculative trilithon from his objective Plan Seven.

Jones died in 1652 and his book was not published until his nephew, John Webb, had it printed in 1655. It was an anticlimax. Few copies were made, sales were slow and what books remained were destroyed in the Great Fire of London in 1666.

John Aubrey had read Jones' work.

In the year 1655 was published by Mr *Web* a Booke intitled *Stone-heng-restored* which I read with great delight; there is a great deale of Learning in it: but, having compared his Scheme with the Monument it self, I found he had not dealt fairly: but had made a Lesbians rule, which is conformed to the stone: that is, he framed the monument to his own Hypothesis, which is much differing from the Thing it self. This gave me an edge to make more researches.[23]

One result of that resolve showed that Aubrey was developing a scepticism about the age of other monuments around Stonehenge. From Inigo Jones he read the dismissive observation about the barbaric Saxons that 'the *Saxons* were buried in huge heapes of earth, to this day visible amongst us'. As a marginal note Aubrey added, '(I pray) why might not the Britons to be buried so too?'[24] It was, perhaps, the first evidence that he was considering the unconsidered possibility that human beings before the Danes and the Saxons and even the Romans could have been responsible for that inexplicable fleshless carcase of sarsen on Salisbury Plain.

Well into the seventeenth century the accepted fact was that the builders of Stonehenge had been foreign invaders: Inigo Jones in 1655 chose the Romans, Walter Charleton in 1663 suggested Danes and Aylett Sammes in 1676 preferred the mercantile traders the Phoenicians. Surprisingly, it was not until 1722 that an obscure German antiquary, Johann Keysler, proposed the Saxons, the very people that had given Stonehenge its name.

The Romans, the Danes, Phoenicians, Saxons, all of them were possibilities as the builders of Stonehenge but never the nameless, savage, naked native Britons. No writer favoured them except for the Reverend Robert Gay of Nettlecombe, near Williton on Exmoor, who did believe that Stonehenge and similar rings were British. The problem was that his 'evidence' was not only faulty but also near lunacy. Yet his book of about 1666 but unpublished until 1725, *A FOOL'S BOLT soon shott at STONAGE*, did influence Aubrey's thinking when it circulated in manuscript from friend to friend.

He asked friends whom the anonymous author was and Andrew Paschall told him in 1690 that he was 'M^r ... Jay of Nettlecomb', who died '(I thinke) 14, or 16 yeares since'. Gay had died in 1672, his successor regretting 'that in his tyme there was a very great failure in registering the baptisms and burials of severall persons'.

'Stonage,' wrote Gay, 'is an old British monument; where, first, I shall briefly shew, who, and what, the old Britons were, and afterward, that this was an old British monument. The old Britons were the first of six Nations, which had the possession of this Land successively, *viz, old Britons, Belgae, Romanes, Saxons, Danes and Normans.*'

Long before those humans a battle on Salisbury Plain was won by Cangic giants from Somerset, the evidence of that 'bloodie battle' lying 'in the numerous traines of burrowes, with mens bones in them, extending from *Stonage* to *Amesburie*'.

Cangi were monsters but were not fictitious. There was evidence of their existence because of 'some huge bones of men, found amongst others, in the said burrowes, as aforesaid, and in other places near *Stonage*'. Sir

Thomas Elliott had described the finds in his *Dictionary*. 'About 30 years since I myself, being with my father, Sir Richard Elliott, at a monastery of regular Canons (three or four miles from Stonage) beheld the bones of a dead man found deep in the ground, which being joyned together, was in length 13 foot and ten inches, whereof one of the teeth my father had, which was of the quantity of a great wallnut.'

'The Cangick Giants having conquered, triumphed over their enemies … they thought it expedient to erect this Monument, as their 'Trophie'. That monument was Stonehenge,' wrote Gay.

His book was erudite, containing evidence that he had seen other stone circles. It was detailed in its descriptions but, unlike Inigo Jones' work on Stonehenge, it was no more than an exercise in escapism.[25]

Jones' conclusions had been erudite, intelligent, logical, and wrong. His book was followed eight years later by Walter Charleton, a physician to Charles II, who contradicted it. Charleton decided that Stonehenge had been the grandiloquent handiwork of Danish courtiers to be 'a royal Court, a place for the inauguration of their Kings', using the learned Danish antiquarian Olaus Wormius as his literary source for references to ancient monuments in Denmark.

Charleton, however, made no attempt to describe Stonehenge itself. Inigo Jones had introduced the reading world to what could be seen at the site. Charleton added only unhistorical wishful thinking in favour of things Danish.[26]

Following Charleton John Aubrey was confronted by an accumulated bewilderment of opinions about Stonehenge from as early as the eleventh century Merlin/magic imagination of Geoffrey of Monmouth to the more recent 'information' about Boudica, Romans and Danes. There was also a blur of local legends.

Aubrey had to assess those tales and also the 'scholarly' theories before examining the disordered stones of the circle themselves to deduce the truth from the monument of Stonehenge itself.

The early nineteenth-century antiquary Sir Richard Colt Hoare had read the still-unpublished *Monumenta Britannica*. He praised it.

This Manuscript, though a *RUDIS INDIGESTAQUE MOLIS* ['a rough, disorganised heavy mass'] is well deserving of the Antiquary's notice, especially as it regards the two celebrated Monuments of British antiquity in our Island viz ABURY and Stonehenge and gives the earliest account of them. much previous to that of the learned D[r] STUKELEY.[27]

That 'disorganised heavy mass', an apt description of the higgledy-piggledy notes gradually assembled by Aubrey as he considered and slowly rejected peasant beliefs about the great ring.

Many local stories were told about the half-wrecked ring. As an embellishment of Geoffrey of Monmouth's medley of giants, Ireland and Merlin some people believed that the stones had been put up as a memorial for Merlin's mother. Or the Devil had stolen the sarsens from the backyard of an old Irish woman, cheating her with false money. Or, other variations claimed, the ring was built of the ossified bodies of nocturnal giants caught in the dawning light of day. And one sarsen had a deep cavity caused by a boulder flung by the Devil at a passing friar.

The most persistent of these credulities was not only that the stones could not be counted but anyone so unfortunate as to compute the number correctly would die.

Numerically, death was unlikely. The disordered stones and stumps were almost uncountable. Some pillars stood, others leaned, or were weathered stumps. With half-buried lintels and fractured bits and pieces from sarsens and bluestones it is unsurprising that the task frustrated so many people. John Evelyn counted ninety-five; Celia Fiennes ninety-one. Daniel Defoe thought a rather slipshod seventy-two. William Stukeley claimed almost double that figure, one hundred and forty.[28]

An earlier numerologist, Prince Charles, had visited Stonehenge in 1651. Years later his companion derided the myth of uncountability: 'The King's Arithmetike gave the lye to that fabulous tale that those stones cannot be told alike twice together.' Samuel Pepys agreed. 'They are hard to tell but yet can be told.' But neither the prince nor Pepys specified a number.[29]

Nor did Aubrey. His own plan simply showed those stones that remained from the sarsens of the outer circle to the surviving trilithons at the heart of the ring. He drew a line through those that had fallen.

His field-survey had been days of hard labour in that hot summer, coats discarded, men hired to hold horses, workers dragging the linked measuring chains across the ring, Aubrey's servant making notes, he himself moving from stone to stone, drafting the first rough plan, insisting on yet one more rechecking of the lengths. The outcome was a triumph.

That plan was good, far better and more objective than Jones'. The ring was measured accurately despite the litter of stones. 'From the circular Trench to the grand circle of stones is thirty-five yards [105 ft, 32 m]. 'The Diameter of the grand circle of stones is thirty two yards ½, [97 ft 6 ins, 27.9 m], a distance that accords within an inch of Alexander Thom's precise survey of 1973, 97 ft 4.9 ins, 29.7 m, forty-five of his Megalithic Rods.[30]

Beyond them was the yet-to-be misnamed Heel Stone 'of which there hath not been any notice been taken'. It was, he decided, 'the remains of the Avenue' like those he had already seen at Avebury and Stanton Drew. Two dotted lines stretching northwards past the Heel 'signifie the imaginarie Walke of Stones which was there heretofore.'[31]

Having disagreed with Jones' hypothesis 'this gave me an edge to make more researches'. At the disputed north-eastern entrance Aubrey's plan, drawn almost fifty years after Jones' investigations, showed only the eastern outer portal. The shattered fragments of the west had disappeared. The Slaughter Stone and its partner remained standing.[32]

But because of the tumbled litter of broken sarsens and bluestones at the centre of the circle he failed to recognise the Altar Stone even though Inigo Jones had drawn it clearly in his own plan. 'He supposed an Altar stone; here are stones fall'n down, this supposed Altar being one of them. Perhaps they used no Altar; for I find the middle of these monuments voyed', referring to the absence of any such stone in any other stone circle that he had seen. It was an uncharacteristic lapse on his part.[33]

He found no stone recognisable as an altar but his keen observation did make him the discoverer of four of the famous pits now named after him, the fifty-six Aubrey Holes. Early in the twentieth century Hawley, knowing of Aubrey's findings, probed with a steel bar and found several of the filled-in pits 'at regular intervals of 16 feet [4.9 m] … To these we have given the name of 'Aubrey Holes' to distinguish them from others which may hereafter be found, and as a compliment to our respected pioneer who left such a useful record'.

They were, Aubrey had written, 'little cavities in the ground, from whence one may well conjecture the stones c, c, were taken [the two remaining Four Stations, 91 and 93]' that he supposed had once been part of a ring around the inner edge of the ditch '(ornamentally) as at Aubury'. His deduction that the pits had held 'stones' made him over three hundred years ahead of modern conclusions.

Sceptics have doubted that he could have noticed such insignificant traces of holes that had been filled for more than four thousand years but the sceptics were ignorant of English history. The year preceding Aubrey's discovery, 1665, had been the time of the Great Plague, and 1666 was the year of the Great Fire of London, two years of insufferably hot summers when prayers were said daily for rain and when Aubrey's earth-filled 'cavities' would have retained some moisture, vegetation and colour unlike the aridly hard, bleached chalk around them.[34]

John Aubrey also mentioned a folk-story about a fallen stone that lay at the west of the ring. 'One of the great Stones that lies downe on the west side, hath a cavity something resembling the print of a man's foot; concerning which the Shepherds and countrey people have a Tradition (wch many of them doe steadfastly believe) that when Merlin conveyed these Stones from Ireland by Art Magick, the Devill hitt him in the heele with that stone, and so left the print there.' The particular 'great' supine pillar was possibly the long, tumbled sarsen 19 at the west of the outer circle.[35]

Aubrey never identified it and it was not until 1771 that John Smith wilfully ignored the legend and, for the sake of his preferred astronomical theory transferred the name from one of the circle stones to the outlying 'solar' Heel Stone which had never lain down and had no sign of a footprint on it. The Devil and sarsens were almost bedfellows in Wiltshire. Villagers claimed there was an imprint of his foot on one of the Broome circle stones, and the fiend lurked everywhere in and around Avebury.[36]

Aubrey did not limit his description to the circle. 'Round about Stoneheng,' he noted, 'one may number/count 43, or 45 Barrowes, some much bigger than others.' Camden had known of them. 'Mens bones have beene digged up here', and his engraving portrayed two treasure-hunters, unearthed skull and bones beside them, trenching into a round barrow, perhaps a bell-barrow in the Cursus group. The engraving was a copy of a sketch of 1575 which 'sheweth wher great bones of men are found'. Camden believed the bones had been buried by the comrades of warriors killed in battles. Aubrey doubted it. 'Soldiers have something else to do.'[37]

Two years after John Aubrey's survey Pepys saw Stonehenge on 11 June 1668. From Salisbury 'to *Stonehege* over the plain and some prodigious great hills even to frighten us. Came thither and them find them as prodigious as any tales I ever heard of them and worth going this journey to see. God knows what their use was. They are hard to tell but yet may be told. Gave the shepherd woman for leading our horses [fourpence].' The guide that took him to the circle received two shillings.[38]

He had stayed at the George Inn on the high street, indignant at the reckoning being so exorbitant for their horses and 7s 6d for bread and beer, total cost £2 5s 6d!

Fourteen years earlier on 22 June 1654 John Evelyn saw Stonehenge 'indeed a stupendous monument, appearing at a distance like a castle; how so many and huge pillars of stone should have been brought together, some erect, others transverse on the tops of them, in a circular area as rudely representing a cloister or heathen and more natural temple is wonderful. The stone is so exceeding hard, that all my strength with a hammer could not break a fragment ...'[39]

John Aubrey had other thoughts about Stonehenge. He mused, 'The Inscription in Lead found at Stoneheng, wch Mr Lilly the Schoolmaster, and Sir Tho. Eliot could not read, might be made by the Druides.' Stukeley added his regrets: 'But eternally to be lamented is the loss of that tablet of tin, which was found at this place ... inscrib'd with many letters.' It had probably been a *defxione*, a 'curse-tablet' stamped on imperishable lead and deposited by some bitter enemy in a place of superstition.[40]

John Aubrey was very much a man of his time, intelligent, educated, but conditioned from childhood by popular beliefs, of fairies, witchcraft, giants, that church bells could drive away thunder, his mind a medley of scientific curiosity and medieval credulity. He recorded without scepticism the local tradition that pieces or grains of sarsen dropped into wells around Stonehenge would drive away toads.

Yet he dismissed the notion that 'no Mag-Pye, Toade, or Snake was ever seen here' as though the animals were terrified of the stones. To the contrary, he explained, weaker birds would not fly over the open plain 'for fear of Hawkes and Ravens', toads would not move far from their spawning-grounds, and snakes and adders preferred the protection of shade and shelter.[41]

John Aubrey's Stonehenge can be left with his words about starlings. 'I thought of *Aves Druidum* when I saw the Stares breed in holes of the Stones of Stoneheng. The Welsh doe call Stars *Sturni Adar y Drudwy*, *i.e. Aves Druidum*, "birds of the druids" because they could talk.' Then came a comment that could have come straight from his *Brief Lives*, a characteristic Aubreyism. 'Pliny tells of a stare that could speake Greek. Why not?'[42]

There is one last thought about Stonehenge. A common belief in those parts of Britain where there are stone circles is that anyone going to them should always walk around the rings, *deasil*, clockwise, following the path of the sun. That way there is fortune.

What must never, ever be done, is to move *widdershins*, anticlockwise. That is the Devil's path, doom-laden, bringing certain misfortune to the misguided.

It is ironical that that is the direction that English Heritage has arranged for visitors to Stonehenge to follow, through the concrete tunnel to the path that turns to the right, against the sun, anticlockwise to the full-stop of ropes and the Heel Stone.

Such misdirection three centuries later could not be known to John Aubrey. What did concern and puzzle him was what the enigmatic circles with their well-spaced stones could have been. They did not look like the remains of dwellings even though Stonehenge with its lintels did resemble the unfinished framework of a house.

But there were no lintels, even pegs for them, in any of the other rings that he knew. There were none at Avebury nor Stanton Drew, nor Clatford nor the slumping stones on Overton Hill. None of them could have been designed to become homes.

And, despite assertions of that great antiquarian William Camden, they could never have been any kind of fortification. They were defenceless. A resolute enemy could have stormed them in minutes. Only the deep ditch around Avebury might have been a defence. But every other site lacked such an impediment.

The circles were not to live in. They were not designed to withstand attack.

They were mysteries unless they had been something unconsidered until the later years of the seventeenth century, strangely unsuspected open-air temples. It was an idea that could be tested against other stone circles if there were any elsewhere in England.

But life for John Aubrey in 1666 was not all Stonehenge and musings about the ancient past. There was a distant tragedy and a disaster much closer and much more personal.

In the late summer a fire started on Sunday night, 2 September, in a bakery on Pudding Lane near the Tower of London. It was in the far east of the city. To the Lord Mayor, Sir Thomas Bloodworth, it was a triviality. 'A woman might piss it out,' he shrugged. He was more than incompetent. He was stupid.[43]

The combination of the long, hot, dry summer and a persistently strong wind from the east spread flames through the crowded, flimsy wooden houses. Day by day the blaze spread westwards right across London up to Temple Bar. John Aubrey's old lodgings on Fleet Street were burnt down.

There was no adequate fire service nor powerful hoses. To create breaks houses were pulled down but the destructive flames flared across the improvised gaps across London and northwards up to Smithfields. An eyewitness described the unceasing destruction. 'The fire gets mastery, and burns dreadfully, and God with his great bellows blows upon it.'[44]

For five long days, from 2-7 September London burned. Eighty-nine churches were destroyed, over thirteen thousand houses, two-thirds of a square mile of that tinder-box of inflammable dwellings. People fled leaving everything behind them. John Evelyn watched the conflagration.

'All the sky was of a fiery aspect, like the top of a burning oven, and the light seen above forty miles round-about for many nights.' When it was over: 'I went again to the ruins, for it was no longer a city'.[45]

It was to become one with sturdier, stronger brick-built houses 'Whereas before they dwelt in low, dark wooden houses, they now live in lofty, lightsome, uniform and very stately brick buildings'.[46]

That was several years away. Through the autumn and winter of 1666 London remained a catastrophe. Samuel Pepys saw the destruction and the despair. He also blamed Bloodworth for the spread of the disaster. On 7 September, the final day of the burning, he wrote, 'People do all the world over cry out of the simplicity of the Lord Mayor in general, and more particularly in this business of the fire, laying it all on him'.

Two days later he was more satisfied. He returned surreptitiously to Mrs Bagwell that night 'and there nudo *in lecto con ella,* lay naked in bed with her did do all that I desired'.

He then went home and had a pleasant chat with Admiral Sir William Penn.[47]

Even when the fire had finally dwindled into a few ashes and scorched wood London remained a desolation. There were ruins everywhere. In many of the abandoned homes there were valuables. Looters plundered. And resisted arrest. And flagrantly robbed any passer-by. In 1667 just a few months after the blaze had died Pepys knew the danger. There were no watchmen to protect the public.

A foul evening this was tonight, and mightily troubled to get a coach home; and, which is now my common practice, going over the ruins in the night, I rid with my sword drawn in the Coach.[48]

It would not be until 1671 that any rebuilding of the devastated city began.

Far from the smouldering wreckage, miles away in Seend, John Aubrey was living through a personal disaster. In 1666 his income was declining. He had neglected his estates and, in desperation, had sold property and thereby lowered his income farther. He was in need of a well-to-do wife. There was Joan Sumner. And disaster.

This yeare all my businesses and affaires ran kim-kam. Nothing took effect, as if I had been under an ill tongue. Treacheries and enmities in abundance against me.[49]

Characteristically, with his moment-to-moment way of living, he almost casually drifted into doom. A marriage was arranged.

On 11 April 1666, the Salisbury Diocesan Registry recorded: 'John Awbrey of Easton Pierse in Kington St Michael, gent., and Mris Joane Sumner of Sutton Benger, sp. Bdmen: Willliam Browne, of Sarum, tailor, and Joseph Gwynne, of Easton Pierse, yeoman. Not attested, but one bondsman signs: Jos G. makes his mark only. Aprile 11, 1666.'[50]

8

1667-81: Antiquarians, Stanton Drew & personal problems

His quick observation, his odd, happy, phrasing, his tenacious, if occasionally straying memory, his wide-ranging friendliness – with these gifts he made himself a figure in his world, and he remains a figure in the history of his time. And it is his friendliness, perhaps, that gives him his footing.

G. M. Young, 1950, 251

He had need of his friends.

For years he was to live through a personal disaster and a decade in England of violence and crime, the Crown Jewels stolen, Catholics and Protestants constantly suspicious of each other, witches persecuted, a highwayman's impossible exploit that intrigued even the king.

For John Aubrey personally the ten years following the end of the 1660s were not good ones during which the problem of stone circles were no more than minor footnotes in a volume of domestic catastrophes. By 1671 he was almost penniless, in debt, and threatened with prison. He was saved only by his natural friendliness that made him a welcome guest to almost everyone that knew him.

Only a few years earlier, in 1666, he had had his portrait painted by the well-known artist William Faithorne the Elder. Aubrey posed, wearing a fashionable wig that reached down to his shoulders. He had a long white shirt with ruffled collar and cuffs under a costly brown jacket, a richly red cloak thrown casually over his right shoulder. Clean-shaven, pensive, he appeared a man at peace with his place in a sociable world. He was also engaged to be married. A dream and a nightmare.

That mismatch with Joan Sumner brought troubles. Late in 1667 he was arrested in Chancery Lane on the Strand, 'at Mr. Sumner's suite'. He had already sold Lower Easton Pierse, and the farm of his home at Broad Chalke, and his mismanagement of those transactions lost him a further £500 in money and £200 in goods and timber. He wandered away like a banished man.

In February 1668, there was a trial at Salisbury over the cause of the failure of John Aubrey and Joan Sumner to marry. The result was in his favour. He was awarded £600 in compensation – 'though divilish opposition against me'.

The Sumners were unforgiving. They loathed him. Five months later on 6 July 1668 he was arrested at Peter Gale's instigation, friend of the Sumners and a man to whom Aubrey owed money. He was released but in March 1669 a further civil trial brought by the relentless Sumners reduced his compensation to £300 from the original £600.

Witnesses alleged that a marriage had been agreed between Joan Sumner and the defendant. She had later reneged because, despite Aubrey's assurances, he had no money and his estates were all mortgaged. He was abusive and, as a husband, would have been extravagant.

The miserable affair worsened. She was litigious. On 7 February 1670 there was an Order in Chancery ordering John Aubrey to stop any further proceedings against her. Illuminating an unattractive aspect of her character, in 1668 she had taken an exactly similar action against Richard Lester, an earlier aspirant for marriage.

No one gained. John Aubrey was ruined. Joan Sumner did not prosper. On 21 March 1671 there was yet another marriage licence, and she and Robert Pope were wed. Nine months later, she died, possibly during childbirth. She survives either a malignant ghost or an innocent woman misled by false promises.[1]

At the end of the bitterness Aubrey had sold all his remaining property and became an indigent wanderer in 'happy delitescency'.

> Anno 1671, having sold all and disappointed as aforesaid of moneys I received [and] with dangers enough, *tanquam canis e Nilo*, [like dogs of the Nile] for feare of the crocodiles, i.e. catchpolls [debt-collectors] – And indeed all that I have donne and that little that I have studied have been just after that fashion, so that I had I not lived long my want of leisure would have afforded but a slender harvest of.

Finally he returned to happiness. Despite bankruptcy he had many good and faithful acquaintants. '[I had] never quiett, nor anything of happinesse till divested of all, 1670, 1671: at what time providence raysed me (unexpectedly) good friends – the right honourable Nicholas, Earl of Thanet, with whom I was delitescent at Hethfield in Kent neer a yeare, and then was invited …; anno … Sarney; Sir Christopher Wren; Mr Ogilby; then Edmund Wyld, esq., R(egiae) S(ocietatis) S(ocius), of Glasely-hall, Salop (sed in margine), tooke me into his armes, with whom I most commonly take my diet and sweet *otium's*.'[2]

During those unsettled years, constantly moving from one friendly home to the next, there were few moments to consider the mysteries of Stonehenge, Avebury or Stanton Drew. But correspondents did send him details of other stone circles that he copied into his collection of letters and jottings.

1671 was the notorious year in which there was an attempt to steal the Crown Jewels. It was not a gentlemanly Raffles-type burglary. It was brutal savagery. On 9 May 1671 an impoverished Irish adventurer, Colonel Thomas Blood, disguised as a parson with three accomplices as clerks entered the Tower, seized its elderly Keeper, Edwards, gagged him and threw a cloak over his head. When he struggled and made a noise, they struck him heavily on the head with a mallet. He moved. Without mercy he was beaten, savagely stabbed and left for dead.

The thugs failed. The royal orb and the sceptre were too heavy and ponderous. The Crown had to be crushed. The Keeper shouted the alarm and they were captured at the Tower's Gate.

Typically amused at their effrontery and shrugging off the violence Charles II pardoned Blood and restored his estates that had been confiscated at the Restoration.

It was rumoured that, always short of money, the king himself had arranged the theft. It would explain the leniency. And the generosity was not unique. When Charles died in 1685 it was discovered that jewels were missing from the coronation crown, replaced by cheap imitations. Courtiers suspected that royal mistresses flaunted the precious originals.

Neither John Aubrey nor Samuel Pepys in his later *Diary* mentioned the Blood affair. In John Evelyn's 'diary' – a better term would have been 'retrospective *Memoirs*' – John Evelyn mistakenly recorded' it as occurring on 10 May 1671. Like so many of his entries, it was written years after the event and full of mistakes.

He remembered dining at the Treasurer's whose guests included 'one Blood, that impudent bold fellow who had not long before attempted to steal the imperial crown itself out of the Tower ... How he came to be pardoned, and even received into favour ... I could never come to understand'.[3]

It was of no concern to a penniless John Aubrey for whom Henry Coley cast a fortune. That well-known astrologer lived in Baldwin's Gardens, Grays Inn Lane. Aubrey often stayed in his cramped house. Coley, who had almost died in the Great Plague, would have been trusted by Aubrey who believed in predictions: 'for we are all governed by the planets, as the wheeles & the weights move the Index of the Clock,' he told Wood.[4]

It was so strong a conviction that he compiled a *Collectio Geniturarum*, between 29 May 1674 and 1677, a vellum-covered notebook containing sixty lives and predictions for friends and acquaintances. Typical of Aubrey's jack-in-a-box mind it also contained some improbable notes such as that for Hooke's niece: 'Mistress Grace hath a hairy mole on her left pappe.' How Aubrey knew this of this intimacy is unclear – perhaps a low-cut bodice; or no more than tittle-tattle.[5]

The 1670s was the decade of the attempt to steal the crown jewels and when three great poets, Herrick, Marvell and Milton, died.

In 1671 Henry Coley drafted Aubrey's horoscope:

> The nativity is a most remarkable opposition, and 'tis much pity the stars were not more favourable to the native [for they] threaten ruin to land and estate; give Superlative Vexations in Matters relating to Marriag, based wondrous Contexts in Lawsuits; all of which vexations, I suppose the Native hath a greater portion of than ever was desired.

He added that Aubrey should be in great danger between the ages of forty and fifty, that is, between 1666 and 1676, a prediction that would be despairingly accurate.[6] John Gadbury, another astrologer, dismissed the report as 'looks no more like Esq. Aubrey than an apple is like an Oyster'.

Aubrey, however, admired Coley and told Anthony à Wood: 'He is a man of admirable parts and as good natured a man as can be'. And late in 1693 he added, 'I forgot to tell you I just called upon Mr. Coley as I was goeing out of Towne; and he is very angry with you, because you terme Astrologers Conjurers.'[7]

It may have been as early as 1668 when Aubrey's financial hardship was becoming known that one of his oldest friends from Middle Temple days, Sir John Stawell, offered him a place on the stagecoach to Salisbury. Stawell lived in Devon and the journey took him through that city. He sent Aubrey a hurried note:

> There are three places in the Salisbury coach on Monday next taken up; no more; so that you may goe with me and make me truly happy in your company. I pray give earnest for a place immediately or goe in my boyes roome, and let him ride your horse (if you have horses sent). I will pay your coach hire. John Stawell.

He added,

> Let me beg your favour in granting this earnest request. I will not admit a denial. Let no slovenly, paltry, pitiful excuse be mentioned. We shall be truly merry on the progress.[8]

It is a short note but it is a vivid picture of the pleasure that Aubrey's cheerful presence provided to his friends. A very few years later after that generous invitation Stawell died only forty-four. It explains the absence of his name from Aubrey's later list of his *Amici*. The list of those men, the friends that he esteemed most highly, is given in Appendix A.

Late in May 1669 Pepys ended his *Diary* for fear that by writing secretly in candlelight late at night he was in danger of losing his sight.

And thus ends all that I doubt I shall ever be able to do with my own eyes in the keeping of my journall, I not being able to do it any longer, having done now so long as to undo my eyes almost every time that I take pen in my hand; and, therefore, whatever comes of it, I must forebear; and therefore resolve from this time forward to have it kept by my people in longhand, and must therefore be contented to set down no more than is fit for them and all the world to know; or if there be anything (which cannot be much, now my amours to Deb [Willett, his wife's pretty young maid whose reluctant body Pepys had lustfully handled but failed to seduce] are past, and my eyes hindering me in almost all other pleasures) I must endeavour to keep a margin in my book open, to add here and there a note in shorthand with my own hand.

He almost kept his word. There was a second 'diary' but it was short, and mainly factual about national events.[9] One of them concerned the rebuilding of London after the Great Fire. Charles II was insistent that it should begin immediately.

London was to be a sturdier, more orderly city with wider streets, more sidewalks, and no open sewers or drains. It was to be rebuilt not in traditional timber but in the far less flammable brick and stone and there were to be four types of houses: of two-storeys in the side-lanes; three in the better streets; four in the principal roads; and great mansions standing in their own grounds.

To kerb any expensive rise in costs and knowing that London's Guilds and City Companies would greedily charge exorbitant rates free-lance builders were also allowed to bid for plots of land.

Late in March 1667 Pepys noticed the beginning of the improvements. 'Thence together to my shoemaker's, cutler's, tailor's, up and down about my mourning; and in my going do observe the great streets in the City are marked out with piles drove into the ground; and if it ever it be built in that form , with so fair streets, it will be a noble sight.'[10]

By September 1671 there had been seven thousand applications for rebuilding, almost twice the number of the original tinder-boxes of timber shacks and by the end of the following year only a few gaps were left except where stone churches and public buildings were to stand.[11]

The reconstruction of St Paul's Cathedral took much longer. After three of Christopher Wren's designs had been proposed and rejected his fourth was accepted and the foundation stones were finally laid in June 1675. Wanting the church to outdo St Peter's in Rome Wren was bravely innovative. St Paul's was completed in 1710 with a 'marvellous and innovative triple-skinned dome'.[12]

Long before that time came the Monument, a structure to commemorate the disaster of 1666. Three men involved in its design were companions of John Aubrey, Robert Hooke, Christopher Wren and Thomas Gale.

Hooke was an old friend, both becoming Fellows of the Royal Society at the same time. Hooke, both scientist and inventor, designed the Monument. 'For about 300 years the Monument has usually been attributed to Wren … but we now know that Hooke was primarily responsible for its design and construction.'[13]

It was erected at the corner of Fish Street Hill and Pudding Lane 202 feet from where the Fire began, and in those days of Imperial measures that was the exact height of the Monument, the equivalent of 61.6 m. The cost was an enormous £13,450, 11s 9d.

Built of fine-grained Portland stone it is the tallest isolated free-standing stone column in the world, encircled by a spiral staircase of 311 steps. At its top is a gilt-bronze flaming urn. Wren, another of Aubrey's friends and who was to find employment for him, wanted a statue of Charles II on horseback placed there but the king objected: 'I didn't start the fire.'

On the Monument is the inaccurate inscription: 'London rises again, whether with greater speed or greater magnificence is doubtful; three short years complete that which was considered the work of an age.' It exaggerated. The column was finished by 1675 but the rebuilding of the city continued until 1700, and St Paul's until 1710.

The Monument had a third connection with Aubrey. Three of the panels at the bottom of the Monument have Latin inscriptions written by his old friend, Thomas Gale, Fellow of the Royal Society, High Master of St Paul's School, and a long, helpful friend of Aubrey's.[14]

Two years later, in 1674, Herrick and Milton died. Robert Herrick was buried on 15 October in an unmarked grave in his churchyard at Dean Prior, Devon. Neglectful parishioners apprehensively feared that his ghost haunted the place.

On 9 November the following month John Milton 'died in a fit of the gout, but with so little pain or emotion, that the time of his expiring was not perceived by those in the room'. He was buried in the church of St Giles, Cripplegate. Earlier that year Andrew Marvell, an old friend, had guided the blind poet through the jostling crowds along the Strand.

Anthony à Wood was promised details of the death for his forthcoming on Oxford's notables. On 18 May 1675 John Aubrey sent him a letter: 'Mr. Marvell haz promised me to write *minutes* for you of Jo. Milton.' There is no record of a note.[15]

Aubrey did, however, include Milton in *Brief Lives*. The poet had had three wives, the first abandoning him. 'His harmonicall and ingeniose Soul did lodge in a beautifull and well proportioned body. … [he was] of a very cheerful humour. He would be chearfull even in his Gowte-fitts, and sing.' Milton would have liked the note.

Gradually in those unsettled years Aubrey was returning to happiness, with faithful friends and his own persistently strong interests. His personal fieldwork was over. He remembered them sadly. 'My head was alwaies working; never idle, and even travelling (which from 1649 till 1670 was never off my horseback, did gleane som observations, of which I have made a collection in folio of 2 quiers of paper + a dust basket, some wherof are to be valued.'[16]

Now, after 1670, he had neither money nor servant but he did have willing correspondents who informed him of stone circles in parts of England far from Wiltshire and Somerset. Over months and years he learned of three main regions: Cornwall; Oxfordshire, and the Lake District. One important source was the *Britannia* of William Camden in its 1637 edition.

That great traveller, born in 1551, was educated at St Paul's school, went to Oxford University and then spent three years travelling in England before becoming a schoolmaster at Westminster School in 1578. Even there he used the school holidays to make journeys into the eastern counties. 'It was not in his power to restrain himself from making Excursions into one quarter or another, in search of Antiquities.' He rose in his profession. He was made Headmaster in 1593 and then appointed as a herald in 1597. Being the Clarenceaux King of Arms greatly facilitated his travels, enabling him to visit many sites.

He accepted no difficulties of language. He already knew Greek and Latin, and painstakingly learned Welsh through his servant. Finding Anglo-Saxon difficult he turned to other scholars.[17]

Even after the publication of *Britannia* in 1586, a pocket-sized quarto with no maps, he still travelled to Wales, Devon, Wiltshire, Somerset, and later to Cumberland and Hadrian's Wall. Yet, determined traveller though he was, he could only offer guesswork about stone circles in his comprehensive description of Britain in that *Britannia*. In it Camden quoted widely from John Leland's *Itineraries*. Almost a quarter of a century later, in 1610, came his *Britain*. It had been turned into accessible English by Philemon Holland, that 'finest translator'.

That translator received many corrections from Camden and in 1637 produced a revised edition. Camden approved. There was still a problem, the unknown builders of stone circles.

Like Camden Aubrey understood that Stonehenge was exceptionally old but the only records about ancient Britain available to him were of little use, reaching back no earlier than a vague 100 BC. The Romans themselves helped – slightly.

Julius Caesar's *The Gallic Wars* provided no useful information about British monuments. The druids, he recorded, were law-givers who held public and private sacrifices. The ordinary Britons dyed themselves with woad, and groups of ten or twelve men had several wives shared together.

A century later another historian, Tacitus, said even less about the Britons except that they had been redoubtable opponents of Agricola, his uncle, who had finally conquered them. It made Agricola's accomplishment all the more laudable.[18]

But neither Caesar nor Tacitus wrote anything about stone-built monuments. In short, there were none. Stone circles were Roman – or even later.

There are always ironies in historical research. Had either Camden or Aubrey read the little-known writings of Diodorus Siculus, a first-century BC annalist, they would have found that a third-century explorer, Pytheas, *c.* 238 – 240 BC, had seen a British 'notable temple which is spherical in shape' and held ceremonies connected with the nineteen-year cycle of the moon'. It was almost certainly the ring of Callanish in the Outer Hebrides around whose islands the adventurer had sailed. The dates of Pytheas proved that it was pre-Roman.[19]

For Camden and Aubrey, however, the writings of Diodorus of Sicily were unknown. Caesar's were not. From them it seemed impossible that his pre-Roman, blue-patterned polygamists could have built great monuments like Stonehenge.

The late sixteenth and seventeenth centuries were years when Europeans were settling in North America, often forcing the natives from their lands. The resentful Indians retaliated. There was blood.

Aubrey compared those wild men with the early people of Britain. 'Let us imagine then what kind of countrie this was in the time of the Ancient Britons ... the inhabitants almost as salvage as the Beasts whose skins were their only raiment ... they were 2 or 3 degrees I suppose less salvage than the Americans.'

In his *Leviathan*, Aubrey's old acquaintance, Thomas Hobbes wrote that those Britons had 'no arts; no society; and which is worst of all, continual fear and danger of violent death; and the life of man, solitary, poor, nasty, brutish and short'.[20]

In Aubrey's time pre-Roman Britain was a wilderness inhabited by skin-clad savages without crops, houses or learning. Culture came to the island only with the arrival of eastern civilisations, Egypt, Greece and Rome, *ex oriente lux*.

It was impossible to believe that primitive Britons had been capable of raising the shaped lintels of Stonehenge onto the tops of the elegantly graceful tall pillars of that ring. Such a well-made monument had to be raised by later inhabitants.

And there was a further problem. The realism of the seventeenth century acknowledged a historical dilemma, the age of the world. There was a chronological wilderness. 'These Antiquities.' wrote John Aubrey, 'are so old that no Bookes doe reach them.'

In his *Annales Veteris et Novi Testamenti* of 1650-4 James Ussher, seventeenth-century archbishop of Armagh, had calculated a date of 4004 BC. A contemporary, John Lightfoot, vice-chancellor of Cambridge, refined it, suggesting that the earth had been 'created by the Trinity on 23 October 4004 BC at nine o'clock in the morning', by not such a coincidence the beginning of the modern university year.[21]

They were not the first chronologists. The Venerable Bede calculated that 3,952 years had passed from the Creation to the birth of Jesus. Medieval scholars, using the Biblical longevities of semi-immortals like Methuselah decided the Creation occurred around 4000 BC. There was theatrical agreement. In his *As You Like It*, written fifty years earlier than Ussher, William Shakespeare had his heroine, Rosalindy, 'The poor world is almost six thousand years old.'[22]

If it were true then it left only some four thousand years for Adam and Eve, Noah and all the other long-lived men as well as the prophets of the Old Testament to have lived before the Romans arrived in Britain.

Aubrey thought that Stonehenge must be centuries later than 4000 BC but the only records about ancient Britain available to him were of little use, reaching back no earlier than a vague 100 BC.

Camden had the same problem. A good historian he distrusted unreliable classical authors with their fantasy of Brutus from Troy coming to Britain. Having no evidence to the contrary Camden rejected a preposterous pre-Roman origin for stone circles.

He used information from contemporary sources like the Elizabethan Society of Antiquaries. Knowing nothing of the years in Britain before the literate Romans came Camden concluded that it had to be those invaders who had set up the rings as triumphal memorials. He recorded some in the south-west of England, one in the Midlands and others in the Lake District. One in Cornwall 'was some trophee (or monument of victorie) erected by the Romans ...' Across the Pennines the ring of Long Meg & Her Daughters had a similar origin; 'verily there is reason to thinke that this was a monuments of some victorie there achieved, for no man would deems that they were erected in vaine'. Circle after circle had the same desperate explanation. The Rollright Stones was 'the Monument of some Victory and haply erected by Rollo the *Dane*, who afterwards conquered *Normandie*'.

There were two sites in Cornwall, the ring of Boscawen-Un at Land's End and, miles away on Bodmin Moor, the cluster of three called the Hurlers.

Boscawen-Un was mentioned in John Speed's Mappe of Cornwall. 'At *Boskenna* upon the south-west of the Promotory is a Trophie erected, which are eighteen stones placed round in compasse, and pitchedt twelve foot each from other: with another far bigger in the very Centre. These do show some *Victorie* there attained either by Romans or King *Athelstan*. ...' Camden elaborated:

> Neere until this' [St Buryan] he wrote, 'in a place which they call *Biscaw Woune*, are to bee seene nineteene stones set in a round circle, distant every one about twelve foote from the other; and in the very center there is one pitched far higher and greater than the rest. This was some Trophee (or monument of victorie) erected by the Romans (as probably may bee conjectured) under the later Emperours, or else, by Athelstan the Saxon, when he had subdued the Cornish-men, and brought them under his dominion.'

Years later Aubrey disagreed. 'In Cornwall at Biscaw-woun stand nineteen stones in a circle, twelve feet distant from each other. In the center is a pitched one far higher than the rest. This Mr Camden believes was a Trophy of King Athelstan: but it agreeing in its architecture with the Temples aforesaid, I presume this also to have been a Temple. I have not (yet) seen this in Antiquity, but it must give such a representation as this fig.. in Plate the IX.'[23] Below the note is a neat plan of the ring.

Boscawen-Un, 'the dwelling by the elder tree on the downs', could be the first stone circle recorded. It may have been the meeting-place of kings of Welsh Wales down to the days of that kingdom's extinction in 926. In the Welsh *Triads*, groups of three statements, the ring of *Beisgawe*, is named as one of the 'three great *gorseddau*' of Britain.[24]

The other Cornish site, a group of stone circles mentioned by Camden, was the group of three rings known as the Hurlers many miles to the north-east on Bodmin Moor. John Speed, the cartographer whose book *54 Maps of England and Wales* was published in 1608-10, in ignorance planned the rings as a square. His plan resembled a chessboard with the white squares missing.

Other chroniclers were more accurate but more interested in the name than the antiquity itself.

The site was composed of three rings on a not quite straight SSW – NNE line erected on a noticeable slope. Their granite stones had been arduously dressed to shape. Similar in size each circle had once had twenty-six to twenty-eight stones. The north was some forty paces across (113 feet 8 inches (34.7 m); and the centre, slightly elliptical, forty-five by forty-four (136 feet 8 inches x 132 feet 11 inches; 41.7 m x 40.5 m). It had a small centre stone, and was neatly floored with small granite crystals. It was connected to the north ring by a narrow paving of stones. The SSW site, now heavily plundered, was thirty-five paces across (104 feet 6 inches (31.9m).

Today the Hurlers are known to be just one of several multiple sites in the south-west peninsula of England.[25]

Being hardly a quarter of a mile from the road the rings had probably been despoiled by stone-robbers long before John Norden saw them at the beginning of the seventeenth century. He was less interested in the rings than why they were called the Hurlers. They were

> certayne stones raysed and sett in the ground of some 6 foote high and 2 foote square; some bigger, some lesser, and are fixed in such straglinge manner as those Countrye men doe in performinge that pastime *Hurlinge*. The manner of the standinge of theis stones is as followeth: [sketch].[26]

Another visitor to the Hurlers was Richard Carew, J. P., born of an old Cornish family. He was a one-time colleague of Camden's at Christ Church. He must have seen the stones shortly after Norden and, like him, was intrigued by what the stones were supposed to be, the petrified bodies of sacrilegious men.

> Not far hence, in an open plain, are to be seen certain stones, somewhat squared, and fastened about a foot deep in the ground, of which some six or eight stand upright in proportionable distance; they are termed the Hurlers. And a like strange observation taketh place here as at Stonehenge, to wit, that redoubled numbering never eveneth with the first. But far stranger is the country people's report that once they were men, and for their hurling upon the Sabbath, that so metamorphosed.

That violent game of 'Hurling' was described as

> accompanied by many dangers, some of which do ever fall to the players' share. For proof whereof, when the hurling is ended, you shall see them retiring home as from a pitched battle, with bloody pates, bones broken and out of joint. And such bruises as serve to shorten their days; yet all is good play, and never attorney nor coroner troubled for the matters.[27]

William Camden knew those reports. He had a more archaeological eye, and suggested different interpretations.

> Many other Stones besides in some sort foure square, are to be seene upon the plaine adjoyning; of which seven or eight are pitched upright of equall distance asunder. The neighbour Inhabitants terme them *Hurlers*, as being by a devout and godly error perswaded, they had beene men sometimes transformed into Stones, for profaning the Lords Day, with hurling the ball. Others, would have it to be a Trophee (as it were) or a monument, in memoriall of some battell: And some thinke verily they were set as

> meere stones or land marks, as having read in those authors that wrote of Limits, that
> stone were gathered together of both parties, and the same erected for bounders.

John Aubrey shrugged, added nothing, almost indifferently repeating: 'The Hurlers also fabulated to be men metaphosed into Stones: but in truth shew a note of some victorie, or els so set, for Land-marks and Bounders.'[28]

Among his friends and acquaintances Aubrey lacked many of their qualities. He did not have the political awareness of Hobbes, the inventive mind of Locke, the naval efficiency of Pepys, the artistry of Wren or genius of Newton.

What he did possess were unlimited interests. He is popularly remembered as the lightweight compiler of anecdotal *Brief Lives* but he also began a *Perambulation of Surrey* before being let down by his sponsor. He wrote the *Natural History of Wiltshire*; the *Antiquities of Wiltshire*; *The Education of Young Gentlemen*; *Remaines of Gentilisme and Judaisme*; *Observations*; and characteristically, *Miscellanea*, that litterbox of everything from 'Magick'; 'Converse with Angels and Spirits', and 'Glances of Love and Malice', all of it while compiling the *Monumenta Britannica* with its page after page and site after site of stone circles. He was a scatterbrain but not a lightweight.

During the late seventeenth century while most people, John Aubrey included, went about their daily, humdrum lives they did find a vicarious pleasure in hearing of the exploits of a few 'gallant' highwaymen. The courteous Claude Duval had been hanged in 1670. Six years later 'Swift Nick' Nevison made history by riding from Gad's Hill in Kent to York, more than two hundred miles in a single day. Having been recognised in a robbery he was desperate for an alibi. The notorious Dick Turpin would later be credited with the exploit but in 1676 Turpin was no more than a loutish butcher's apprentice.

Just as the first quarter of the eighteenth century was to be a golden age for pirates so the mid-seventeenth century were rich years for the 'gentlemen of the road'. Particularly in Britain. They flourished. Across Western Europe there were regular military patrols along the highways. Not in Britain. It was not until 1692 that a Highwayman Act offered a £40 reward for the capture and condemning of a highway robber.

Nevison had robbed some sailors from Chatham of pay about four o'clock in the morning. In his *A Tour through the Whole Island of Great Britain*, the pamphleteer Daniel Defoe described what followed.

Thinking that one of his victims knew him Nevison rode off on a bay mare – not the romantic 'Black Bess' – and galloped through Essex to Chelmsford, where he took a half hour break. Then on to Cambridge, and

Huntingdon and another hour's rest. Exhausted he reached York in the late afternoon having ridden an 'impossible' distance in fourteen hours.

Having changed his creased, workaday clothes he walked to the bowling-green where he had a casual conversation with the mayor around eight o'clock that evening. When, much later, he was arrested and put on trial the jury acquitted him. It was impossible for anyone to have reached York from Kent in a single day.

Nevison later met Charles II to whom he confessed as the law would not allow him to be retried. Amused, the king gave him the name or title of 'Swift Nicks' instead of 'Nicks'. Defoe added, 'But these things, I say, I do not relate as certain.'[29]

There was to be a coincidence. Over-confident, Nevison was finally caught, condemned and hanged in York in 1684. Dick Turpin was executed in the same city fifty-five years later.

Sadly, the 'ride' may be taking the reader on a wild goose chase. The rider may not have been Nevison. There may never have been a ride.

In his book of 1719, *A Compleat History of the Lives of the Most Notorious Highwaymen*, 'Captain' Alexander Smith wrote a short life of Nevison but did not mention his exploit. That was only included as an afterthought in another 'Life' of 'Captain Dudley, Murderer and Highwayman'. There 'Swiftnicks' robbed a man of 560 guineas at five in the morning and reached York by six o'clock that evening.

In 1926 the editor of Smith's *Lives*, Arthur Hayward, added a footnote suggesting that 'Swiftnicks' could have been John Nevison, a surname already accepted by Defoe, Macaulay and Dickens. Smith's *Lives* has been described as 'one of the most readable and least reliable history books ever written'.[30]

In brief, the rider is uncertain, the ride is uncertain, there was no Dick Turpin and there was no Black Bess. Everything could be fictitious. Legends grow like weeds in the garden of wishful thinking.

Neither John Aubrey nor Anthony à Wood mentioned that equestrian will o' the wisp. In 1676 both men were occupied with realities.

Aubrey had read what Camden had written about the Rollright Stones, the well-known circle in the Midlands, and on 1 February 1675, he wrote to Wood asking that when he next went to Oxfordshire to stay with Ralph Sheldon, 'you may informe me concerning Roll-rich stones, viz. the Diameter, how many yards or paces, and the height of the stones and the number' and Wood promised that 'God willing, I shall view more severely the Roll rich Stones'.

It was an easy undertaking. Ralph Sheldon had homes both in Beoley, Worcestershire, and Weston Park, Warwickshire, just north of Long Compton and only two and a half miles from the stone circle across the county border of Oxfordshire.[31]

Aubrey was intrigued because Camden was describing sites far away from Wiltshire and Somerset in the old kingdom of Wessex. Some were much more distant in Cornwall. Camden added others on Exmoor.

> This river [Exe] hath its head, and springeth first in a weely, and barren ground named *Exmore*, neere unto Severn sea, a great part whereof is counted within Sommersetshire: and wherein, are seene certaine monuments of anticke worke, to wit, Stones pitcht in order, some triangle wise, others in a round circle.[32]

Such rings were many miles away to the west and south of Avebury and Stanton Drew. Now there was another a hundred miles to the north in Oxfordshire. Camden described the Rollright Stones. The Evenlode river

> passeth by an ancient Monument standing not farre from his banke, to wit, certaine huge stones placed in a round circle (the common people usually call them *Rolle-rich stones*, and dreameth that they were sometimes men by a wonderfull *Metamorphosis* turned into hard stones. The draught of them, such as it is, portrayed long since, heere I represent unto your view. For, without all forme and shape they bee, unequall, and by long continuance of time, much impaired. The highest of them all, which without the circle looketh into the earth, they use to call *The King*, because he should have beene King of England (forsooth) if he had once seene *Long Compton*, a little Towne so called lying beneath, and which a man, if he goe some few paces forward, may see: other five standing at the other side, touching as it were, one another, they imagine to have been knights mounted on horsebacke, and the rest the Army. But loe the forsaid Portraiture. These would I verily thinke to have beene the Monument of some Victory and haply erected by *Rollo* the Dane.[33]

Three hundred years before Camden's account a description of the circle had been added to a list of the Wonders of Britain. It was a cry of desperation. '*Sunt magni lapides in Oxenfordensi pago …* In the Oxfordshire countryside are great stones, arranged as it were in some connection by the hand of man. But at what time this was done, or by what people, or for what memorial or significance, is unknown.' In 1637 that remained true.[34]

Over the years the circle accumulated a medley of local superstitions: the stones were a petrified army; they could not be counted; at midnight they turned into men and at dawn into stone again; also at midnight they went down the hill to drink at a spring; at that time fairies dance in the circle, 'little folk like girls to look at'. Chippings from the stones brought good luck. Welsh cattle-drovers took them. A soldier going to India had one. It did him no good. He died of typhus.[35]

John Aubrey partly paraphrased Camden but added his own, more sceptical comments:

Roll-rich Stones in Oxfordshire

This Monument consisteth of certain huge stones placed circularly. The common people call them by the name abovesaid, and dreame that they were sometimes men by a wonderful metamorphosis turned into hard Stones. The draught of them portrayed long since I doe here present to your view. [His sketch copied Camden but omitted the man and the windmill]. For, without all forme & shape, they be unequall, and by long continuance of time much impaired. The highest of them all, which without the circle looketh into the earth, they call the King, because he should have been king of England (forsooth) if he had once seen Long-Compton, a little Towne so called, lying beneath, and which a man, of he goes some four paces forward, may see. Other five standing on the other Side, touching as it were one another, they imagine to have been Knights mounted on horse-back; and the rest the Armie. These would I verily thinke to have been the monument of some Victorie. & haply erected by Rollo the Dane, who afterwards conquered Normandie.

The stone ā [the King Stone] have been part of an avenue: as at Aubury and Kynet; two such stones are remayning at Stoneheng, without the circle.

The stones at b resemble the monument in one of the little circles at Aubury, fig ... [the Cove inside the north ring].

Ralph Sheldon of Beoley Esq (my honoured Friend) told me, he was at some charge to digge Aᵈ167. [year unspecified] within this Circle, to try if he could find any Bones: but he was sure that no body was buried there: but had he digged without the circle, and neer to it: it is not unlikely he mought have found Bones there: as at the Temple above Kynet aforesaid.', the ring now known as the Sanctuary on Overton Hill near Avebury. [A plan in perspective was included here, showing the circle, the King Stone and the Whispering Knights.]

Except 1, 2, the rest of the stones are not above four foot and a half high, one with another. This monument is circular, but Mr. Camden hath rendred it in perspective. But there is a better draught of this place donne by Mʳ Loggan in yᵉ Discription of Oxfordshire by Dʳ R. Plott.³⁶

Aubrey scribbled some accounts of sites while staying in the comfortable homes of one or other of his friends. It is unlikely, however, that he took a copy of Camden's 1637 *Britain* with him. That leatherbound volume of more than a thousand large pages was the size of a small suitcase and the thickness of a man's hand. It weighed more than half a stone (6+ kg). It was not hand luggage.

He probably used that book in his London lodgings. The arrangement also had the advantage of enabling him to read the accumulated letters that people had sent him about distant stone circles.

Also in London a great poet died. Andrew Marvell, Member of Parliament for Hull, had been leaving that city for the capital when he contracted a fever, perhaps malaria. Reaching his home he was examined by a stupidly dogmatic doctor who rather than prescribing quinine decided to bleed him and put his patient under heavily hot blankets. Marvell sweated, drifted into a coma and died on Friday 16 August 1678.[37]

The death was so unexpected that there were hints of murder. John Aubrey wrote, 'Some suspect that he was poysoned by Jesuites, but I cannot be positive.'

The suspicion had come from a rumour that during his time as a Cambridge undergraduate those fanatical Catholics had tried to persuade him to join their faith. According to an earlier biographer of his, 'They used all the arguments they could to seduce him away, which at last they did.' If so, he quickly relapsed, returning to the Church of England. That was in 1640. It is unlikely that his would-be converters waited forty-six years to assassinate him.[38]

There is an ironical coincidence. Quinine was known as 'Jesuits powder' because it had been brought to Europe by those missionaries.

Andrew Marvell was buried at St Giles-in-the-Fields, under the pews 'near the middle of the south aisle by the pulpit', in a grave, a 'fine and private place', from which he could gaze on those 'vast deserts of eternity' of which he had warned his reluctant lover in the greatest poem of seduction in the English language.

Just a few years after that sad event John Aubrey visited the Lake District to see the well-known stone row of the Devil's Arrows (Appendix B). He also visited the stone circles of Mayburgh and, possibly, Long Meg & Her Daughters. John Leland saw neither. William Camden provided only unhelpful accounts, describing Mayburgh near Penrith, 'a little towne, and of indifferent trade, fortified on the West side with a castle of the Kings, which in the reigne of King Henry the sixth was repaired out of the ruines of a Romane fort thereby called *Mayburg*'. For an antiquarian of his ability it was nonsense.

John Aubrey was much more descriptive. Near the earthwork known as King Arthur's Round Table, he wrote:

> upon a meane ascent is a great circular Bank of stones and earth ... and neer to the centre thereof are erected four stones of great magnitude, the biggest of them conteining eleven foot in highth above the earth, and six foot in breadth one way, and four foot in thickness standing equally distant in a quadrangular form about 50 foot asunder.
>
> These stones are very unshapen, hard boulder stones, not being capable of being wrought in any proportion. On each side of the entrance, which is upon the south side therof and 50 foot wide is fixed a very great stone of the same kind standing in a strait line with two of the aforesaid stones. This place is vulgarly called *Mabrough-Castle*.[39]

Fieldwork in days before gazetteers and guidebooks was haphazard, frequently missing the greater for the lesser. Both Camden and Aubrey described the enormous stone circle of Long Meg & Her Daughters six miles from the market town of Penrith. Yet there was an even more intriguing stone circle at Castlerigg by the roadside only a couple of miles from the larger and more important county town of Keswick. Neither man mentioned the ring.

Camden provided a description of the Long Meg ring. Near Penrith and alongside the River Eden,

> at the less *Salkeld*, there bee erected in manner of a circle seventy seven stones, every one ten foot high, and a speciall one by it selfe before them, at the very entrance riseth fifteene foot in height. This stone the common people thereby dwelling, name Long Megge, like as the rest, her daughters. And within that ring or circle, are heapes of stones, under which, they say, lye covered the bodies of men slaine. And verily there is reason to thinke that this was a monument of some victory there achieved, for no man would deeme that they were erected in vaine.[40]

It is not clear whether Aubrey himself had seen that enormous ring or whether he had just made notes from a description omitted carelessly from a book about Cumberland. He was, however, sufficiently curious to ask a local minister for more details.

> From Sᵣ Will. Dugdale Clarenceaux: but 'tis not entred in his *Visitation of Cumberland*; but was forgot by his servant.
>
> In Cumberland neer Kirk-Oswald is a Circle of Stones about two hundred in number, of severall Tunnes. The Diameter of this Circle is about the diameter (he guesses) of the Thames from the Herald's Office, which by Mᵣ J. Ogilby's *Mappe of London* is ... foot. In the middle are two Tumuli or Barrowes of cobble-stones, nine or ten foot high.

Aubrey augmented the description of the ring from information he had received from yet another of his myriad correspondents:

> From Mᵣ Hugh Todd Fellow of University college in Oxford, a Westmorland-man.
>
> In little *Salkeld* in Westmorland are Stones in an orbicular figure, about seventie in number, which are called *Long Meg & Her Daughters*. Long Meg is about ... Yards: and about fifteen yards distant from the rest.
>
> Quaere Mᵣ *Robinson* the Minister there, about the *Giants bone* and *Body* found there. The body is in the middle of the orbicular stones.[41]

One very important question about the possible builders of stone circles had been resolved. At the onset of his searches Aubrey had been misled by uninformed 'authorities' who were certain that stone circles had been erected for varying reasons either by the Romans, or the Saxons or the Danes. Now he knew from Camden's account of Cornwall that one of those sources could be deleted. There had been no Danish settlement in Cornwall.

The Romans had had tin-mines there. Both they and the Saxons had set up milestones along the roads. But the Danes had done nothing more than send intermittent piratical expeditions along the Cornish coasts.

Some of those plunderers had settled in West Wales. In 845 one group had been involved in a battle at *Hengestedune*, 'Stallions Down', near Callington. It failed. The Saxon king of Wessex, Ecbert, 'put to flight' both native Britons and intrusive Vikings.[42] No Danes had lived in Cornwall and none had erected any stone circle there. And if not there, why anywhere else?

Everywhere in England where stone was plentiful there were probably tantalising stone circles. That was England. John Aubrey needed informants about rings, if any, in Wales or Scotland. And there was a further problem.

In a short piece, 'A Digression' John Aubrey called it, about the 'terraqueous world', he doubted the Biblical statement in Genesis, VI, 7 – VIII, 19, that life on earth had begun with Noah's Flood. The world was older.

His friend Robert Hooke had given a lecture to the Royal Society in which he argued that the earth's irregular surface had been caused by a succession of earthquakes, not by the Flood alone. This went against contemporary teaching that the Mosaic account of Creation began with Noah but Aubrey 'was not, however, inclined to read the sacred writings too literally', a dangerous attitude in his time.

He avoided heresy. 'This Hypothesis,' he wrote, 'is Mr. Hookes.'[43]

It left stone circles in a chronological vacuum.

9

1682-95: Edward Lhwyd, Anthony à Wood & James Garden

JOHN AUBREY Esq; a Member of the Royal Society, with whom I became
acquainted at Oxford when I was a sojourner there … was the only person that I ever
then met, who had a right notion of the Temples of the Druids, or indeed any notion
that the Circles so often mention'd were such Temples at all: wherein he was intirely
confirm'd, by the authorities which I show'd him; as he supply'd me in return with
numerous instances of such Monuments, which he was at great pains to observe and
set down.

John Toland, *A Critical History of the Celtic Religion*[1], 1726 (3rd ed, 1814, 146)

By the year 1682 England was, at last, a safer place for Roman Catholics.
No more of their peers were executed. None of their less distinguished
people was imprisoned. No ordinary houses were damaged, few of
their religion were spat at in the street. It was the first peaceful year
for Catholics since 1678. And certainly so for both Ralph Sheldon and
Anthony à Wood.

Quite unaffected by those religious disturbances John Aubrey continued
with his now-desultory search for antiquities.

Sheldon was considered a friend by both Anthony à Wood and John
Aubrey but that did not prevent him from having adverse opinions about
both of them. Wood had often overstayed his welcome at Sheldon's house,
so much so that in the end his host frequently abandoned him, returning
home only when Wood had departed.

He also told Wood he had met Aubrey in London in June 1679.
'Yesterday came to me honest John Aubrey, whose head is so full it will
not give his tongue leave to speak one word after another. I assure you,
he is to my appearance as mad as anyone almost in the university of
Bedlam.'[1]

Sheldon had been imprisoned only the year before for being a Roman
Catholic. In August 1678 a self-seeking scoundrel, Titus Oates, told the
King of a 'Popish Plot' to assassinate him. Charles was unimpressed. He

laughed at the ill-looking rogue, a short-necked, wide-mouthed and beak-nosed man, a money-grabber and a perjurer. He dismissed him as a fool.

Oates, son of an Anabaptist preacher who served in Cromwell's New Model Army, had been to Cambridge, taken holy orders, become a curate and then a naval chaplain, only to be dismissed for 'infamous practices' and drunken blasphemy. In 1677 Oates joined a Jesuit seminary. He was expelled for misconduct. His character did not change but his ambitions developed into dangerous fantasies.

That contact with Catholics and their aspirations to have one of them on the English throne led Oates to concoct the 'narrative of a horrid plot' of a Catholic rising to massacre Protestants and murder the king, before an invading French army would have Charles' brother, the Catholic Duke of York, crowned in his place.

After Charles II had dismissed it as hysteria Oates found another outlet, making a sworn disposition about the perils of a Popish Plot to a London magistrate, Sir Edmund Berry Godfrey. Some days later Godfrey's body was discovered in a ditch on Primrose Hill, seemingly impaled on his own sword. Doctors thought he had been strangled. They were misled. Godfrey had been neither throttled nor impaled. He had been kicked to death.

The public reaction was a boon to the self-seeking Oates. He was innocent of the murder. The popular belief was that it had been a Catholic crime to suppress any whispers of the planned treasonable conspiracy.

Instead, Godfrey's killer may have been the young but vicious Philip Herbert, Earl of Pembroke, who had been found guilty of another murder by a Middlesex jury headed by Godfrey. Pembroke had his revenge before dying of drink and syphilis two years later.[2] But Godfrey's death made Oates a national celebrity.

There was panic and an anti-Catholic hysteria. Oates was acclaimed as a hero. Many Catholics were imprisoned and Oates himself was involved in at least thirty-five 'judicial murders' including several Catholic noblemen.

In churches sermons attacked the Catholics. Wood being a friend of Sheldon's had realised as early as 1671 that it could prove to be a dangerous acquaintance. 'Now Mr. Sheldon, being a zealous Papist, and A. W. afterwards often in his company, must be esteem'd a Papist also, as he was by many snivelling saints, who make it a most horrible thing to be seen in the company of any of them.'[3]

Seven years later the words had been prophetic. In late November 1678 Wood wrote of suspicions against himself:

> Dr. John Wallis took way all writings and registers that I have had in my keeping 18 yeares for feare that they might be seized on, he supposing that I might be in the plot because Mr. Sheldon was lately clapt in prison – A man that is studious and reserved is popishly affected.

> Dec. 1, Sunday, about 1 of the clock in the afternoone Dr. John Nicholas, vicechancellor, with a bedell and his two men, taking my lodgings in their way to St. Marie's church, he (the said Dr. Nicholas) came up into my chamber and there told me in my eare that he had lately received command from above to enquire after all such under his government that are supposed to be popishly affected and to search their chambers and studies for any papers or writings relating to the plot. Hereupon I told him very freely that I should submit to his will.

Nicholas found nothing incriminating. Wood showed him Sheldon's letters, the last as recent as July 1678. In them the suspicious vice-chancellor found only expressions of kindness and friendship.

Nevertheless, he ordered Wood to take the loyal Oath of Allegiance to the Crown. On Monday 2 December at ten o'clock in the morning Wood took that oath and another to the Supremacy. He was promised a Certificate.[4]

Wood was exonerated in 1678 when Catholicism was almost a crime. He was reprieved. Four years later Titus Oates was condemned. There had been a reaction as common sense replaced irrational fears. Courts that had almost automatically condemned Catholics were now dismissing the accused.

Oates, who had been awarded a comfortable allowance, had it withdrawn. Desperate, and going too far, he accused the Duke of York of being a traitor. He was promptly fined a fortune, £100,000, that he was unable to pay. He was sent to prison. In court in May 1685 he was found guilty of perjury, had his awards withdrawn, sent to the humiliating pillory where jeering louts bombarded him with filth, and then, for three successive days, whipped through the streets of London before being imprisoned for life. 'Cheats never prosper' was the comfortable public opinion.

During that religious Protestant 'Reign of Terror' no one had been safe from suspicion. The Gunpowder Plot of 1605 was a persistent reminder that Roman Catholics could not be trusted because they could be disguised as loyal subjects. Even the elderly Samuel Pepys was sent to the Tower because of his suspicious years of service at the Admiralty under the command of the 'popish' Duke of York. It took a tedious month and a half before he was set free.[5]

1685, when Titus Oates was flogged and imprisoned, was also the year of the death of Charles II. Suffering an apoplectic fit on the Sunday he died on Friday 7 February. 'I am sorry, gentlemen, for being such an unconscionable time a-dying,' he joked on his deathbed. Even then he remembered the women who had given him pleasure. John Evelyn heard that he had urged his brother, the Duke of York, 'to be kind to his Concubines The DD: of Cleveland & especially Portsmouth, & that Nelly might not starve'. She did not. Nell Gwynn died twelve years later leaving 'a considerable estate to her son, the Duke of St Albans'.[6]

Charles had had no legitimate son. There was a bastard, James Scott, later Duke of Monmouth, born of Lucy Walters, a Welsh exile, in April 1649. John Evelyn described her as a 'Brown, beautiful, bold but insipid creature'. She died, neglected and penniless, in 1657.[7]

Charles having no lawful heir the throne passed to his brother, the Duke of York, who was an avowed member of the Church of Rome. That fraternal sequence was a rare coincidence in England. There were few precedents. As kings a Plantagenet brother had followed brother when John succeeded Richard the Lionheart. As queens the Catholic Mary Tudor was succeeded by her sister, the Protestant Elizabeth. Both successions had been relatively peaceful.

In 1685, however, when James, Catholic Duke of York, succeeded his brother, members of the Roman Church were suspected. Resentful of being deprived of his birthright Charles' illegitimate son, the Protestant Duke of Monmouth, led a rebellion against his uncle, that newly appointed Catholic king. There was a battle in the West Country at Sedgemoor on 6 July 1685. John Aubrey was in the wrong place at the wrong time.

He was staying with an old friend, Andrew Paschall, rector of Chedzoy in Somerset. He told Anthony à Wood what happened.

Broad Chalke Aug. 3, 1685. I went from London Tuesday in Whitsonweeke into Somerset to an ingeniose friend of mine, and came just that night as Monmouth began his Rebellion. It was not without danger that I came hither: Monmouth's soldiers came into my friends's house and tooke away horses and armes and came into my bed chamber as I was abed. But *Deo Gratias*, that cloud is overblown. Within this fortnight I shall goe thither againe, where I shall be glad to serve you.[8]

Monmouth's rebellion failed. A night attack on the royal army failed and next day the rebels were routed. Monmouth was captured and taken to the house of one of Aubrey's *Amici*, Anthony Ettrick. Being the Recorder for Poole he sent Monmouth for trial. Condemned, the illegitimate heir was executed on the scaffold.

Several hundred of the rebels were hanged in the notorious Bloody Assizes ruled over by Judge Jeffreys. A thousand were transported as slaves to the West Indian plantations. Others were flogged, pilloried, fined, imprisoned or mutilated.

John Aubrey had written a 'Life' of the Duke of Monmouth. It is lost. That biography together with another about James I were among the many writings that Aubrey had entrusted to Wood. As early as 1680 he had sent them:

London, June 15, 1680. Sir! I have, according to your desire, putt in writing these minutes of lives tumultuarily, as they occur'd in my thoughts or as occasionally I had information of them. They may easily be reduced to order at your leisure by numbring them with red letters, according to time and place etc. 'Tis a taske that I never thought to have undertaken till you imposed it upon me, sayeing that I was fitt for it by reason of my generall acquaintance, having not only lived above halfe a centurie of yeares in the world, nut have also been much tumbled up and downe in it which hath made me much knowne.

In November 1692 Wood returned only Part II of those contributions to his 'Oxford Notables' and even those sheets were mutilated. On the back of one the normally equable John Aubrey wrote indignantly:

This part the second, Mr. Wood haz gelded from page 1 to page 44 and other pages too are wanting wherein are contained Truths, but such as I entrusted no body with the sight of but himselfe. There are severall papers that may cutt my throate. I find too late *Memento diffidere* was a saying worthy of the Sages.

'Take care to distrust' was an apt quotation. Characteristically, Aubrey had included indiscretions, some dangerous if made public, in the notes he sent assuming, naively, that Wood would consider them confidential. Wood did not. The affair was to be the cause of a great quarrel between them.[9]

As late as 1688 Catholics were still suspected to be treacherous. John Aubrey told Wood that when in Oxford 'coming one time out of All-Soules, the Gapeabouts at the gate pointed at me and one said, "Romano-Catholicus". I pray God bless and deliver you from such affronts. You know my Fate haz hindred me from study and reading much, so that I pretend but to little Learning, but for what I have donne by way of Excerpts, and preserving things from being lost, you know best of any one.'[10]

During that semi-barren time one person who was able to help Aubrey with his on-and-off investigation into the problem of distant, unseen stone circles was the great Welsh scholar Edward Lhwyd, a surname that has also been spelled 'Lhuyd', even 'Lhwyd' or Llhwyd. He became a very helpful friend who preserved many of Aubrey's imperilled papers. Born in Cardiganshire, western Wales, he was educated at Oxford and, in 1690, succeeded Plot as Keeper of the Ashmolean Museum there.

In 1693 he wrote to Aubrey telling him that he had made a catalogue of Aubrey's books and manuscripts, generously adding that 'in case you are disposed to dedicate your Collections of Letters to the Museum, I will take care to have them bound out of hand: unless you have been at that charge yourselfe'.[11]

Both men had a deep curiosity about ancient monuments, thinking far beyond the unthinking, copycat explanations of past scholars. Both Lhwyd and Aubrey individually made field-visits to see the sites for themselves. And both, where such journeys were geographically impossible, wrote to local people about information.

Lhwyd was aware of the ignorance about the prehistoric past for which there were no written records. The physical remains – megalithic tombs, cairns, standing stones and circles – were the only evidence. 'He determined to think sensibly about pre-Roman Britain and reconstruct what it was like, and his successes win him an eminent place in the history of field archaeology.'[12]

Lhwyd, who could be a difficult man to deal with, was a committed polymath: philologist, natural historian, geologist and antiquarian. He was influenced by Aubrey's thinking about the past, 'for instance, on the role of the Druids in British prehistory. Aubrey was an older man, with first-hand acquaintance with the great sites of Stonehenge and Avebury, as well as having family ties in Wales. He and Lhwyd were kindred spirits, sharing a scientific interest in natural history, and by the time of their friendship in the early 1690s Aubrey had written his unpublished essay claiming that the primitive stone monuments were pagan temples used by the Druids.'[13]

From his determination to investigate those blank pre-Roman ages Lhywd inspected megalithic monuments in Wales, England, Scotland, Ireland, even Brittany. In 1695, the same year that Gibson's updated *Britannia* was published, Lhwyd ambitiously advertised his *Archaeologia Britannica*, a book intended as a description of Britain's forgotten past. To gather material for it he planned a Great Tour of Britain, Ireland and Brittany. From May 1697 until mid-1701, Lhwyd and three assistants embarked on 'the fatigue of five years' travels through the most retired parts of Her Majesty's Kingdoms' and farther.

Fortitude and fortune were needed. Had they known of a poem written almost three centuries later they would have recited it to each other, groaning, as they struggled over unlaid roads harshly rutted in summer, mud-deep in winter.

A cold coming we had of it,
Just the worst time of the year
For a journey, and such a long journey:
The ways deep and the weather sharp,
The very dead of winter …
Sleeping in snatches,
With the voices singing in our ears, saying
That this was all folly.   T. S. Eliot

Despite adversity it had not been folly although maps were scarce and unreliable. Accommodation varied from the hospitable to the disgusting. Strangers, especially those with unusual accents, were at best ignored, sometimes suspected, often treated with hostility.

There was unseasonably bad weather, hail in May and June 1697, hail and snow over Easter in 1698. In 1720 Killarney bandits threatened them. At Helston, Cornwall, the party was accused of being thieves and taken before a Justice of the Peace. Worse followed. At St Pol de Léon in northern Brittany they were arrested as spies and suffered eighteen undignified days in a filthy prison at Brest.[14]

By April 1701, laden with notebooks, folders of sketches and plans, weary but triumphant they returned to Oxford having travelled at least three thousand miles by land and sea.

Anticlimax followed triumph. Lhwyd's manuscripts were prepared by 1703 but the University printers were slow and the first – and only – volume of the *Archaeologia Britannica* was not issued until 1707. Disappointingly for antiquarians it consisted only of scholarly notes on etymology.

After Lhwyd's death in 1709 the work was to be finished by his assistant, David Parry, but he had become an obstructive drunkard, refusing to show scholars Lhwyd's papers. Nor did he do anything himself.

Anti-climax followed anti-climax. Lhwyd had left debts and to settle them the university took his books in payment. In 1715 the manuscripts were sold to Sir Thomas Sebright of Worcestershire. A Welshman groaned:

> I am told no manner of care is taken in preserving Mr. Edward Lhwyd of the Museum's manuscripts in the Seabright family ... What a pity that such a treasure should fall into the hands of the English, who know no more how to value it than the dunghill cock in Aesop that of the jewel.[15]

It was prophetic. Most of those irreplaceable documents were destroyed in fires. Only by fortune the same did not happen to the fragile papers of John Aubrey.

Just as Aubrey was doing Lhwyd augmented his own discoveries by corresponding with colleagues, being informed in 1693 of the megalithic tomb of Arthur's Stone in a letter from John Williams. John Aubrey had already seen Arthur's Stone in 1656 and later made a rather forgetful record of it.

> As I rode from *Brecknock* to *Radnor*, on the top of a mountain (I think not far from *Payn's-castle*) is a Monument like a Sepulchre but much bigger than that at Holyhead: the stones were great and rudely plac't. I think they called it *Arthur's chaire*, or such a name. But this Monument did no more belong to Him, did that called the Round-Table in Cumberland.[16]

In the margin was a note: 'see S^r Jo. Hoskyns for this.' Hoskyns of Herefordshire, who lived quite near the site, was one of Aubrey's *Amici*. Five years earlier than Aubrey's visit Hoskyns had visited Venice and in a letter to Aubrey mentioned seeing the city's famous courtesans. Unfavourably. 'Their beauty is only fatness and what is an easy product of it, "impudence". Pray get me some of Mr. Hobbs his future books before the Hangman burns them.'[17]

That was in 1651 in the mid-seventeenth century. Towards its end John Aubrey was being informed by Lhwyd of unknown Welsh circles.

In his description of the Gwern Einion portal-dolmen near Bangor Lhwyd called it Coetan Arthur standing near Gwen Engiawn. 'On ye North of it hath been a Carnedh [cairn].' Stone circles were little easier. Often they were bewilderingly described as *y meini hirion*, incomprehensible to readers outside Wales but very much more musical than the pedestrian English equivalent, 'the standing stones'. And now Aubrey had accounts of some of those far-off rings of stone. Many of those descriptions by Lhwyd were later published in the 1695 edition of Camden's *Britannia*.

Among them were the Bryn Gwyn Stones in Anglesey not far from the Menai Straits. Lhwyd wrote:

> There are stones pitcht on end, about 12 in number, whereof three are very considerable, the largest of them being twelve foot high, and eight in breadth where 'tis broadest; for 'tis somewhat of an oblong oval form. These have no other name than *Kerig y Bryngwyn* (*or Bryngwyn stones*) and are so called from the place where they are erected. On what occasion they were rais'd, I cannot conjecture, unless this might be the burial place of the most eminent Druids.[18]

And there was also a description of one of Wales' most evocative circles now known as the Druid's Circle high on the slopes of Penmaenmawr above Conwy Bay.

> It was the most remarkable monument in all Snowdon, called *Y Meineu hirion*, upon the plain mountain ... It's a circular entrenchment, about 26 yards diameter; on the out-side whereof, there are certain rude stone-pillars pitch't on end; of which 12 are now standing, some 2 yards, other 5 foot high, and these are again encompass'd with a stone wall. It stands upon the plain mountain, as soon as we came to the height, having much even ground about it; and now far from it are three other large stones pitch't on end in a triangular form.[19]

Unexpectedly, Aubrey made no note of either of those splendid rings although it is likely that Lhwyd told him of them. What mattered was that he now knew that outside England there were more of those perplexing circles as far away as western Wales. Lhwyd knew of some in Pembrokeshire;

'There are in this County several such circular Monuments.'

Just as fulfilling was that other informants were writing to him about similar settings as far away as Ireland. Lhwyd himself had learned where one had stood, the destroyed ring of Crom Cruaich, in Co. Cavan.

> We meet with several in *Anglesey* and some in other parts of *Wales* called *Kromlecheu*. Now that these Monuments have acquired this name from *bowing*, as having been places of worship in the time of Idolatry, I have no warrant to affirm. However, in order to farther enquiry, we may take notice, that the Irish Historians call one of their chiefest Idols *Cromcruach*; which remain'd till St. *Patrick's* in the plain of *Moy-sleuct* in *Bresin*. This Idol is decrib'd to have been *aura argento caelatum*, [decorated with gold and silver] and said to be attended with twelve other Idols much less, all of brass, plac'd round about him. *Cromcruach*, at the approach of St. *Patrick* fell to the ground, and the lesser Idols sunk into the Earth up to their necks .... We may from hence infer that this circle of stones (which are mentioned by the name of Idol's heads) was before the planting of Christianity in this Country, a place of Idolatrous worship. And if this be granted, we may have little reason to doubt but that our *Kromlechs*, as well as all other such circular Stone-monuments in Britain and Ireland (whereof I presume that there are not less than 100 yet remaining) were also erected for the same use.[20]

John Aubrey copied that extract from the *Britannia*. He had already been told by others that there were indeed stone circles in Ireland. 'I have heard Persons of quality and worthy of Beliefe averre, that in the Kingdom of Ireland (especially in Ulster) are severall Monuments of the like nature.'[21]

'Mr. Gethyng of the Middle Temple assures me, that in Ireland are severall Monuments of stones standing circularly as at Stoneheng Kynnet &c.'[22] Gethin, whose home was in Co. Cork, also informed him of the wedge-tomb of Labbacallee with its enormous capstone. Yet, although legally educated, he was credulous. Aubrey added:

> Mr ... Gethin of the Middle Temple London, told me that at Killian-hill (or a name like it) in Ireland, is a monument of Stones like those at Stone-heng: and from whence the old Tradition is that Merlin brought them to Stone-heng by Conjuration.

Aubrey knew that that was nonsense. (See Appendix C for the magical fictions of Geoffrey of Monmouth).[23]

Another friend was more scholarly. 'Mr. Toland assures me that in the northern parts of Ireland are several such monuments of Stones standing circularly, set in the quarter-land of Rathseny in the parish of Clonmeny and in severall other places.'[24]

Toland was both a scholar and a critical deist, questioning much of the accepted 'truths' in the Bible. A copy of his book, *Christianity Not Mysterious* of 1696, was ordered by Parliament to be publicly burnt by the common hangman.

John Aubrey had now collected information about the existence of stone circles from north to south in England, in Wales, and in Ireland. He waited for information about the possibility of more in Scotland.

> The right Hon[ble] John Lord Yester and S[r] Robert Moray doe assure me (as also severall other learned Gentlemen of Scotland) that in that Kingdom are severall Monuments of the fashion before shewen: nay, in the middle & most northern parts of that Country where the Romans had no dominion. S[r] George Macensi in his *Historie of Scotland* pag. 2, affirmeth that Scotland was never conquered by the Romans.
>
> S[r] Robert Moray promised me, to send me an account of some of these Temples, and how the vulgar called them: but sudden death prevented him. He was a Courtier, that would doe Courtesies for Friendship-sake.[25]

Moray died in 1673. Aubrey had to wait almost twenty years before he found a reliable source of information about those rings in the far north of Britain. He had already convinced Lhywd that the Welsh circles he had seen, and others in Scotland that he had not, were temples, were pre-Roman, and had been centres of worship by the priesthood known as the druids. In his contribution to the additions to 'Penbrokeshire' in the 1695 *Britannia* he wrote that Dr James Garden, Professor of Theology at King's College, Aberdeen, in Scotland

> was the first that suspected these Circles for *Temples of the Druids*. I find that in several parts of that Kingdom they are called Chapels or Temples; with this farther Tradition, that they were places of worship in the time of Heathenism, and did belong to the *Drounich*. Which word some interpret as the *Picts*; but the Dr. suspects it might denote originally the *Druids*; in confirmation whereof, I add, that a village in Anglesey is called *Tre'r Driw*, and interpreted as the *Town of the Druids*.[26]

For the very first time in a printed book, the 1695 *Britannia*, readers learned that the mysterious stone circles were druidical places of worship. Edward Lhwyd, however, was mistaken that James Garden was the first to make that interpretation. It had been John Aubrey exactly thirty years earlier. Garden and Aubrey had been exchanging letters about the problems of the mysterious rings of stone in Scotland since 1692 and Aubrey had told him of his conclusions about those controversial monuments.

Aubrey's druidical deductions had been written down many years earlier. At that time he personally had seen only a few rings, all within riding distance of his home at Broad Chalke. But from the 1637 *Britannia* and other writings he already knew that there were stone circles elsewhere in Britain, even in Ireland although he had no details about them. One source was the 1655 *History of the Church of Scotland* by the former chancellor of Scotland, John Spottiswood.

In his neat but small handwriting Aubrey stated:

> Arch-Bishop Spottsiwood pag. 3 saieth (out of Hector Boetius and G. Buchanan) that the power of Druides in those daies was so great, that it did a long time give a stop to the propagation of the Christian Religion.

Aubrey continued:

> Now to wind up this Discourse: the Romans had no Dominion in Ireland or (at least not far) in Scotland: therefore these Temples are not to be supposed to be built by them: nor had the Danes Dominion in Wales: and therefore we cannot presume the two last mentioned Temples to have been Works of Them. But all these Monuments are of the same fashion, and antique rudeness; wherefore I Conclude, that they were Works erected by the Britons: and were Temples of the Druids.
>
> Broad Chalk [Easton Piers *deleted*] 1665.
>
> FINIS [27]

During that scholarly time of archaeological exploration and research there had been political eruption in England. In only two short years, 1688 and 1669, the Catholic James II had been forced into exile in France and a foreign Protestant, William of Orange, had been invited to come 'to defend the liberties of England'. He came but only on promise of being made king. He was crowned in 1689.

By 1692 Anthony à Wood was in trouble. In June 1691 he had published the first volume of his *Athenae Oxonienses*, about the dignified worthies of Oxford University. The second volume was promised for the following year.[28]

The work caused indignation and rage in the scholarly university colleges. His 'warts-and-all' approach would have been acceptable to a blunt person like Oliver Cromwell but learned scholars, as well as one very highly-born nobleman, expected gentler descriptions. Wood's near-puritanical virtue-cum-vice of expressing the explicit truth – as his restricted, humourless mind considered it – would damage him.

With justification. Some of the 'Lives' were ill-natured, slanderous and unnecessary. John Gadbury, a respected astrologer, was infuriated by an entry in the 'Life' of Sir George Wharton, a Royalist Captain of Horse, that included 'John Gadbury, born at Wheatley ..., son of William Gadbury of that place farmer ...' That exposure of his lowly birth was a gratuitous insult. It was also an irrelevance. Gadbury had never been to Oxford University.[29]

Trouble followed in 1692. In that claustrophobic academic world the book was disliked. Some picked holes in it, that it contained 'a great deal of popery', had 'bad sense in many places', and was 'not fit to wipe one's arse with'. The 'book deserves to be burnt in every college quadrangle'.

On Friday 18 November 1692 Wood was summoned to the Vice-Chancellor's court where he was found guilty of libel, fined £40 and humiliatingly expelled from the university.

Offending passages in his two books were to be publicly burnt. The following year on Monday 31 July, at ten in the morning, 'Andrew Skinner the parator [Summoning Officer of the Ecclesiastical Court] made a fire of two fagots in the Theater yard, and burnt the 2d volume of Ath. Oxon.'[30]

It was a symbolic gesture of rejection but there were many other copies and one was read by a man with sufficient power to endanger the life of John Aubrey. In December 1692 Aubrey complained to Wood that the Earl of Clarendon had accused him of libel.

In his still – unpublished *Brief Lives* Aubrey had written one of Judge David Jenkins stating that 'tis pity he was not made one of the judges of Westminster-hall; and he might have been, he told me, if he had given money to the Chancellor – but he scorned it.'

Aubrey told Wood of this in a letter as early as January 1672. Insensitively, Wood quoted this almost word for word in his own 'Life' of Jenkins in Book II of his *Athenae Oxonienses*. 'After the Restauration of King Charles II 'twas expected by all that he should be made one of the Judges in Westminster Hall, and so he might have been, would he have given money to the then Lord Chancellor'.

It was tactless. It was dangerous. The father of a powerful person had been accused of taking bribes. That venal Chancellor had been Lord Clarendon and his son of the same title succeeded him. He was outraged and the University of Oxford agreed with him.[31]

John Aubrey was horrified and he was scared. On 3 December 1692 he wrote to Wood that Lord Abingdon had informed him that

The Lord Clarendon hath told me [Abingdon] that Mr. Wood had confessed to him, that he had the Libell (*Advice to the Painter*) from me; as also the other informations: I doe admire that you should deale so unkindly with me, that hath been so faithfull a friend to serve you ever since 1665, as to doe so by me: the Libell was printed, and not uncommon. Could you not have sayd that you bought it? or had it of George Ent: or somebody that is dead? To be short my Lord is resolved to ruine me ... I must be faine to fly some whither ere long.[32]

It could be no more than a coincidence but only four months later in London Aubrey wrote that on 'March 20, 169?, about 11 at night robbed and 15 wounds in my head'.[33] It was months before they healed.

Hired thugs were commonplace in Stuart England, paid to do anything from intimidation, assault, murder, to assassination. Only payments differed. The assault may have been Clarendon's retribution. 'Revenge,' says the proverb, 'is a dish that is best eaten cold'.

If so, it was for its exposure rather than its accuracy that Aubrey's accusation of Clarendon's acceptance of bribes was punished. The accusation had been correct. Clarendon had been exiled among other reasons for corruptly selling offices, taking bribes and selling grants for patents. He spent the rest of his life in France.[34]

Anthony à Wood was prosecuted by the same man, Henry, 2nd Earl of Clarendon, for that libel against his father, Edward Hyde. Obsequiously, Wood promised to make changes to the offending book.[35]

Finally, having satisfied his enemies, in June 1695, Wood was pardoned by the university.[36] He died the following year diagnosed by his doctor as suffering from 'a Total Suppresson of Urine'. He lingered in pain but stoically for eleven days until 28 November. His callous physician, Dr Robert South, joked that if his patient could not make water then he must make earth. To which Wood remarked, 'It was South's custom to suffer neither sacredness of place nor solemnity of subject to restrain his vein of humour.' The doctor must have been one of those inadequate persons who were psychologically compelled to make jokes about other people's misfortunes while resenting any jests about their own errors.[37]

In a letter to the young Thomas Tanner who had earlier successfully pleaded with Aubrey to allow some of his descriptions about antiquities to be published in the 1695 *Britannia*, Aubrey wrote on 19 March 1696:

> I am extremely sorrowful for the death of my deare Friends and old correspondent Mr Anthony Wood: who (though his spleen used to make him chagrin and to chide me) yet we could not be asunder, and he would always see me at my Lodgeing, with his dark Lanthorne, which should be a relick ... I am glad that you have all his papers and will be faithful to him and finish what he left undon.[38]

Despite his comparative youth Tanner was faithful. He had been appointed Wood's literary executor and he performed that responsibility properly. Seventeen years after Wood's death he published a third volume of the *Athenae Oxonienses*. It contained almost five hundred more lives.

In 1695, just a year before Wood died, Professor James Garden of Aberdeen University sent John Aubrey the last of nine very long and expensive letters about druids and stone circles in the neighbourhood of Aberdeen.[39]

It cost three pence to send a letter from Aberdeen to Edinburgh and a further five to reach London. It was paid for on delivery. Eight pence was a lot of money in the years when a farm labourer only earned twelve, a shilling, for a full day's work and when a pound of the best beef cost three pence. For writers of long letters a pound's weight of a small bundle of short-lasting rush-candles cost five.

To reach London there were regular post-houses in England with fast galloping horses every ten miles. It took about nine or ten days from the date of writing to being postmarked in London.[40]

There were no envelopes. Garden's missives would be carefully folded, sealed, addressed to Aubrey at the address of his present host, for the first letter, Edmund Halley.

> For his honoured friend
> Master John Aubrey
> To be left with
> Master Edmund Halley
> At Gresham College, London.

Halley, an astronomer, was one more of Aubrey's distinguished friends. The comet named after him had been noticed in 1583. Halley observed it for himself in 1682. With mathematical assistance from Newton he was able to predict that it had a seventy-six-year cycle. It reappeared in 1758 sixteen years after Halley's death.

He had been Aubrey's host when Garden's first letter of 15 June 1692 was delivered. Aubrey had written to Garden, telling him of his belief that stone circles were temples of the druids but he lacked information about similar rings in Scotland. In reply Garden was able to inform him of many stone circles of which Aubrey had never heard including some very distinctive forms in north-eastern Scotland.

He was replying to Aubrey's letter of 9 April that year. Garden replied that he had visited six or seven sites near Aberdeen. One kind was the unusual recumbent stone circles of north-eastern Scotland with their distinctive long stone lying flat at the south of the ring. By mistake Aubrey had written to Garden's brother, a minister of the gospel. James Garden asked that future letters be directed to himself, 'Professor of Theologie in the King's College of Aberdene'. Aubrey did so.

Garden described the circles near Aberdeen. 'What the Lord Yester and Sir Robert Morray told you long ago is true, viz. that in the northern parts of this Kingdom many monuments of the nature and fashion described you are yet extant. They consist of tall bigg unpolished stones, sett upon end & placed circularly not contiguous together but at some distance. The obscurer sort (which are the more numerous) have but one circle of stones standing at equal distances; others, towards the south or south-east; have a large broad stone standing on edge, which fills up the whole space betwixt two of those stones y^t stand on end; and is called by the vulgar the altar stone.'

Garden had visited two seven miles south of Aberdeen in Kincardineshire: Auchquorthies, 'field of stones', and Old Bourtreee bush. In his letter he wrote his only detailed description of a recumbent ring:

> Two of the Largest and most remarkable of those monuments that ever I saw, ar yet to be seen at a place called Auchincorthie, in the shire of Mernis and five miles distant from Aberdene. One of them has two circles of stones, whereof the exterior circle consists of thirteen great stones besides two that are fallen and the broad stone toward the south about three yards high above ground, betwixt seaven & eight paces distant from on from another; the Diameter being 24 large paces the interior circle is about 3 paces distant from the other, and the stones therof 3 foot high above ground. Toward the East from this Monument at 26 paces distance ther is a bigg stone fast in the ground … The other Monument (which is fully as large if not larger than that which I have alreadie described, and distant from it about a bow shott of ground) consists of three circles having the same common center. The stones of the greatest circle are about 3 yards, and those of the two lesser circles 3 foot high above ground, the inner most circle 3 paces diameter and the stones standing close together.
>
> James Garden, June 15, 1692

It is a good description of the recumbent stone circles of north-eastern Scotland, correctly placing the long, prostrate slab in the south arc of the ring.

Garden added that here was 'a tradition that the preists caused earth to be brought from other adjacent places upon peoples backs to Auchincorthie, for making the soile thereof deeper, which is given for the reason why this parcel of land (though surrounded by heath and moss on all sides) is better and more fertile than other places thereabout'. Even today the rings are placed on good, deep soil.

There were similar circles in Banff and Nairn and more than a hundred in Aberdeenshire itself.

'The generall tradition throughout the Kingdome concerning this kind of Monuments is, that they were places of worship & sacrifice in heathen times … In this part of the country the are called Standing Stones.' Some were known as chapels.

'Albeit from the general tradition that these monuments were places of Pagan worship, and the historicall knowledge, we have that the superstition of the Druids did take place in Brittaine, we may rationally collect, that these monuments have been Temples of the Druids' – something that Aubrey had already told him. And at the end of his letter he mentioned 'that some persons who are yet alive, declare that many years since they did see ashes of some burnt material digged out of the bottom of a little circle (sett about wt stones standing close together) in the center of on of those monuments which is yet standing near the church of Old Keig'.

Garden was referring to the small ring at the centre of the low cairn around which the stones of the circle of Cothiemuir Wood stood. Centuries later an archaeological excavation proved that the ashes were those of a human cremation.[41]

In his second letter of 22 January 1693, mainly about bards, poets and druids, Garden answered one of Aubrey's questions about local customs of the highlanders.

But having made enquiry about the peculiar customes of our Highlanders, I find that what has been reported to you about their making a curtesie to the new moon is not altogether without ground; for I am informed that in the shire of Ross the vulgar use when they first see the new moon turning their faces that way to pull off their caps and say God bless the new moon.[42]

Over a hundred and fifty years before Garden, Hector Boece, Principal of King's College, Aberdeen University, also known as Boethius, the 'Father of Lies', had published his unreliable but popular *Scotorum Historiae* in 1527. He included a folk-memory about recumbent stone circles. It had a reference to the moon.

He wrote that 'huge stones were erected in a ring, and the biggest of them was stretched out on the south side to serve as an altar, whereon were burnt the victims in sacrifice to the gods'. The new ritual 'included a monthly sacrifice to Diana, goddess of the moon, 'and that is why the new moon was hailed with certain words of prayer, a custom which lingered very late'.[43]

Boece was correct both about human cremations and the moon but it would be five hundred more years, late in the twentieth century, before those rings' unexpectedly precise arcane lunar astronomy was explained.

That Boece more than four hundred years earlier should have had a vague knowledge of the significance of that orientation is, to the writer, the most positive evidence for a surviving verbal record of a prehistoric custom performed by people without writing, a custom that by Boece's time was already at least three thousand years old.

In between that time, around 1500 BC, when the recumbent stone circles had been abandoned there had been later prehistoric peoples, a partial Roman occupation, the advent of Christianity, and then centuries of disruptive medieval history. That folk-memory should endure so many demographic disruptions is astonishing. But Boece did write those equally astonishing words.

Neither Garden nor Aubrey understood the implications of such esoteric lunar astronomy. Aubrey should have consulted Edward Halley.

In his seventh letter of May 1694 Garden remembered that Aubrey had told him that a gentleman at a meeting of the Royal Society claimed that the 'circular monuments of stone in Orkney were made by the Danes'. Garden scoffed, 'Albeit the Danes made sundry descents into Scotland, yet they never had footing in it much less were they masters of it', nor time to build monuments of lasting stone.[45]

And in his final letter of 31 July 1695, Garden told Aubrey that in a letter from an acquaintance in Orkney he had learned of two imposing stone circles there.

> There is a Booke intituled *A Description of the Isles of Orkney* by M[r] James Wallace late Minister at Kirkwall printed in Edinburgh anno 1693. In it he makes mention of two rounds sett about with high smooth stones or flags about 20 foot above ground, 6 foot broad and a foot or two thick, and ditched about: whereof the largest is 110 paces diameter and reputed to be high places of worship & sacrifice in Pagan times, this he confirms from a passage in Boeth [Hector Boece]. 'He makes mention of these rounds of stone & saith they are called by the people the ancient temples of the Gods.[46]

The two circles were the Ring of Brodgar and the Standing Stones of Stenness, Brodgar being the larger.

In London John Aubrey had moved from one friend's house to another, Garden's following letters were addressed:

> For his honoured friend
> Master John Aubrey to
> Be left with Doctor Gale
> Schoolmaster of Pauls School
> In Paul's Church-yard in London.

Those letters were about the priestly caste of druids in Scotland. The third letter of 6 February 1693 stated that in the northern parts of Scotland there had been bards and poets, and so it was likely there had also been druids.

In Ross the popular opinion was that the 'stone monuments ... were places of worship ... And that they belonged to the Drounich or Trounich. Now if it be true that these monuments were places of worship in heathen times, and that before Christianity was planted in this Kingdome, the superstition of the Druids prevailed therein, as well as in England'.

For Garden the problem was that no old author whether Julius Caesar or later when describing druids ever mentioned a stone circle although they did describe the groves in which druids worshipped. Only many centuries later did Hector Boece write about the circles.

And despite general belief of the same ancient writers that Stonehenge was erected as a memorial to slaughtered Britons 'their wavering and uncertainty ... [was] not based on good authority'. The same was true of Scottish stone circles. They were no more cemeteries than a Christian church was a cemetery because it stood in a graveyard.

In his fifth letter of 6 March 1693 James Garden returned to the puzzle of groves without any stone circles. There was no evidence in his time of druidical groves near stone circles. 'The cutting down of the Druid-groves (which consisted of oaks which could be putt to many profitable uses) was both an easier and a mor profitable work than the demolishing of the temples or ston-monuments from which no benefit could be reaped.'

Later having become Christians people 'might leave these Temples to be monuments and memorialls to posterity of the gross idolatrie which sometime defiled this Isle'.[47]

What neither Garden nor Aubrey nor anyone from Stuart times up to the late nineteenth century could have known was that the druidical caste that Romans encountered in both Gaul and Britain was at least three thousand years, a hundred and fifty short-lived generations, later than the time when stone circles had been set up in Britain.

From Garden's long letters John Aubrey copied the parts mentioning particular stone circles in Scotland. He added some paragraphs Garden had written about druids. It was only selective extracts that he added to his collection of pages about his *Templa Druidum*. Letters Eight and Nine were not included.

Garden satisfied John Aubrey that there were stone circles in Scotland. Consequently Aubrey's bran-tub of a mind picked out two more titbits of enquiry for his helpful correspondent, one far-fetched, the second foolish: the question of second sight and, then, the possibility of transportation by an invisible power. Both those debatable subjects were to be included with other fripperies such as 'Converse with Angels and Spirits' and 'Glances of Love and Malice' in Aubrey's only book to be published in his lifetime, his *Miscellanies* of 1696.

The poet John Dryden had wanted his own publisher to sell it but he refused so 'I am advised to do it by Subscriptions, which doe begin pretty luckily'.[48]

Aubrey's letters asked Garden about information on both second-sight and transportation. Patiently the rector replied that there were some reported occurrences of Scottish clairvoyance. He had heard that a nobleman had been magically transported. Garden wrote that the man said he had been caught up in a whirlwind and carried by fairies to a place where he slept, only to wake up in the presence of the king. 'Its said the King gave him the cup which was found in his hand & dismissed him.'

Aubrey copied this and one or two other stories related by Garden into his book of *Miscellanies*.[49]

Garden continued:

This being all the information which I can give at present concerning transportation by an invisible power; I'm sorry yt I am able to contribute so little to the publishing of so curious a piece as it seems, your hermetick philosophie wilbe. As for my letters concerning 2nd sighted men yow know there is litle in them besides some written relations which I received from others out of which if yow please yow may call the most remarkable passages and set ym down in your own stile and in case of publishing the intire letters I desire my name may be spared as well as in them as in those relating to the Druid-temples.

Courteously, the rector thanked Aubrey for his present of the *Transactions* of the Royal Society. Garden would arrange for an Aberdeen merchant to pick up the book from Dr Gale's where Aubrey was lodging.

The four-year-long correspondence finished. On 31 July 1695 Garden's last letter to Aubrey ended:

What I have already written hath wearied me & will, I doubt not weary you in the perusall. Wherefor I shal add no mor but that I still am
Your affectionat faithfull friend
Ja: Garden
Old Aberdeen. July 31 -96
For his honoured friend
Master John Aubrey
To be left with Doctor Gale, Schoolmaster
of Paul's school in Pauls churchyard
London.[50]

It was over. The long years of searching had discovered what Aubrey had been wondering about ever since seeing Avebury forty-seven years earlier. That ring and other stone circles were not Danish, Saxon or Roman. They were earlier. And they had been the temples of the druids. It would all be included in his *Templa Druidum*.

Having discovered Avebury by accident in 1649 and astonished and curious why such great stones had been set up, and when, he had begun to gather facts about prehistoric rings. Learning that many were in parts of Britain such as north-eastern Scotland, western Wales, even Ireland where Romans, Saxons or Danes had either never reached or settled he realised that the rings must be earlier than those times.

I am perswaded that the monument was built long before the Romans ever knew Britaine ... a work of a people settled in their country and therefore 'tis odds, but that these ancient Monuments (sc. Aubury, Stonehenge, Kerrig y Druidd &c) were Temples of the Priests of the most eminent Order, viz, Druids, and it is strongly to be presumed that Aubury, Stoneheng to be as ancient as those times.

It was an insight that proved seminal to the study of megalithic rings.

There have been several Books writt by learned men concerning Stoneheng: much differing from one another: some affirming one thing, some another. Now I come in the Rear of all by comparative Arguments to give a clear evidence that these Monuments were Pagan-Temples: which was not made-out before, and also (with humble Submission to better judgement) offere a probability that they were *Temples* of the *Druids* ...

Now my presumption is, That the Druids being the most eminent priests (in order of Priests) among Britons' tis odds, but that these ancient Monuments (sc. Aubury, Stonehenge, Kerrig y Druidd &c) were Temples of the Priests of the most eminent Order, viz, *Druids*, and it is strongly to be presumed, that Aubury, Stoneheng & &c. are as ancient as those times.

This Inquiry I must confess is a gropeing in the Dark: but although I have not brought it into a cleer light; yet I can affirm, that I have brought it from an utter darkness to a thin Mist: and have gonne farther in this Essay than any one before.[51]

It was not a boast. It was a statement that could only have been made after years of drudgery, visiting some rings, enquiring by letter after letter about many others.

John Aubrey was Britain's first prehistorian, an archaeological alchemist who converted the dull lead of superstition into the gold of truth about stone circles.

10

1695-97: *Britannia & Monumenta Britannica* 1980-82

It is hardly too much to say that modern antiquaries owe their knowledge of the great Celtic temple, at Avebury, in Wiltshire, entirely to Aubrey ... Aubrey too was the first whose published opinion pronounced this monument, with Stonehenge and similar stone circles, to be religious monuments raised by the British Druids ... On this point, as in most of his theories ... Aubrey's views were generally useful, practical, and rational.

John Britton, 1845, 3-4

In 1695 the new edition of Camden's *Britannia* appeared and at last some of John Aubrey's records of stone circles were printed. The book was a big volume of over a thousand pages and, unusually, each of the two large pages in the open book, left and right, *verso* and *recto*, was divided into two columns, separately numbered, odd on the left, even number on the right.[1]

The 'Preface to the Reader' explained the need for a new edition. 'The space of sixty or eighty years must make a strange alteration in the face of things'. The Preface assured its readers that the 1695 *Britannia* had kept an exact translation of the previous Camden but there were also 'Additions' by contemporary authorities at the end of each Chapter to bring the book up to date.

The revised book was the production of two young men with the contributors whom they had enticed to write sections. Those editors were not established elderly scholars. They were in their twenties, undergraduates of Queen's College, Oxford. Edmund Gibson was the older in his mid-twenties. His colleague, Thomas Tanner, was an academic year behind him. Having gained their degrees Garden went to London. Tanner stayed in Oxford.

For their ambitious enterprise they inveigled some thirty correspondents including young Tanner, who was only twenty-four. The oldest was the ageing John Aubrey, almost seventy. Among others were several of

Aubrey's friends: Anthony Ettrick offered notes on Dorset; John Evelyn on Surrey; Samuel Pepys on naval matters; predictably, Edward Lhwyd on Wales.[2]

John Evelyn contributed a substantial piece for Surrey. Almost twenty years earlier he had told Aubrey that 'Surrey is the Country of my Birth and my delight', and in 1691 he had made notes for the revised edition of Aubrey's *Perambulation of Surrey*. He told Anthony à Wood he wished he made them earlier 'soon after my Perambulation, whilst the Idea of them was fresh and lively; I should have then have given it more Spirit'. For the 1695 *Britannia* his additions were almost double the length of the entry in the earlier edition.[3]

The editors debated whether to present the new edition in scholarly Latin or the more accessible English. Samuel Pepys insisted on English. He contributed 'the account of the Arsenals for the Royal Navy in Kent with the additions to Portsmouth and Harwich so far as they relate to the Royal Navy'.[4]

Another scholar invited was the Irish thinker, John Toland, who was known to John Aubrey. Aubrey was, for Stuart times, one of the most advanced of thinkers, unusually radical even amongst his intellectual acquaintances and it is not surprising that he became acquainted with Toland whose deistic beliefs had alarmed orthodox Christians. Toland's *Christianity Not Mysterious* of 1696 was compared with John Locke's *The Reasonableness of Christianity* of the previous year. Locke thought him likely to go wrong through 'his exceeding great value of himself'.[5]

Locke was prophetic. Toland was prepared to contribute to the *Britannia* but on his terms, without amendments because what he submitted would be correct. Gibson, the editor, considered him conceited; the two fell out. Toland contributed nothing.

Edward Lhwyd was different. To make archaeological additions for the 1695 *Britannia*, he journeyed to South Wales, his 'Camden Tour', from mid-August to mid-November 1693. Impoverished he worried about the cost. The journey, he wrote on 16 June, 'would take up more time and expences than Mr. Swalle (yᵉ Bookseller concerned) is willing to allow'. Another man's sloth was already dooming Aubrey's own work to centuries of precarious survival.

On page 111 of the new *Britannia*, three-quarters of the way down the column is a sentence: 'About half a mile from Silbury, is Aubury, a monument more considerable in it self, than known to the world.' A marginal note explains who the author was: '*Aubury*. Aubr. Monument. Britan. MS.'

The reference to Avebury had been taken from the scattered sheets of John Aubrey's disordered *Monumenta Britannica*. It was a perishable manuscript. Only centuries later was it edited and rearranged in two books.[6]

Edmund Gibson, by then settled in London, pestered Aubrey to allow him to send the bundle of papers to Tanner in Oxford for him to edit. By persuasion and persistence he got his way and was, grudgingly, given the package to be despatched to Oxford. Aubrey fretted. The sheets had no copies.

It is understandable that Aubrey was a reluctant contributor to the new *Britannia*. He had spent over forty years gathering his material with no acknowledgement except for the praise of his friends. To allow Gibson and Tanner to print anonymous contributions was quite unacceptable and it took many weeks for any agreement between the three men. He was finally persuaded but only on the sworn promise of an acknowledgement for each entry: 'Aubr. MS' or 'Aubr. Monument. Britan. MS' or a similar entry giving his name and the source of the entry.

With Aubrey involved there was inevitable procrastination but the scribbled pages were finally despatched to Oxford for Tanner to arrange and then return to Gibson in London.

More delay followed. But in reverse. Gibson was being pestered by Aubrey for news of what had happened to that irreplaceable manuscript. Tanner should have sent them to London earlier. Gibson wrote to Tanner on 21 March 1694 asking whether there was any good excuse for delay. Surely Tanner had nothing better to do. He had never been a gadabout. Just arrange, edit and return.

> If you were to trot every day along *Cat-Street*, and after a turn or two in the Schools quadrangle, to adjourn to Tom Swift's, I could excuse you for not sending your papers sooner. But when a man's cloystered up in an old Monkish Lodge and the very Phys of his chamber is nothing but antiquitie itself; for such a one to make delays, is a little intolerable. If you knew how I am persecuted, you would not keep me a mom[t] longer; old John Aubrey is dayly upon me, and the blame is as dayly layd upon poor Mr. Tanner.[7]

But when Gibson did finally receive Aubrey's *Monumenta Britannica* he was dismayed.

> The accounts of things are so broken and short, the parts so much disorder'd, and the whole a mere Rhapsody, that I cannot but wonder how that poor man could entertain thoughts of a present Impression.[8]

As his biographer Anthony Powell wrote, 'Aubrey's method of writing, on some scrap of paper that came to hand, any item of interest that might at a given moment drift into his head – combined with his inability to stick to the point and habit of toying with a piece of work for thirty-five or more years – of necessity makes any brief attempt to describe the final accumulation of his work somewhat irregular in form.'⁹

The twentieth-century editors of the *Monumenta Britannica* were to experience exactly the same difficulty.

For the 1695 *Britannia* its editor, Gibson, struggled with the chaotic pages and ended with a compromise. Aubrey's disordered rhapsody was tediously edited into a form suitable for the new Camden. There were entries for many sites but most had been paraphrased by Gibson from Aubrey's original notes, mainly about Wiltshire but with others from Somerset, Oxfordshire and Dorset.

A typical entry and acknowledgement was the one for the circles at Avebury:

> About half a mile from *Silbury*, is *Aubury*, a monument more considerable in it self, than known to the world. For a village of the same name being built within the circumference of it, and (by the by) out of it's stones too; what by gardens, orchards, inclosures, and such like, the prospect is so interrupted, that 'tis very hard to discover the form of it. It is environ'd with an extraordinary *Vallum* or Rampart, as great and as high as that at Winchester; and within it is a graff of a breadth and depth proportionable: from which Mr. *Aubrey* inferrs, that it could not be design'd for a fortification, because then the graff would have been on the outside. From the north to the south port are 60 paces, and as many from the west port to the east. The breadth of the Rampart is 4 perches, and that of the graff the same. The graff has been surrounded all along the edge of it, with large stones pitch't on end, most of which are now taken away; but some marks remaining give one the liberty to guess they stood quite round. *Aubury** Aubr. Monument. Britan. M.S.

That description was followed by others about the Kennet avenue and the stone circle at its far end at the top of Overton Hill known today as the Sanctuary:

> There was a walk that has been enclose'd on each side with large stones, only one side at present wants a great many, but the other is almost, if not quite, entire; above which place, on the brow of the hill is another Monument, encompass'd with a circular trench, and a double circle of stones, four or five foot high, tho' most of them are now fallen down; the diameter of the outer circle 40 yards, and of the inner 15. Between *West-Kennet* and this place is a walk much like that from *Aubury* thither, at least a quarter of a mile in length. Aubr. ibid. West Ken-net.

The entry was followed by a short account of the human bones discovered around the circle, presuming they were the remains of Saxons and Danes killed in the battle of Kennet fought in AD 1006.

In the 'Additions' to Somerset there was an account of Stanton Drew:

> A mile east from *Chue-Magna*, on the south-side of the river *Chue* lies *Stanton-Drew*,
> where is to be seen a monument of stones like those of *Stone-henge* in Wiltshire: but
> these not being altogether so big as the *Stone-henge* ones, nor standing in so clear a
> plain, the hedges and trees mix'd amongst them have made them less taken notice
> of.

On the *recto* sheet the adjacent columns 81 and 82 provided additional
tales about the little-known site. It was an unfortunate trait in the 1695
Britannia. The editors accepted Aubrey's entries but then added other
information, a medley of the out of date, guesswork, legend and simple
nonsense.

> Between *Bathe* and *Bristol*, a little river runs into the *Avon*, upon which is *Stanton-*
> *drew* , whereof the latter part might seem to point out some relation to the old Druids,
> but that *Drew* is the name of an ancient family in the western parts; and the monument
> there, called the *Wedding*, would strengthen such a conjecture. The occasion of the
> name *Wedding*, is a tradition which passes among the common people, *That a Bride*
> *going to be married, she and the rest of the company were chang'd into these stones.*
> They are in a circular form, 5 or 6 foot high, and the whole monument is bigger than
> *Stonehenge*, the diameter here being 90 paces; tho' no appearance of a ditch.
> Stanton-Drew. *Aubr. MS.

The entry shows the problem of editorial changes made by editors with
neither knowledge nor understanding of archaeological matters. What was
printed had both changed and abbreviated what Aubrey had presented. The
1695 entry was not as informative as the years-old related description in
Aubrey's manuscript notes in his *Templa Druidum*. It was also intermixed
with descriptions from the previous *Britannia* without any indication of
which was the more reliable.[10]

Regrettably, the same is true of the entry for Stonehenge, 'a piece of
Antiquity so famous, as to have gain'd the admiration of all ages ... 'Tis
of itself so singular, and receives so little light from history, that almost
everyone has advanc'd a new notion'.

In the 1695 *Britannia* the tedious account of the world's most famous
stone circle occupied almost three entire columns, 108, 109 and 110, some
of it no more than medieval nonsense about Merlin and Irish giants but,
characteristically, through editorial archaeological ignorance, Aubrey's
perceptive information about Stonehenge's previously unrecognised pits
that had once held bluestones from Wales was omitted. The cavities only
became known and called the Aubrey Holes in the early twentieth century
when more were recognised during an excavation. Today their tops are

visible because the encroaching grass has been removed exposing the underlying white chalk.

As well as the 'Additions' for the counties of Wiltshire and Somerset there were others by John Aubrey for Oxfordshire and Dorset.

The Rollright Stones near Chipping Norton in Oxfordshire had its first anonymous entry on pages 253-4 of the new *Britannia* with an illustration of a windmill, and four visitors inside the ring and three more at the megalithic tomb of the Whispering Knights.

In the 'Additions' there were two contributions, the first from Dr Plot, the second from John Aubrey.

Plot wrote:

More to the North is the Monument of *Roll-rich*, a single Circle of stones without *Epistyles* or *Architraves*, and of no very regular figure. Except one or two, the rest of them are not above four foot and a half high. What the occasion of this monument might be, is not hinted by any Inscription upon the stones, or by any other marks about them: which seems to make it probable at least that it was not erected in memory of any pesons that were bury'd there. For if so, we might hope (as in other places in this kingdom) to met with a Cross or something of that kind implying the design, if Christian; but if Pagan, one would expect to find barrows at some small distance. Plot, p.319.

Then Aubrey's piece was added:

Besides, that curious Antiquary *Ralph Sheldon* Esq, making a diligent search in the middle, after anything that might lead us to the first design of it, and particularly *bones*; found himself disappointed. Though if we make an estimate of this from another of the like nature, the bones (if any are any) may more probably be met with without the circle as they were some years ago at a little distance from that at *Kynet* in *Wiltshire*, and have been formerly at the famous *Stone-henge*. Aubr. MS

Typical of the 'new' *Britannia* that frequently mingled good descriptions with long out-of-date material the two sensible accounts of what could be seen, even found, at the Rollright Stones, followed by a long paragraph repeating the medieval nonsense of Rollo the king, his army, his traitors and the malevolent witch who petrified them all.

The editors admitted it could all be nonsense but:

though it be upon the whole ridiculous enough, yet it may (as we so often find in such traditional tales) have something of truth at the bottom. For why may not that large stone at a little distance, which they call *the King*, be the *Kingstolen* belonging to the Circle of stones rais'd usually for the Coronation of the Northern Kings (as *Wormius* informs us:) especially since the learned Dr. *Plot* has observ'd from the same *Wormius*, that this *Kingstolen*, though ordinarily in the middle, was yet sometimes at a distance from the Circle?[11]

If John Aubrey ever read that nonsense he may have remembered how thirty-two years earlier, in 1663, in the presence of the king his colleague Walter Charleton had made the same Danish argument about Stonehenge being a monument erected by Danish noblemen for coronations.

Charleton's 'ghost' intruded farther into the *Britannia*. On its page 831 even the sprawling circle of Long Meg & Her Daughters near Penrith suffered. Both that ring and the Rollright Stones

> may seem to be monuments erected at the solemn Investiture of some Danish kings, and of the same kind as the *Kingstolen* in Denmark and *Moresteen* in Sweeden.

The justifications for that archaic nonsense were the 'reliable' sources of Wormius and Dr Plot's *Oxfordshire*.

Clearly the editors of the new *Britannia* either did not know or had rejected the fact that by 1695 it had been proved that stone circles had been built many centuries before the Danish occupation of England and were pre-Roman temples of the druids.

Aubrey's last site to be acknowledged was the Nine Stones at Winterbourne Abbas in Dorset:

> Aubr. Mon. Brit. MS. 'Not far from hence is *Winterbourne* in the parish whereof, within an inclosure near the London-road, there stand certain stones, nine in number, in a circular form. The highest of them is seven foot, the next highest almost six foot; the rest are broken, and now not above a yard high ... The stones of both these monuments seem to be petrify'd lumps of flint.[12]

John Aubrey was now in his late sixties and his health, never good, deteriorated. In 1694 he had suffered an apoplectic fit but a month later he was well enough to send a friend a hand-written copy of his 'Education of a Young Gentleman'. The Earl of Pembroke had already approved of it.

The following year Aubrey 'had been ill of a great cold since St Paul's tyde' but there was worse, his eyesight was failing. 'Ever since I came from Oxon I have a *mist* in my *eies*.' A doctor assured him that he would recover 'but I must forebeare reading. Indeed I can hardly read a letter'. He went on, 'my eies are hardly anything mending but I can write by guess'. In August he told Lhuyd 'my eieis do not mend but very slowly'. And his years-long drinking companion with whom he had passed many bibulously merry evenings was ill, 'Edmund Wyld growes very weak and I feare cannot long continue'. His friend died in December.[13]

A year later, 1696, Aubrey's pot-pourri of idiosyncratic interests, his *Miscellanies,* was published. It was successful and went into further editions with alterations and additions. Amongst its scatter of topics: 'Days Lucky and Unlucky'; 'Magick'; 'Corps-candles in Wales'; there was a section on 'Dreams', one of which could just as easily have been written for his *Brief Lives.*

> Mrs. C.-, of S.-, in the county of S-, had a beloved daughter, who had been a long time ill, and received no benefit from her physicians. She dreamed that a friend of hers deceased, told her, that if she gave her daughter a drench of yew pounded, that she would recover; she gave her the drench, and it killed her. Whereupon she grew almost distracted: her chamber maid to complement her, and mitigate her grief, said surely that could not kill her, she would adventure to take the same herself; she did so, and died also. This was about the year 1670 or 1671. I knew the family.[14]

That gullible, semi-hysterical mother had crushed yew berries and mixed the juice with water. She should have read Nicholas Culpeper's *Colour Herbal,* published twenty years earlier. Yew, he wrote, 'has no place among medical plants. The leaves and berries are poisonous to man and beast'.[15]

Aubrey's *Miscellanies* were published but the scholarly, archaeologically important *Templa Druidum* had not. Yet it was a wonderland of stone circle information. It provided concepts that eradicated long accepted, arid beliefs about ancient monuments. John Aubrey knew that much of what he had documented about old places was irreplaceable. Decay and neglect were erasing the past.

'Force this in here,' he scribbled at the top of a page about a different kind of antiquity, '(though it being foreign to the County) to preserve it from being lost and forgotten.'[16]

He had visited sites, corresponded up to his death with other antiquarians and he learned about others, many of which have since disappeared. The result was a collection of invaluable though disordered notes, his bits-and-pieces *Templa Druidum,* that survived perilously unpublished for almost three hundred years after his death. Scholars plunder them to this day.

They nearly disappeared. As early as 1673 Aubrey had told Wood that 'My *Templa Druidum* is with Dr. Locke at my Lord Chancellor, who is much importunate with me to print it.' Years later, on 24 April 1690, Aubrey wrote to his friend, Anthony à Wood, announcing in relief that the work had been finished. 'By the beginning of October last I had made an end of my *Monumenta Britannica,* 3 volumes, and one other vol. of *Miscellanea,* all of which I shall send you, God willing, next weeke.' Instead, that October everything was entrusted to Robert Hooke.

Time drifted. The draft of John Aubrey's little 'history', written 'at a gallop', 'was worn-out with time & handling, and now, me thinks, after many years lying dormant, I come abroad like the Ghost of one of those Druids'.[17]

It had been given dedication after dedication, the first to Charles II who died in 1685. Other mortal dedicatees followed: Sir William Turnbull, then Sir Walter Long, death after death down to Thomas, the Earl of Pembroke. It was almost a curse as each subsequently honoured name died.

In 1692 the *Templa Druidum* was offered for private subscription at a price of eighteen shillings, nine down, nine on publication a year later but there were only just over a hundred takers, too few to be profitable for a publisher. Three years later in 1695 Awnsham Churchill, a rich but dilatory London bookseller who had published Gibson's enlarged edition of Camden's *Britannia* that year in partnership with a Mr Swalle, was still considering publication of Aubrey's manuscripts which he had already kept 'shamefully long'.

Aubrey had already made additions to the new *Britannia* and he was anxious that his hard-accumulated researches should not now be stolen by some impostor.

'I would have a man hanged,' he wrote to Anthony Wood in July the previous year, 'should print anothers booke under his own name.' Already he had one of his discoveries of a medicinal spring claimed by the unprincipled Benjamin Woodroffe, no less than the Master of Gloucester Hall in Oxford. 'Lord!' Aubrey wrote to Wood the following year in September 1695, 'what snatching & catching there is of other men's discoveries.' He himself had told Woodroffe of the spring![18]

Nor was any publisher ready to edit the confusion of the *Templa Druidum* and print it. Awsham Churchill had had the pages in his 'safe-keeping' since 1690. And did nothing. That a publisher actually had them in safety was little more than a raindrop in an ocean. Aubrey worried: 'I see what becomes of Mens writings when they are deceased.' His anxiety was justified. On Aubrey's death in 1697 the procrastinating Churchill still had the only manuscript, perishable, uncopied and unpublished.

He never did anything. The pages were inherited by his son, another Awnsham. From 1755 to 1780 it was held by an equally unenterprising nephew of the same name. By 1817 it was owned by another indifferent Churchill, a William. Ultimately it went to a Colonel William Greville who finally sold the papers to the Bodleian Library in Oxford, in 1836. 'How these curiosities would be quite forgotten,' Aubrey had mused, 'did not idle fellows such as I putt them downe.'[19]

Then he himself was put down. In June 1697, 'surprized by age', he died in Oxford's Holywell Street only a quarter of a mile from Trinity, his old college. He had perhaps suffered another attack of apoplexy, maybe while boarding for a night or two with Christopher White, a chemist and friendly acquaintance.

Much later the antiquary, Dr Richard Rawlinson stated in his unreliable Memoir for Aubrey's *Perambulation of Surrey* that Aubrey had died on his way to Draycot, some miles south of Oxford, going to the home of Lady Long, widow of his old friend Sir James Long. She is known to have helped Aubrey in those later times of need.[20]

Aubrey died intestate. And almost forgotten.

For the very time and place of his burial was forgotten, and not for one hundred and fifty years was an entry uncovered in the Register of the Church of St Mary Magdalen – '1697, JOHN AUBERY A Stranger was Buryed June 7th'. A 'Stranger' meant no more than a non-parishioner for whose burial an extra fee was demanded.

His funeral was arranged by Thomas Tanner, by then a Fellow at All Souls College, Oxford. Aubrey's body was laid somewhere in the south aisle, nicknamed 'Trinity aile', where those collegiate scholars were buried. There was no tomb, no gravestone, and there was no inscription despite Aubrey's clear instructions:

> I would desire that this Inscription should be a stone about the bigness of a royal sheet of paper scilicet, about 2 foot square. Mr. Reynolds of Lambeth, Stonecutter (Foxhall) who married Mr. Elias Ashmole's Widow will help me to a Marble as square as an imperial sheet of paper for 8 shillings.[21]

Nothing was done.

Oliver Lawson Dick, the editor of a fine *Brief Lives*, amended the lacuna. He had a commemorative stone plaque set up at the end of the church's south aisle facing the supposed grave.[22]

There is another plaque in Aubrey's childhood church of Kington St Michael. Unfortunately the year of his birth is given as 1625 rather than 1626, an error caused by the confusion between the calendar year beginning in January and the ecclesiastical which started on the variable occurrence of Easter.

That brass plaque is set below a stained-glass St George window made in memory of Aubrey and his later biographer, John Britton, 'for both these Wiltshire antiquaries were born in this place. Neither is buried here, but both owed their inspiration to Wiltshire and its antiquities'.[23]

In October 1698 John Gadbury, astrologer and old friend of Aubrey's, wrote to Tanner thanking him for the news of Aubrey's death.

He went on: 'He was a learned honest gentleman and a true friend, whose loss I really mourne, as having a more than XXX years acquaintance with him, a time sufficient to experience any man's integrity.'[24]

Years earlier John Aubrey had wished to be buried alongside a small prehistoric round barrow on the crest of Knowle Hill a mile south of Broad Chalke.

> On the South-downe of the ffarme of Broad-Chalke on the top of the plaine, is a little Barrow (not very high) called by the name of Gawen's Barrow. I was never so sacralegious as to disturbe, or rob his urne: let his Ashes rest in peace: but I have often times wish't, that my Corps might be interred by it: but the Lawes Ecclesiastick denie it. Our Bones, in consecrated ground, never lie quiet: and in London once in ten yeares (or thereabout) the Earth is carride to the Dung-Wharfe.

Early in the nineteenth century Sir Richard Colt Hoare rode by the mound. 'Pursuing my road northwards towards Broad Chalke, I pass by a small barrow on high ground', the one that enticed John Aubrey. Hoare knew that the land had belonged to the powerful Gawens since the thirteenth century but the name had nothing to do with the distant people who had raised the little mound. Hoare continued, 'that must be raised before the Christian religion was thoroughly established'.[25]

It was probably heaped up in the Early Bronze Age three or four thousand years ago. Inconspicuous, slowly weathering and settling, it survived the Romans, the coming of Christianity, the Saxons, medieval farming and the agrarian revolution. As late as 1953 Leslie Grinsell described it as about forty-five feet across and nine inches high (*c.* 14 m x 0.2 m).[26] The present writer saw it from the roadside in the 1980s.

It was needlessly ploughed flat a year or two later.

It symbolised the fate of John Aubrey's physical associations. His homes, Easton Piers and Broad Chalke, have gone. Most of his London lodgings were destroyed during the Great Fire. Many of his friends died before him. The second part of his North Division of Wiltshire was borrowed from the Ashmolean by his brother, William, 'some years after Aubrey's death; and with the inconsequence of his family, failed to return it to the library'.[27] It was auctioned in 1835 by the bookseller Thorpe, and sold. It has never reappeared. Even Gawen's Barrow has gone.

But there is the *Templa Druidum*. It is John Aubrey's unique archaeological memorial. He reminisced: 'Surely my starres impelled me to be an Antiquary. I have the strangest luck at it that things drop into my mouth.'

It is also the world's good fortune.

Appendix A:
Aubrey's 'Amici' & His Friends Today

John Aubrey was elected to the Royal Society in January 1663 and 'he was soon on good terms with many of the Fellows ... and after the weekly meetings, he usually adjourned with a group of friends to a coffee house, where discussion continued, often till late at night'.

Balme, 10.

Many of them became such close acquaintances that he listed fourteen of them as his special *Amici*. In this Appendix the names, as given by Aubrey, are italicised and are followed by more details of the men concerned.

A Ettrick, Trin. Coll.
Anthony Ettrick. (in Will). *c.* 1622-1701. At Trinity, 'a very little man', `Middle Temple, judicious. Dissatisfied with the outcome of a witch-trial in Salisbury, 1649. Appointed Recorder of Poole in Dorset he later quarrelled with Wimborne people and left them a riddle. He informed them that at his death he would lie neither in nor out of their minster. When he died his oak coffin in its case of black slate was placed in a niche of the wall, neither underground nor above ground, neither in nor out of the church.

M. T. – John Lydall
A year older than Aubrey they first met at the Middle Temple. Later he became a Fellow of the Royal Society. Aubrey often mentioned him in letters. In 1650 Lydall wrote to his credulous friend because Aubrey had heard of weirdly inexplicable noises at Woodstock Manor near Oxford, plausibly caused by the Devil or witchcraft?

Neither, replied the matter-of-fact Lydall. Parliamentary Commissioners had officiously evicted the owners only in turn for indignant natives to throw them out themselves, soundly thrashing one, who had drawn his sword, with his own weapon. That was the cause of the noises, not Satan nor any of his hags. Aubrey deeply regretted Lydall's death in 1657, only thirty-two years old.

FR Potter of 666, letters
Francis Potter of C.C.C., wrote on 666, the Number of the Beast. Mechanically skilled. JA knew book but did not meet until 1649, friends till death 1678. 'I never have enjoyed so much pleasure, nor ever so much pleased with such philosophicall and heartie entertainment as from him.'

Sir J Hoskyns, baronet
John Hoskyns, Baronet. Trinity and Middle Temple. Very ugly. Brief Life intended but not included, perhaps purloined by Wood? Good friends, joked about JA's love affairs and the courtesans of Venice.

Ed Wyld, esq. of Glasley Hall, quem summae gratitudinis ergo nomino
Edmund Wyld. Esq. of Glazely Hall. Christ Church, Ox, 1633, barrister, Middle Temple, provoked, killed man in London. FRS. When Aubrey was impoverished Wyld 'took me in his armes, with whom I most commonly take my diet and sweet otiums. [leisure]'. Many over-indulgent but enjoyable drinking-bouts together.

Mr Robert Hooke, Gresham College
Robert Hooke, Gresham College. Chemist, physicist and architect. Friend since the Middle Temple. In 1682 generously offered to pay for the publication of Aubrey's *Templa Druidum.* That disorganised book was not to be completed for another ten years, nor was it published until 1980.

Mr Hobbes, 165-
Thomas Hobbes. Political philosopher whose famous book *Leviathan* was published in 1651. An old friend of Aubrey's since the latter's childhood. He received the longest entry of all the *Brief Lives,* well over 20,000 words. The shortest contained just two. Hobbes, born in the year of the Armada, 1588, died in 1679.

A Wood, 1665
Anthony à Wood, a friend since 1665. He and Aubrey had a long, sometimes bad-tempered acquaintance, their incompatible natures causing constant misunderstandings despite their collaboration over Wood's forthcoming book on the worthies of Oxford.

Sir William Petty, my singular friend
An economist. Charles II appointed him Surveyor-General of Ireland. As well as their long friendship and Petty's generosity Aubrey remembered a remarkable achievement of Petty's: '*Anno Domini* 1650 happened that memorable accident and accident of the reviving Nan Green …'

Anthony à Wood provided more details: 'a servant maid, who was hang'd in the castle of Oxon for murdering her bastard-child. After she had suffer'd the law, she was cut downe, and carried away in order to be anatomis'd by some young physicians, but Dr. William Petty finding life in her, would not venter upon her, only so farr as to recover her life. Which being look'd upon as a great wonder, there was a relation of her recovery printed, and at the end several copies of verses made by the young poets of the Universitie were added.'

Sir James Long, Baronet, of Draycot
Went hawking with him. Hospitable, when Aubrey was penniless promised him cloth to make a warm winter coat and also four famous cheeses from Draycot in northernWiltshire. 'A gentleman absolute in all his numbers.'

Mr Ch. Seymour, father of the d of S
Charles Seymour, … Of the d. of s. Brother of Francis, 5th Duke of Somerset, Charles became 6th in 1678, 'my honoured and faithful friend'. Had Aubrey's portrait, became Lord in 1664 but died the following year.

Sir J Stawell, M. T.
Sir John Stawell of Bovey Tracy, Devon, was of the Middle Temple where Aubrey met him. He later generously offered the penniless Aubrey a place in the Salisbury stagecoach. He was knighted in 1665. He died in 1669, aged only forty-four. His sister married William Bull, the astronomer, also of the Middle Temple.

Bishop of Sarum
Seth Ward, Bishop of Salisbury. 'His genius lay much in mathematiques.' In his *Diary* for Sunday March 17, Samuel Pepys recorded that as well as the Bishop of Hereford Ward was 'one of the two Bishops that the King doth say he can not have bad sermons from'.

Dr W Holder
William Holder, a later friend and kind host of Aubrey's. He was 'very musicale both theoretically and practically and hathe a sweete voyce'. As the sub-Dean of the Chapel Royal he was a severe disciplinarian, gaining him the soubriquet 'Mr. Snub-Nose'. At the beginning of January 1693 Aubrey thanked him for the New Year gift of 7*s* 6*d* that had been spent on 'a couple of good fowles as ever I did eate and we had the rest in wine (very good).

The fourteen men were those listed as Aubrey's *Amici*.

And today

This Appendix is also dedicated to those recent, determined explorers who have followed John Aubrey in the search that has no ending.

It does not include the misguided escapists who have fantasized about Eygptians, Phoenicians, Romans, Danes, Martians, giants, witches, ley-lines and other escape-holes from reality. And certainly not Geoffrey of Monmouth, nor the ungrateful William Stukeley.

Nor does it contain those enthusiasts who have chosen to confine their search to a single site.

The Appendix is for those committed scholars who since 1900 plodded their way to distant circle to even remoter circle, and tediously read ancient journal after even older journal, compiling lists of sites present, decaying and gone, discovering neglected stones that the world had forgotten.

Some of these discoverers have been students of regions, or of mineralogy, or numerology, geometry, astronomy, architecture. They have all contributed to megalithic knowledge, and include in alphabetical order:

John Barber and the stone circles of Cork and Kerry; John Barnatt and the stone circles of Britain; Isabel Churcher, the stone circles of southern Leinster; Fred Coles, the stone circles in Scotland; John Conlon, the stone circles of County Cork; Oliver Davies, the stone circles in northern Ireland; H. St G. Gray, the stone circles of eastern Cornwall; W. F. Grimes, the stone circles of Wales; Leslie Grinsell and the legends and folk-stories of stone circles and other megaliths; Sir Norman Lockyer, megalithic astronomy; Rosemary McConkey and the stone circles of Ulster; Leslie Myatt and the stone rows of northern Scotland; Sean O'Nuallain, the stone circles of Ireland; Gerald and Margaret Ponting, the stone circles of the Outer Hebrides; Clive Ruggles and the astronomy of stone circles and stone rows; Alexander and Archie Thom on the arithmetic, design and astronomy of stone circles and stone rows; E. K. Tratman and the lost stone circles of Somerset; John Waterhouse and the stone circles of Cumbria.

Surprisingly, very regrettably, no French archaeologist, neither male nor female, has undertaken a comprehensive study of the splendid cromlechs of Brittany. From palaeolithic painted caves to Roman aqueducts the literature overflows but standing stones, whether single, in rows or circles, have been no more than minor footnotes to 'more rewarding' subjects. Nor has anyone in France even catalogued the other stone circles of that megalith-rich country. *Hélas*!

A final note of gratitude to John Fowles, Bill Hoade and Rodney Legg for their rearranged, annotated publications of the 1980 and 1982 *Monumenta Britannica*. Their labours have made that invaluable work of John Aubrey's available to the general public. It had lain restless but rarely touched in the Bodleian Library's archives for almost three centuries. Only scholarly enthusiasts knew of it.

Today, thanks to that hard-working trio, despite the work's shortcomings of intermixed pagination and occasional misidentification of sites, John Aubrey's stone circles have been published and the book stands in daylight, expensive, bulky, but there for anyone to read. Aubrey foresaw it.

> Now, me thinks, after many years lying dormant, I come abroad like the Ghost of one of those Druids.

Appendix B:
The Devil's Arrows stone row, Boroughbridge, Yorkshire

A friend of mine hath invited me into Yorkshire as far as Ripon.

John Aubrey, 5 January, 1687.

The stones of the Devil's Arrows are not a circle. They stand in a line and would have no place in this book were it not for the surprising fact that no fewer than eight people, directly or indirectly, told John Aubrey about the row, far more in number than any group of informants for a stone circle, including Stonehenge.

Aubrey's eight correspondents ranged from Mr Aston, a secretary of the Royal Society who read a letter from a Dr Lister about the stones to members on 4 January 1681, to Dr William Watts, a local clergyman, at Boroughbridge, who paced out the stones at Aubrey's request and wrote him a letter about the distances between the stones.

What was seen in 1681 is what can be seen today. The 'Arrows' stand in a 570 foot (174 m) long row, very unevenly spaced, arranged in a NNW – SSE line a quarter of a mile from the River Ure. The heaviest of them, the southernmost, weighs over thirty tons.

The three increase in height from north to south, 18 feet, 22 feet and 22 feet 6 inches (5.5 m, 6.7 m, 6.9 m), the tallest of them only surpassed in these islands by the Rudston pillar which stands 25 feet 6 inches (7.8 m) high. By megalithic coincidence both pillars are in Yorkshire although fifty miles apart.

They are exceptional. Even the highest of the Stonehenge sarsens and the towering stones at Puncheston and Longstone in Co. Kildare are shorter.

Although standing in a region of sandstone the Devil's Arrows are millstone grit probably dragged from the vicinity of the high and despairing Lover's Leap cliff at Plumpton Rocks near Knaresborough nine miles south of Boroughbridge.

They are not rough blocks but 'dressed' as posts would have been if set up by carpenters. Like many prehistoric rows in Britain they stand close to water. The stone at the end was set at right-angles to others as though to act as a 'blocking-stone'. Arguments continue about how many there were originally, their age, their function, even whether they are the remnants of an enormous stone circle.

They are unevenly spaced. From the NNW to the central stone is 198 feet (60 m), and then much wider gap to the tallest at SSE, a further 360 feet (110 m).

A fourth had stood between the central and SSE pillars. It was removed in the late seventeenth century to become a bridge over the River Tutt running through Boroughbridge.

The local inhabitants neglected it. On 9 January 1621 an official letter warned them that they had not honoured their commitment to repair the bridge, and they were threatened with a fine of £5.00 'to constreyne them speedily to re-edifye the same bridge according to the said payne of v^{li} in that case formerly made'.[1]

A twentieth-century typically accurate but despairing survey of the row was made by Alexander and Archie Thom:

> These 3 large menhirs are not in a straight line and it is reported that one has been re-erected and so we do not know the azimuth. Looking to the south there are trees but we guessed the altitude to be about 0°.4. this with the approximate line of he two south stones gives the approximate lunar declination of -29.°5 but until archaeologists can tell us which stone was re-erected this is almost valueless.[2]

There has been no recorded archaeological excavation at the site to determine whether there had once been more stones or posts in between the wide gaps.

The Devil's Arrows not only keep their secrets but have encouraged a clutter of folk-stories and legends about their origin. They were satanic and malevolent. Known locally as the Devil's Bolts, the Three Greyhounds and the Three Sisters the missiles had been aimed by the Arch-Fiend at the town of Aldborough from How Hill near Fountains Abbey eight miles to the west but they fell a mile short and embedded themselves just outside Boroughbridge. Dissatisfied, but determined to make use of his stones, Lucifer decided to kill his grandmother. Local people pointed to the weathered grooves in the tops of the pillars, marks left by his noose.

It was rumoured that to walk around the line anticlockwise twelve times at midnight would raise the Devil. An overseas visitor did start, but for some unexplained reason abandoned that defiant stroll after his eleventh circuit.[3]

In the early eighteenth century an annual St Barnabas Fair at the summer solstice may have succeeded less Christian medieval superstitious ceremonies at the Arrows.

It was not until the sixteenth century that objective reports were added to the folklore. The indefatigable Tudor traveller John Leland saw the Arrows in the 1540s.

On his 'Laboriouse Journey and Serche' of the antiquities of England Leland came to north Yorkshire and saw the astonishing Devil's Arrows.

A little withowt this towne on the west parte of Wateling-Streate standith 4. great maine stones wrought above *in conum* by mannes hand.

They be set in 3. feldes at this tyme.

The first is a 20 foote by estimation in higheth, and an 18. foote in compace. The stone towarde the ground in sumwhat square, and so up to the Midle, and then wrought with certen rude bol[tells] *in conum*. But the very [toppe thereof is broken] of a 3. or 4. foote [by estimation]. Other 2. of like shap stand in another feld a good But Shot of: and the one of them is bigger then the other: and they stand within a 6. or 8. fote one of the other.

The fourth standith in a several feld a good stone cast from the other ii, and is bigger and higher than any of the other 3. I esteem to the waite of a 5. Waine Lodes or more.

Inscription could I none find yn these Stones: and if ther were it might be woren owt: for they be sore woren and scalid with Wether.

I take to be *trophea â Romanis posita* in the side of *Watheling-Street*, as yn a place moste occupied yn Yorneying , and so most yn sighte.

They stonde [all] as loking *ab occident[te in orientem]*.[4]

Many years later the Elizabethan antiquary William Camden saw the row.

Not farr beneath, there standeth by *Ure* a little towne called *Burrow bridge*. Neere unto this Bridge Westward, we saw in three divers little fields, foure huge stones, of Pyramidall forme, but very rudely wrought, set as it were in a streight and direct line. The two Pyramides in the middest, whereof the one was lately pulled downe by some that hoped, though in vaine, to find treasure, did almost touch one another: the uttermore stand not farr off, yet in almost equall distance from these on both sides. Of these I have nothing else to say, but that I am of opinion with some, that they were Monuments of victory erected by the Romanes, hard by the High Street, that went this way. For I willingly overpasse the fables of the common people, who call them the *Devils Bolts* which they shot at ancient Cities and therewith overthrew them. Yet will I not passe over this, that very many and those learned men thinke that they are not made of naturall stone indeed, but compounded of pure sand, lime, vitriol (where of also they say there be certaine small graines within) and some unctuous matter. Of such a kinde there were in Rome cisternes, so firmely compact of very strong lime and sand, as *Plinie* writeth, that they seeme to be naturall stones.[5]

There were only slight changes to this in the 1695 edition of the *Britannia* but an Appendix by an anonymous informant offered different suggestions about the 'Pyramids that the common people call the 'Devil's Arrows'.

Both Leland and Camden had already referred to 'Bolts' or Arrows. That legend was already well established by the early sixteenth century.

It was doubtful, wrote the unnamed contributor, that the stones had a Roman origin.

> But whether our Author's conjecture of their being set up as Trophies by the Romans may be allowed, is not so certain. A * later Antiquary, [*Hill. *Staff*. p398] seems inclin'd to conclude them to be a British work; supposing that they might be erected in memory of some battel fought there, but is rather of opinion that they were British Deities, agreeing with the learned *Dr. Edward Stillingfleet*.

In his *Origines Sacrae* of 1662 Stillingfleet had suggested that the unpolished pillars represented 'British Deities in the same manner that early visitors to Britain had 'set up unpolish'd stones instead of images to the honour of their Gods'.[6]

Not yet having seen the stones for himself it was from those reports and from letters written by a variety of correspondents that John Aubrey learned of the Devil's Arrows. He had already seen the entry in Camden's earlier 1637 *Britannia* and, knowing his enduring combination of curiosity and wide reading, he may also have known Leland's account of the stones.

Needing more specific details he turned to his friends. He learned that Dr Martin Lister, a Fellow of the Royal Society, then living in York, had sent a letter about the well-known and nearby Arrows to the Society. Mr Aston, its secretary, had it read to the Fellows at a meeting on 4 January 1681. Aubrey heard of the occasion and decided to ask another Fellow, Mr Rich. Waller who had attended, about the talk.[7]

There was an even more enticing but frustrating target than mere words, a chance of seeing a faithful drawing of the Arrows by an assistant of Wenceslaus Hollar, the famous engraver. His man Collins, also an engraver, 'tooke a draught of these stones, but it cannot be heard of'. Probably sketched some time in the 1670s it disappeared.

Aubrey wrote a pleasant account of Wenceslaus Hollar in his *Brief Lives*. Of the artist's death he said,

> He was a very friendly good-natured man as could be, but shiftlesse as to the world, and dyed not rich. He married a second wife, 1665, by whom he has severall children. He dyed on our Ladie-day (25 Martii), 1677, and is buried in St. Margaret's church-yard at Westminster neer the north west corner of the tower. Had he lived till the 13th of July following he had been just 70 years old.[8]

There were letters from other informants about the perplexing row, two from Dr Thomas Gale, a notable antiquary and the headmaster of St

Paul's School in London. He was a long friend of Aubrey's:

> Formerly they say, there were 5 of those pillars (Arrows) now they speake but of 4. and of those 4 I think one was whilome converted into a Bridge. Coins, Aquaducts, urnes, Bricks, polished Stones are here found sans number. T. Gale.

John Aubrey added:

> Dr Thos Gale July 1692 hath lately received a letter from the present Rector of Aldborough [who was his Pupill) that there were five arrows.

Even the number was debateable, three at present, four reported, even a fifth mentioned.[9]

Finally there were specific details about the row by Dr William Watts, who had known Aubrey since 1656 when Watts had been a canon at Hereford Cathedral. The two had maintained a correspondence over the years and in 1679 he sent Aubrey a letter in his nearly illegible old-style scrawled handwriting. It gave Aubrey the detailed information that he needed.

> Sir
> Attending to your desire I paiste it out and betwixt the 3 grey hounds and the first stone in 670 yards and to ye second 100 yds to ye third 70' nothing else'.
> I am Sir y^{rs} to Command. Borrowbridge.

He added that he would be glad to accompany Aubrey when he came to Yorkshire and go around the stones with him.

His letter of 15 August 1679 was sent to Aubrey's lodgings at Mr Kent's house at the 'three Black polts [pestles] in Suffolk Street near Charing Cross. London'.[10]

Aubrey finally saw the controversial stone row for himself in September 1687. He wrote a description of what he had seen and what he had deduced.

> The Devill's Arrows.
> In Yorkshire neer Burrough-brig on the west side of the Fosse-way about a quarter of a mile [in the Lordship of Aldburgh] stand three pyramidish Stones called the Devills arrows. The Arrow standing toward the South is seaven yards and ½ in heighth. The compasse of it five yards and ½. The middle arrow seaven yards ½, in compasse six yards. The arrow towards the north in height five yards and a halfe, in compasse seaven yards. Here was another stone that stood in a straight line at D that was taken downe, and a Bridge made of it.
> [Let this stand in the Margine; This survey was takeby a Workman, by the procurement of Mr Gilbert Minister of Aldburgh April 17th 1669].

They are a hard kind of Ragge-stone: and not much weatherbeaten: their position is is as in Fig. Plate ... they are distant from one another about fourty yards. The stone that was taken downe to make the Bridge, was the farthermost stone at D.

These Stones seeme to be the Remaines of a Temple of the like nature with the former.

I did not perceive of a signe of a circular Trench, as at other Monuments before mentioned: The fields here are ploughed with deep furrowes and far worne-out.

The three Stones that remaine, their Sides doe stand parallel to one another: and (so they tell me) the side of that Stone at D, which was converted into a Bridge.

In Plate the XIth I give the Iconography of the Arrows whose sides are placed parallel to one another as in fig ... A. B. C. D. and I have drawne two imaginary circles in which it may be supposed those stones were placed as at Aubury, Stonehenge &c: perhaps there might be more Stones in each circle, than I have fancied. I had not a right Idea of this Antiquity, till I sawe it myselfe, Sept 1687. The Stones doe stand almost in a direct, direct, except that neer the three Greyhounds marked A which wants about three yards and a halfe of being in a right line: as in the fig ...1.

The Arrows are strinted [constricted] from the top downward two foot + as if those furrowes had been worne by droppings of raine. They are entire Stones, grown hard by the weather. I should be enclined to believe these Stones were artificiall, for a kind of ornament.

70b. Sketch. Plate XI, remains of a theoretical concentric circle.

Bottom of the page. 1. 'The Arrowe next to the three Greyhounds'.

2. 'The Prospect of the Arrowes from the Roade by D. King'.[11]

There has to be a warning for present-day visitors. Unevenly spaced lines of stones deceive the modern eye. Stones could have been removed to become doorsteps or gateposts. Today's spaces may not have held stones but perishable posts. Those posts could have been carved or painted. The viewer today may be seeing tattered remnants.

The Alignement du Moulin near St Just, Ille-et-Vilaine, Brittany, still has lines of standing stones but the uneven gaps once had tall posts standing there, even a flimsy shed. All vanished several thousand years ago. What is seen today is a fragment, and what is worse, a deceptive fragment from which all colour has been washed away by the weather over some thousands of years. The stones are solid but they are no more than ghosts, as unsubstantial as the minds of the men that raised them.[12]

John Aubrey's *Miscellanies Upon Various Subjects* of 1696 was his only book to be published in his lifetime. In his formally written Dedication to the Right Honourable, James, Earl of Abingdon, John Aubrey explained the difficulty and frustration of ever understanding the complete truth about monuments raised so many years ago:

The matter of this collection is beyond human reach: we being miserably in the dark, as to the oeconomy of the invisible world, which knows what we do, or incline to, and works upon our passions and sometimes is so kind as to afford us a glimpse of its praescience.

The row of the Devil's Arrows provides a reason for such realism[13].

Appendix C
Geoffrey of Monmouth's 'Stonehenge'

1. INTRODUCTION

In his search for the truth about the origins of ancient monuments such as Stonehenge one of the worst of John Aubrey's obstacles had been the persistence of long-established legends that had to be considered and tested against what was certain. The truth was frequently elusive. From the very beginning of his interest in the age and purpose of stone circles Aubrey was confronted by one of the strongest pieces of medieval fiction, Geoffrey of Monmouth's 500 year-old fabrication about the building of Stonehenge.

Aubrey had gradually realised that many long-held beliefs about old monuments were guesswork rather than knowledge. There was literally no written history or reliable folk-stories about them whether from any Roman, Saxon or Danish chroniclers.

> The memorie of Things have become obliterated. Bookes (if any of such Remarks) perisht, and Tradition was forgot.[1]

Stonehenge was no exception. For more than half a millennium before Stuart times the circle was believed to have been the work of giants – with considerable magical assistance from the Arthurian sorcerer, Merlin.

In his early twelfth-century manuscript, *Historia Regum Britanniae*, *The History of the Kings of Britain*, circulating around AD 1130, the monk Geoffrey of Monmouth claimed that an oral tradition about Stonehenge stated that its stones had been transported from a far distant place.

Geoffrey was a churchman in Oxford. Around 1136 his famous, or notorious, best-selling and widely accepted book appeared. He had selectively plundered old chronicles such as Gildas' angry mid-sixth century *De Excidio Britonum, the ruin of Britain*, and the disorganised ragbag of facts, folk tales and fictions in Nennius' *Historia Britonum, the history of Britain*, three centuries later.

Geoffrey's *History* was cleverly constructed, its convincing first half containing only long-accepted history about famous men like Julius Caesar, the Roman occupation, and its abandoning of Britain in AD 410. The early fifth century became an age when petty local rulers squabbled against each other in between fighting the persistent invasions from north and west of Picts and Scots. In despair the fatal decision was taken to invite Saxons from overseas to help them. That decision had been made by an 'arrogant commander', *tyrannos superbus*, Vortigern.

It was only after the recital of those well-known historical facts that the fabulous stories of Arthur and Merlin the Magical appeared in Geoffrey's *History*. The Stonehenge story was even later, not appearing until a full four-fifths of the way into the book in Sections 10-12 of Book VIII.

It informed readers that the stones had been brought to Salisbury Plain from a place very far away.

Geoffrey obtained much of the 'information' from the erratic early – ninth-century mishmash of memory and myth of the monk Nennius, who wrote that in the mid-fifth century AD three hundred British nobles had been treacherously massacred at a feast by their hosts, knife-concealing Saxons.

In grief, Vortigern, 'arrogant tyrant' of those Britons, commanded that a fitting cenotaph be raised in their memory. His Christian archbishop of Chester told him, 'If there is anyone anywhere who has the ability to carry out your plan, then Merlin, is the man to do it. There is no one else in your kingdom who has greater skill, either in the foretelling of the future, or in mechanical contrivances.'[2]

It was not history. It was 'faction'. What 'history' there was for Geoffrey to use came from the selective mid-sixth-century writings of the monk Gildas, who had not been making a historical record of known events but what is best described as a 'sermon' to leaders and churchmen of his time about the mistakes and sins of the rulers of Britain in the previous century. The worst of those men had been an unnamed 'proud commander', to be known later to the Venerable Bede and then to Nennius as 'Vortigern'. Very few reliable facts about him have survived.

2. HISTORY

Before Geoffrey of Monmouth in the early twelfth century there were four major sources with information about Vortigern. One did not give the ruler's name, preferring a derisive pun on it, *wor-tigernos*, 'overweening despot'. In receding chronological order the references were the most recent, the *Anglo-Saxon Chronicle*, then Nennius, the Venerable Bede, and finally, the earliest, Gildas.

The *Chronicle* in variant forms was compiled late in the ninth century during the reign of Alfred the Great but included material from much earlier annals, their reliable entries beginning around AD 379. Vortigern was mentioned in the years 449 and 455.

In the first he 'invited the Angle race here and they then came to Britain in three ships at the place *Heopwines fleot* [Ebbsfleet]. The king Vortigern gave them land in the south-east of this land on condition that they fought against the Picts. They then fought against the Picts and had victory wherever they came.'

Six years later they were fighting the Britons.

> 455. Here Hengist and Horsa fought against Vortigern the king in the place that is called *Aegaeles threp* [Aylesford] and his brother Horsa was killed. And after that Hengist and Aesc, his son, succeeded to the kingdom.[3]

There is no further mention of Vortigern in any version of the *Chronicles*.

Around AD 858 the monk Nennius added some titbits. He wrote that Vortigern fell in love with Hengist's daughter, 'a beautiful and very handsome girl'. To gain Hengist's approval he gave the Saxons all of Kent even though it belonged to one of his own British tribal leaders.

In his Preface he explained where he had gathered information about that distant period.

> I Nennius … have undertaken to write down some extracts that the stupidity of the British cast out; for the scholars of the island of Britain had no skill, and set down no record in books. I have therefore made a heap of all that I have found from Roman and Christian sources and out of the traditions of our elders.
>
> … pardon me for daring to write so much here after so many, like a chattering bird or an incompetent judge.

After that charming naïveté he included a gloss to the *Chronicle*'s account of the battle of Aylesford in which the Britons had been commanded by the eldest of Vortigern's sons, Vortimer. With him was his younger brother, Cateyrn, who, like Horsa, was killed there.[4]

Chronologically, the more distant in time a writer was from Gildas the more unreliable he became. Nennius was writing more than three centuries later than Gildas when many 'facts' had already distorted into fantasy. In consequence he amassed a collection of untrustworthy history and folk tales.

Far later still, in 1576 more than six hundred years after Nennius and a thousand after Gildas, William Lambarde, the London lawyer mentioned in Chapter 4 about the sarsens of Stonehenge, added a gloss to Nennius's account. In his *Perambulation of Kent*, Lambarde attempted to explain the presence of otherwise inexplicable ancient monuments by his supposed association with known historical events.

One was the death of Vortigern's son, Catigern, slain at Aylesford. On a hillside above Aylesford, the lawyer wrote, was the denuded megalithic tomb of Kit's Coty House, 'Citscote House', three thick chest-high stones, covered by a heavy ten-ton capstone. Locally it was believed that three witches from nearby Blue Bell Hill had set up the standing stones, a fourth hag lifting the capstone.

A little lower down the hill from Kit's Coty is the prostrate White Horse stone on which some people have imagined faces. Tradition claimed that Hengist and Horsa had raised their Saxon standard by it.

Many years after Lambarde's mention the tomb was not forgotten. In March 1669 Samuel Pepys went 'to see a Saxon monument, as they say, of a king; which is three stones staying upright and a great round one lying on them, of great bigness, although not so big as those on Salisbury-plain, but certainly it is a thing of great antiquity, and I mightily glad to see it; it is near to Aleford'. Even more entertainingly he then went to Captain Allen's house where he met Mrs Rebecca Jowles. Had he had the opportunity he would have taken her away for the night, she very willing, 'for ella is a whore, that is certain, but a very brave and comely one'.[5]

Elsewhere, John Aubrey, unaffected by such diversions, also learned from Thomas Gale of the imagined connection between Kit's Coty and Catigern. 'Catigern was interred on that plain … his monument remains. Being four vast stones pitcht somewhat after the manner of Stonehenge on Salisbury plain but of greter depth than they though not so thick or long whereby it appears like a small sheepcote and is vulgarly styled Cits-Cotshouse.' 'In the same field is another large stone sunk into ye ground.' Aubrey added

Mr John Evelyn R. S. P. tells me that neer Ashford in Kent is a monument of Stones something resembling Stoneheng, or such stones as those of Stonehenge: *Quaere* D^r Jo. Wallus *de hoc* I believe it is Kits-Cotyhouse.[6]

Kit's Coty's imaginary connection with Vortigern was nothing but a delusion fabricateded by Lambarde.

Returning to the 'chronicle' of Nennius that 'historian' added an event that would provide the foundation for the Stonehenge story in Geoffrey of Monmouth.

Pretending that they were weary of the constant struggle in which so many men had died the Saxons claimed that all they longed for was peace and asked for a meeting to be arranged in which a lasting agreement for the end of fighting could be made. As the Britons also wanted no more war it was agreed that the two sides should come together, unarmed, to agree upon terms.

> But Hengest told all his followers to hide their daggers under their feet in their shoes, saying, 'When I call out to you and say "English, draw your knives", take your daggers from your shoes and fall upon them and stand firm against them, But do not kill the king, keep him alive, for my daughter's sake, whom I wedded to him, for it is better for us that he be ransomed from us … and all the three hundred Seniors of king Vortigern were murdered, and the king alone was taken and held prisoner. Enough has been said of Vortigern and his family.[7]

Some seventy years earlier than Nennius the Venerable Bede in his *History of the English Church and People* wrote nothing as dramatic as that. He wrote history and was much more reliable about the events of Vortigern's time.

> The Angles or Saxons came to Britain at the invitation of King Vortigern in three long-ships and were granted land in the eastern part of the island on condition that they protected the country: nevertheless, their real intention was to subdue it.

Many others came, Saxons, Angles, Jutes, their first chieftains being Hengist and Horsa. 'The latter was subsequently killed in battle against the Britons, and was buried in east Kent, where a monument bearing his name still stands', clearly not Kit's Coty's House.

Bede continued that for their persistent sins the Britons were crushed, 'doomed to lifelong slavery even if they escaped instant massacre'.

The only other mention of Vortigern in Bede's *History* was that the tyrant had asked Hengist 'and his son, Oeric', to help Britain.[8]

Almost all the information about Vortigern came from Gildas' *De Excidio Britanniae*, *The Ruin of Britain*, completed in the first decades of the sixth century AD. But he never named Vortigern, alluding only to a *superbo tyranno*, 'proud despot', whose arrogance had ravaged a land that had once been civilised under Roman rule and blessed with Christianity.

> Then all the members of the council, together with the proud tyrant, were struck blind; the guard – or rather the method of destruction. – they devised for our land was that the ferocious Saxons (name not to be spoken!) hated by man and God, should be let

into the island like wolves into the fold, to beat back the people of the North. Nothing
more destructive, nothing more bitter has ever befallen the land.

That bitter complaint was followed by a cry of despair. All the great
towns had been ruined, priests and commoners slaughtered, buildings
burnt, and 'no burial to be had except in the ruin of houses or the bellies
of beasts and birds'.

It was all that Gildas had to say about the 'reign of Vortigern'.[9]

There was nothing in that work or in the Venerable Bede or in Nennius
about giants, Ireland, Merlin or Stonehenge or the magical transportation
of enormous stones across the sea to Salisbury Plain. In those works there
was only Vortigern, Saxons, treachery and the remnants of reliable record
tainted by forgetfulness and exaggeration. Modern scholarly histories
have clarified many of the uncertainties.

In all probability Vortigern was a real person, a ruler of southern
Britain from Wales to East Anglia in the early fifth century several
decades after the Romans had abandoned Britain, 'an overlord of
some sort, who had a general control over military matters for the
territories of a group of southern civitates or overlords of cities and
towns'.[10]

3. Geoffrey of Monmouths's *History of the Kings of Britain*

That wonderful book made persuasive writing to twelfth-century readers
indoctrinated in the certainty that there had once been a time of supernatural
powers when unearthly beings and superhuman giants lived.

Such readers were entirely ignorant of a megalithic age, those distant,
prehistoric years in Britain when stone-built tombs and circles were built,
which began before 3000 BC, flourished and finally died fifteen hundred
years later.

By the following Iron Age folk-memories of that lost period had been
distorted into myth and imagination. To people of the time of Caractacus
and Boudica and Hadrian's Wall Stonehenge's roofless structure must
have been built by inhuman monsters for reasons that no man could
understand.

Over a long, mutating period as Wiltshire natives were infiltrated
by outsiders there were centuries of change to the legend: omissions,
persuasive exaggerations about the decaying circle, where its stones had
come from, how the ring had been built.

An entire hundred generations had lived and died between the ending
of the prehistoric Stonehenge and the Norman years of Geoffrey of

Monmouth. Languages changed from the native vocabulary of Bronze Age Wessex to the poly-lingual Iron Age. Then it was overlaid with a veneer of Latin. Later, from AD 550, what villages and farms had been called in Wiltshire were given Saxon place-names, Scandinavian words infiltrated, then Norman French and monkish Latin. That was the time when Geoffrey chose to 'translate' what survived of the original story.[11]

In every one of these transformations the Stonehenge tradition had been adapted to suit its new audiences.

That ever-changing 'history' was first written down by Geoffrey of Monmouth fewer than a hundred years after the Battle of Hastings. It was a period of historical, geographical and geological ignorance when the world was known to be flat and when a careless captain could find his ship falling fatally over the edge of the sea. Fearsome giants inhabited a mythical Africa.

It was an age when the sun went round the world. Men could be burnt alive for denying it. Even worse for fallible mankind it was also certain that an eternity of Hell's flames and sadistic devils' pitchforks awaited sinners.

It was in those superstitious years that Geoffrey of Monmouth stated that Stonehenge was built by the command of Vortigern. Massive stones had to be discovered, transported and erected in a circle on Salisbury Plain as an everlasting cenotaph to his murdered followers.

Just one or two of his mostly acquiescent contemporaries ridiculed his story. 'The father of historical criticism', William of Newburgh, author of the *Historia Regum Anglicarum, the History of the Kings of England, c.* 1198, condemned Geoffrey. 'A writer in our times has started up and invented the most ridiculous fictions … no one but a person ignorant of ancient history, when he meets that book which he calls *The History of the Britons,* can for a moment doubt how impertinently and impudently he falsifies in every respect. For he only who has not learnt the truth of history indiscreetly believes the absurdity of fable.'

He went on:

Geoffrey of Monmouth writes of giants. There have been none since the time of David and Goliath. He says that there were three archbishops at London; Caerleon and York, but there was none before St. Augustine in Canterbury. In his 'History' he praises the virtuous qualities and loyalty of the Britons but he is contradicted by proper historians such as Gildas and the Venerable Bede with their reliable accounts of the brutal Saxon settlement and the invading Jutes in Kent.

Since, therefore, the ancient historians make not the slightest mention of these [Geoffrey's] matters, it is plain that whatever was published of Arthur and Merlin are mendacious fictions, invented to gratify the curiosity of the undiscerning.

'It was a thunderclap of courageous and devastating criticism' but 'most succeeding medieval chroniclers stopped their ears'. Wishful thinking about wizardry would withstand honest history for hundreds of years. John Aubrey would be confronted by the problem.

A fellow-cleric, Gerald of Wales, *Giraldus Cambrensis*, also doubted the reliability of the 'history'. He wrote a parable. It was the story of a Welshman who could foretell the future but who was tormented by demons.

> When he was harassed beyond endurance by these unclean spirits, Saint John's Gospel was placed on his lap, and then they all vanished immediately, flying away like so many birds.
>
> If the Gospel were afterwards removed and the *History of the Kings of Britain* by Geoffrey of Monmouth put there in its place, just to see what would happen, the demons would alight all over his body, and on the book, too, staying there longer than usual and being even more demanding.

Others shared the scepticism. A Benedictine monk of Chester, Ranulf Higden, compiling facts about England in his *Polychronicon* of 1342 two hundred years after Geoffrey's *Historia Regum Britanniae* was equally scathing. 'I would have included in this history other things which are included in this [Geoffrey's] book had I believed them to be true'.

He did not repeat Geoffrey's fantasia about Stonehenge. Instead, he preferred Henry of Huntingdon's choice of that circle as one of the four wonders of England, the others being whirlwinds in the Peak District, subterranean caves at Cheddar Gorge, and rain at any time across the country. It was that medley that William Caxton also included in his *Description of England* of 1480.[12]

It is sadly surprising that a much better historian and antiquarian, the Tudor William Camden, in the first English edition of his *Britannia* rather half-heartedly accepted that Geoffrey of Monmouth was probably right about Stonehenge. 'The common saying is, that *Ambrosius Aurelianus*, or his brother *Uther* did reare them up by the art of *Merlin* that great *Mathematician*, in memorie of those Britaines who by the treachery of the Saxons were there slaine at a parley.' It repeated what he had first stated in his Latin edition of *Britannia* in 1607.[13]

What neither Camden nor any of his predecessors could have known was that the famous wizard 'Merlin' was no more than a creature of Geoffrey of Monmouth's imagination. There was no such man. Even the name was wrong. It should have been *Myrddin*.

In Celtic mythology there had been two men called that. One was driven mad in Scotland. The other, from the same country, was adopted by the Welsh. 'He' may not even have been a human being but a place, to Romans the town of *Maridunum*, to the Welsh, Carmarthen.

Geoffrey even changed the name to avoid offence. Aware that his book, written in Latin, would be read aloud to Norman-French listeners, almost all of whom were illiterate, the Latin form of *Myrddin* would have *Merdinus* from the classical root, *merda*, 'excrement' or 'shit', a word not suitable for Geoffrey's audience.

Myrddin became *Merlinus*. That, to a warlike race of men accustomed to the joys of hunting, would have had pleasant associations with the tiny bird of prey, the merlin. And 'Merlin the magician' became an established part of popular folklore.[14]

It was such conflicting details that John Aubrey encountered as he read about Stonehenge and other stone circles. He groped through a bewilderment of guesswork for the truth about a prehistoric mystery for which there was no written history. The combination of Vortigern, Merlin and magical spells was just one of a multitude of contradictions.

To question that story of Vortigern and Stonehenge several separate matters must be considered. Geoffrey's account of the origin of Stonehenge is in four distinct parts: the stones; their origin; their transportation; and their magical powers.

The stones are enormous and there is no one alive strong enough to move them.

Geoffrey of Monmouth emphasised their size and weight although he may never have seen Stonehenge. He might only have learned about their enormity from earlier clerics crossing Salisbury Plain on their way to Ireland.

A later chronicler, Henry of Huntingdon, wrote 'stones of extraordinary dimensions are raised as columns, and others fixed above, like lintels of immense portals; and no one has been able to discover by what mechanism such vast masses of stone were elevated ...'[15]

It may seem surprising that Henry should write in such a way. By the mid-twelfth century imposing early English churches and cathedrals were being built. Henry would have seen the master-builders, the scaffolding, the winches, 'foreign' stone like Purbeck Marble transported over miles of land.

Geoffrey of Monmouth would have been just as aware of the medieval masons and their methods. In Oxford alone Saxon and Norman churches were being redesigned. Osney Abbey was founded in 1129 just before he arrived in Oxford, and Christ Church chapel, now Oxford Cathedral, was begun in 1122.

They are architectural illusions. Those churches, even abbeys and cathedrals, were composed of thousands of relatively light stones of a ton or so. Even the apparently sturdy round pillars supporting the roof inside the church were optical deceptions. Their neatly cylindrical exterior was no more than a shell, the outer face of a hollow tube filled with rubble. The size and weight of even one of the Stonehenge sarsens would have bewildered any medieval church architect.

That stone circle was different from any church. Its 'walls' had gap after gap. It lacked a roof. Such an unworldly framework was mystifying, never the work of ordinary men. Geoffrey explained. The magician Merlin had casually dismantled an imposing stone circle far away from Britain and lifted its stones overland to a port where they could be sailed across the sea and dragged across hills and valleys to Salisbury Plain where Merlin would re-erect them supernaturally.

Those were Geoffrey's imaginary stones. He was merely repeating what many others had already remarked about Stonehenge, the massively tall sarsens on the circumference of the ring, and the even higher, heavier horseshoe of trilithons rising above them at the ring's heart. It was that body of impressive pillars that stood out starkly to astonish any gaping passer-by.

Geoffrey explained where those stones had come from. Vortigern was advised to

> Send for the Giants' Ring which is on Mount Killaurus in Ireland. In that place there is a stone construction which no man of this period could ever erect, unless he combined great skill and artistry.[16]

'Mount Killaurus' was the present-day Hill of Allen a few miles north of Kildare. In the Middle Ages it was the residence of the kings of Leinster, and earlier, in prehistoric times, the home of a mythological hero, the supernatural Finn mac Cumhail, leader of the Fianna warband. Around his hill the entire region was a pagan landscape with shrines of ancient gods and spirits, standing stones, and magical wells.

'Mount Killaurus' was already known to John Aubrey. He had been told of it by a colleague named Gethin or Gethyn from Co. Cork.

> Mr ....Gethin of the Middle Temple London, told me, that at Killian-hill [or a name like it] in Ireland, is a monument of Stones like those at Stoneheng: and from whence the old Tradition is that Merlin brought them to Stoneheng by Conjuration. Tacitus in the life of Agricola saieth that the Religion of the Irish was the same with the British.

Aubrey added a cautious Latin quotation from Sir James Ware's *Antiquities of Ireland.* 'An Saxa illa ...: I cannot state for certain whether the huge stones which are to be seen everywhere on the plain near Naas ... were set up by the Danes.'[17]

It was an interesting aside, all the more significant to Aubrey because a colleague of his, Dr Walter Charleton, was confident that Stonehenge itself was a Danish monument.

Both Ware and Charleton were writing in the seventeenth century years after Geoffrey of Monmouth when there were quite different ideas about Stonehenge and its sarsens. In the English version of his Latin *Britannia*, the 1637 *Britain,* William Camden, who half-believed in Geoffrey's fiction, more sensibly observed that the circle stood in the stone-less landscape of Salisbury Plain and wondered whether its 'stones' could possibly have been artificially made of sand glued together. They were not. They were natural boulders that men had shaped.

According to Geoffrey of Monmouth Merlin had brought them from the plain of Naas near the Hill of Allen. Just a few miles from that hill was the abbey of Kildare, a double monastery of nuns and monks, founded by St Brigid in the fifth century. That 'saint' was of pagan origin, adopting the name of a pre-Christian goddess, born, rumour said, in the home of a druid.

Saint Brigid had been religiously transformed from that triple goddess of fertility and childbirth, Brigid, whose great day, the ancient festival of Imbolc, 1 February, became the Feast Day of her Christian embodiment. Unable to eradicate that irreligious hag from people's awed minds the Church adapted her as a saint!

Her abbey possessed a beautiful illuminated gospel-book; Gerald of Wales saw it, enthusiastically describing it as 'that wonderful book which they say was written at the dictates of an angel during the lifetime of the virgin'.[18]

There was nothing unusual about a Welsh archdeacon visiting the Kildare monastery. From the eleventh century English churchmen had been travelling to it. In reverse, Irish clergy had been going to England since Norman times when Lanfranc, the Archbishop of Canterbury, had proclaimed the widespread authority of the Church of Rome and demanded obedience from the Irish bishops.

Prelates travelled to Ireland from as far away as south-east England, from Canterbury, St Albans and other religious houses, and they followed the Harroway, the 'hard' or 'old' road, a gradual linking of age-old local tracks that followed higher ground, avoiding swamps and forests, crossing England from coast to coast. Part of it is now Chaucer's Pilgrims' Way to Canterbury but it was far more ancient than that medieval road. Prehistoric merchants had known it as they carried their wares from settlement to settlement.

The Harroway led for miles westwards. Along it ancient tall stones stood as landmarks. From Canterbury, St Albans and other religious houses the well-ridden road led mile after tedious mile into Wiltshire and the River Avon. There, at Bulford, another stone marked the safe crossing-place of a ford whose marshy banks were ragged with pink robin flowers.

Beyond the river was the pillar of the 'Cuckoo Stone' and then, uphill, the isolated Heel Stone before that amazement of Salisbury Plain, Stonehenge. Marvelling bishops and passers-by stared at the impossibly high, weathered pillars, understood nothing about them.[19]

What they never remarked on were the dwarfed bluestones. Even a fanciful fourteenth-century sketch shows Merlin handling a sarsen lintel into place, 'more easily than anyone would believe', in sight of two astonished onlookers. But not a single bluestone is shown. It was that megalithic miracle, the skeletal sarsen structure that passers-by remembered as they reached the coast and the sea-crossing to the port of Dublin.

The ecclesiastical traffic was constant. Bishops with their sumptuously apparelled entourages, groups of lesser clerics, monks and priests with a following of servants on foot plodded through the landscape.

The road from Dublin, through Naas to Kildare was almost a monkish thoroughfare but those medieval travellers did not have the advantage of today's half-hour drive along a smoothly metalled motorway.

A thousand years ago there was no more than a two- to three- mile-wide meander of fairly firm tracks attempting to avoid the trampled-into-mud, hoof-rutted trails of past years. In the distance all around that ever-changing route were dozens of prehistoric pillars, now out of sight from today's road, but very visible to wandering medieval clerics on horseback as they plodded on to Kildare.

The reality of Geoffrey of Monmouth's 'Giants' Ring' was that it had never been anything but a scattered collection of standing stones within a few short miles of Naas. Today the most conspicuous survivors are the lofty Craddockstown West, 14 feet 6 inches [4.4 m] high to the south-east; Longstone Rath, 17 feet 6 inches [5.3 m] to the east-north-east; and tallest of all, Punchestown, a soaring 19 feet 6 inches [5.9 m] high slender granite pillar two and a quarter miles south-east of Naas. Amongst them, even today, are lesser ones, many almost as high as a Stonehenge sarsen. Once there had been hundreds. But it had been the outstanding megalithic monsters that deceived the monks and priests of Geoffrey's time, believing them scattered remnants of Merlin's robbery, remnants of a once-awesome circle built by giants that had been denuded to provide the pillars of Stonehenge.[20]

Many of those once-numerous idolatrous objects were later destroyed on the orders of fanatical priests or, more mundanely but constructively, toppled decade by decade and taken away for lintels, door-jambs and gate-supports, leaving only the highest, heaviest, as too dangerous to attack.

Geoffrey recorded that the magician Merlin told Vortigern about the Irish Giants' Ring and the king sent his men across the sea to collect the pillars.

'Of extraordinary dimensions' shows that the geologically ignorant Geoffrey was describing the ponderous twenty-six-ton sarsens, three times the height of a man, on the circumference of Stonehenge, and the even higher, heavier horseshoe of trilithons rising above them at the ring's heart. It was that mass of impressive pillars that would have been very obvious to any astonished passer-by.

Ireland, however, was a long way from Salisbury Plain where Stonehenge stands. Having been told of its marvellous circle Vortigern sent thousands of men to bring the stones to Salisbury Plain.

> They all set to with every conceivable type of mechanism and strove their hardest to take the Ring down. They rigged up hawsers and ropes, and they propped up scaling-ladders each preparing what he thought most useful, but none of these things advanced them an inch.

The inventive Geoffrey of Monmouth explained that it was obvious that ordinary men could never have brought those impossibly heavy stones across miles of land and sea. Magic was required. Merlin provided it.

> When he saw what a mess they were making of it Merlin burst out laughing. He placed in position all the gear he considered necessary and dismantled the stones more easily than you could ever imagine. ... He put the stones up in a circle round the sepulchre in exactly the same way as they had been arranged on Mount Killaurus in Ireland.[21]

Stonehenge's silicious 'hard' sandstones were locally known as sarsens from the Anglo-Saxon word *sar-stan* or 'troublesome stone' because of the manner in which those crowded blocks had obstructed the plough on the Marlborough Downs in Wiltshire.[22] They came from the 'giants' beds' strewn across the downs near Avebury, some nineteen miles north of Stonehenge. John Aubrey had seen them: 'These Downes look as if they were sowen with great Stones, very thick, one might fancy it to have been the scene where he giants fought with huge stones against the Gods.'[23]

Unlike many of his contemporaries he had become entirely sceptical of Geoffrey of Monmouth's statements.

The tradition amongst common people is that these stones were brought from Ireland as aforesayd by the conjuration of Merlin ... whereas indeed they are of the very same kind of stones with the Grey-weathers about fourteen miles off: that tract of ground towards Marleborough.[24]

It was fieldwork rather than guesswork. The stones of Stonehenge were local.

Those sarsens were heavy. The 'small' thirty-five lintels each weighed just under seven tons. The thirty circle-stones each weighed between twenty-three and twenty-six tons. Of the inner 'horseshoe' of five trilithons the heaviest stood at the south-west, Stone 56, the one still standing, was well over forty tons in weight.[25]

For those seventy-five sarsens almost one thousand, four hundred tons of unyielding sarsen had to be dragged eighteen to twenty miles to Salisbury Plain and then erected. It was a muscular work-load.

It is probable that this was the epic undertaking that was remembered and repeated over long years in the farms and hamlets around Stonehenge, the pain, the injuries, the tedious years of stone by stone until the final triumph of the world's most famous stone circle. Geoffrey of Monmouth's Stonehenge had another virtue. Its stones had healing powers.

These stones are connected with certain secret religious rites and they have various properties which are medicinally important. Whenever [giants] felt ill baths should be prepared at the foot of the stones; for they used to pour water over them and to run this water into baths in which their sick were cured. What is more, they mixed the water with herbal concoctions and so healed their wounds. There is not a single stone among them which hasn't some medicinal virtue.[26]

It was only after the mundane matters of size, origin, transportation, even conflict, were described that the arcane healing powers of the stones were mentioned by Geoffrey of Monmouth. Those benefits came from a combination of stone, water, 'baths', and herbal concoctions. The presence of recipes for herbs in the story is unsurprising. The value of certain herbs had been known almost since Adam and Eve. Greeks and Romans had herbalists. Ordinary country people had long been aware that some plants and herbs were beneficial, some innocuous, others lethal. Monastic almoners used many herbal prescriptions for sick brothers, something that Geoffrey of Monmouth would have known well.

Five hundred years after him, in 1649, England's first comprehensive recipe book appeared when the puritanical Nicholas Culpeper published his best-selling *The Complete Herbal* in which he recommended the use of native rather than foreign plants. He chose adder's tongue for tending wounds, maiden's hair for soothing coughs, wild tansy to eradicate troublesome worms. It is unsurprising that such well-known 'herbal concoctions' should have been included in the Stonehenge legend.[27]

Stonehenge's curative properties: the stone, the water, the 'baths' had a local explanation. John Aubrey provided it. There was a known connection for that esoteric mixture with the Stonehenge sarsens. Geoffrey of Monmouth had written:

> ... baths should be prepared at the foot of the stones, for they used to pour water over them, and to put this water into baths ...

It does not explain into what receptacle the water was 'poured' before ladling it into the 'baths'. Allowing it to splash uncontrollably down the stone would have been wasteful and ineffective. The probability in this half-remembered description is that water was poured into cavities in the sarsens. Stonehenge has many.

Sarsen was formed over millions of years by grains of embryonic sandstone sinking through water and settling on a rough bed of chalk. Eventually the solidified sandstone was exposed to erosive weather. It fragmented, leaving those prostrate blocks with a relatively smooth upper surface and a coarse underside of lumps and hollows made by the ruggedly uneven chalk on which it had formed.

When the Stonehenge sarsens were erected, their builders chose to arrange the smoother sides to face the interior of the circle. Over long centuries of weather on the exposed Plain soft chalk in the crevices of the rough, exposed faces of the blocks was washed away leaving a clutter of 'solution holes', visible on many stones. Some are very obvious on the prostrate Stone Twelve at the south-east side of the ring.

Shakespeare's rascally Autolycus was not the only 'snapper-up of unconsidered trifles'. Wiltshire also had one. The inquisitive and observant John Aubrey noticed the holes. The 'high Stones at Stonehenge are honeycomb'd so deep that the Stares [starlings] doe make their Nests in the holes ... the holes are towards the tops of the jamb-stones.'[28] Such holes would explain the conjunction of stone and water in the story but not the 'baths' which were to be prepared 'at the foot of the stones'.

This tantalising therapeutic account of stone, water and 'baths' had an ancestry at least two and a half thousand years old when Geoffrey of Monmouth came across it.

So many changes to the original folk-story had been made over hundreds of long centuries that the complete truth seems irrecoverable.

'Giants' can be excluded as mythical monsters in the medieval mind. Stone, water and 'baths', however, remain as basic elements in what was once known. It is fortunate, therefore, that five hundred years later in his Stonehenge jottings, John Aubrey left a hint of the skeletal truth behind the fictitious flesh, adding a gloss in the *Templa Druidum* section of his *Monumenta Britannica*.

He recorded a Wiltshire local custom. 'It is generally averred hereabout that pieces (or powder) of these Stones putt into their Wells doe drive away the Toades, with which their Wells are much infested, and this course they use still.'[29]

It explains the otherwise 'inexplicable' mixture of stone, water, and 'curative power'. Over time two simple country ideas had become linked: a 'down-to-earth' well had been metamorphosed into a 'bath' for giants; and water scooped from the solution holes had probably been mixed with herbs as a rural remedy for a variety of illnesses.

That was the prehistoric stone circle of Geoffrey's fairy story. There was no Merlin. There were neither giants nor baths for their ailments. There were only stones and ordinary human beings.

That was the truth but it was a seventeenth-century truth. Since the early twelfth century the long-known 'truth' about Stonehenge had been Geoffrey of Monmouth's mélange of monsters, Merlin and magic. And like medieval measles it was contagious. Just a few years after the appearance of the *Historia Regum Britanniae* an Anglo-Norman monk in Paris, Robert Wace, wrote a French version of that fantasia. At the very beginning of the thirteenth century an English priest of Worcestershire, Layamon, composed the first English translation of the fairy story.

More copies of Geoffrey's *History* followed, four more in that century, three in the next, a further four in the still-credulous sixteenth, even two more in the seventeenth, even one by an Irish prelate, Bishop James Ussher of Armagh, who proclaimed his support for Geoffrey's never-never land of nonsense.

It was untrue. But even six hundred years after Geoffrey of Monmouth some still believed it explained the origins of Stonehenge. Enquiring minds like John Aubrey's were needed to reveal the real truth.

Yet even today Geoffrey's Irish statement can be quoted as a misunderstanding of the origin of the Welsh bluestones. Despite his story's many blunders 'underneath though are the critical ideas that some at least of Stonehenge was brought from a land far to the west'.[30]

The 'underneath' is simply that Geoffrey wrote what he did because he had read that trustworthy clerics had seen stones similar to Stonehenge in Ireland, a source over a hundred miles farther to the west than Wales.

Geoffrey believed that Merlin had helped their passage – but not to the Preseli mountains of Dyfed in south-west Wales.

Notes

[n.b. References to Pepys' Diary, 1660 to 1669, are from the Latham & Matthews edition of 1995.]

INTRODUCTION

1 John Collier, *The Scandal and Credulities of John Aubrey*, Peter Davies, London, 1931: Overall's wife, 51; MS Aubrey 8, fol. 93; Clark, II, 116.

2 'Twelve' Apostles: Burl, 2000, 197.

3 'for what purpose': Henry of Huntingdon, *Historia Anglorum*, 'The History of England', trans. T. Forester [1853], facsimile, Llanerch, Felinfach, 1991, 7.

4 'at what time': T. H. Ravenhill, *The Rollright Stones and the Men who Erected Them*, Cornish Brothers, Birmingham, 1932, 3, 54.

5 'absolutely nothing': W. Black, *A Princess of Thule*, Sampson Low, London, 1893, 88.

6 Aubrey, TG, c.24, 26b; MB, I, 25.

7 Aubrey, TG, c.24, 25a, b; MB, I, 22-3.

8 Aubrey, TG, c.24, 78b; MB, I, 127.

9 Petty: MS Aubrey 6, fol. 12; Clark, II, 141, 149-50; Elizabeth Broughton: MS Aubrey 6, fol. 101; Clark, I, 127.

10 'Head always working …': Barber, 1893, 11.

11 Evelyn on Aubrey's *Surrey*: Powell, 1682, 165-6.

12 Pepys and Mrs Bagnall: *Diary* IX, 2 June 1668, 221. John Smith's translation of the entire *Diary*: C. Tomalin, *Samuel Pepys. The Unequalled Self*, Penguin, 2002, 382-3.

13 Evelyn and the Duke of Norfolk's wife: G. de la Bédoyère, *The Diary of John Evelyn*, Boydell, 2004, 258; Upshott, *ibid*, 13-15. Dress-patterns or fires: Dobson, I, viii.

14 'deluge of Historie:', Aubrey, TG, c.24, 30b; MB, I, 32.

Chapter One

1 Genealogy: Britton, 1845, family tree, 24; Powell, 1988: Chart 1, Aubrey's family, 296-7; Chart 2, Aubrey's relations.

2 Early childhood: Dick, xxiv, xxviii, xxxi.

3 Buckingham at Stonehenge: Mrs Mary Trotman, wife of tenant farming Stonehenge land in the 1620s. Aubrey, TG, c.24, 90b, MB, I, 95; the Fallen stone 55, TG, c.24, 89b, MB, I, 76; the pit, TG, c.24, 89b-90b, MB, I, 93, 95; bugle, TG, c.24, 93b, MB, I, 100. The barrow, probably Amesbury 37a, a round one in the New King barrows group, Grinsell, 1957, 151.

4 Early sicknesses: Dick, xxiv.

5 William Stumpe: Dick, xxx.

6 The nunnery: A. Mee, *King's England, Wiltshire*, 1929, 202-3. Grandfather's day and manuscripts: Britton, *Nat Hist*, 1847, 79; Ponting, 1969, 79.

7 Shervill and destruction: Dick, xxxvii.

8 Avebury's rood-loft: M. Pitts, *Footprints through Avebury*, 1985, 46-51; Pevsner, *Wiltshire*, 1975, 101-2.

9 Stumpe and misuse of manuscripts: Britton, 1847, 78, 79; Ponting, 1969, 79.

10 Balloon flight: Dick, cvii; Aubrey, *Miscellanies*, 'Transportation by an invisible Power'.

11 The Lancashire witch-trials: Scott, 1975, 216-37, 'Witchcraft'.

12 Witches and horse-shoes: Aubrey, *Miscellanies*, 'Magick', 106. An afflicted wife: *British Archaeology*, 107, 2009, 7.

13 Aubrey's illnesses, 1633 and 1634: Dick, xxiv.

14 Robert Latimer: Powell, 19-20.

15 John Hampden: M. Ashley, *England in the Seventeenth Century*, Penguin, Harmondsworth, 1954, 66-7; Schama, 77, 100, 102.

16 Burnett manor house: Aubrey, TG, c.24, 52a [deleted]; MB, I, 65.

17 Love of antiquities: Aubrey, TG, c.24, 23b; MB, I, 17.

18 Stanton Drew: Aubrey, TG, c.24, 50?; MB, I, 46-7.

19 The legend of the petrified dancers: Aubrey, TG, c.24, 52b; MB, I, 66 stones uncountable; Westwood, 26: petrifaction: Grinsell, 54, fiddler replaced by Devil, 56, accurate counting meant misfortune, 63; Stanton Drew, 139-40. Stones drank at the river: G. Strong, *Stanton Drew and its Ancient Stone Circles*, Wooden Books, Glastonbury, 2008, 44.

20 Blandford school: Ponting, 1969, 79, 80.

21 Aubrey's memories of himself as a schoolboy: Dick, xxxi.

22 Horse accident: Clark, I, 37.

23 Declaration of Civil War: Clark, I, 37.

24 Oxford, plague and Broad Chalke: Powell, 50-1.

25 Hopkins: C. Cabell, *Witchfinder General. The Biography of Matthew Hopkins*, Sutton, Thrupp, 2006; the 'water test': P. Hughes, 2004, 176-7; ruinous church: A. Mee, *King's England, Essex*, 1940, 53.

26 Aubrey in London and back to Oxford: Powell, 57-9.

27 Aubrey's father fined: Tylden-Wright, 55.

28 Poets mentioned by Aubrey, see Dick: Herbert (Jane Danvers), 137; Lovelace, 93; Suckling, 289; Vaughan, 303-4.

29 'Blottynge papyr': William Horman, *Vulgaria*, 1519, 80b.

30 Rochester: G. Hopkins, *Constant Delights*. Rakes, *Rogues and Scandal in Restoration England*, Robson, London, 126-46. see also J. Lamb, 2005.

31 Sword attack on Aubrey in 1673: Dick, xxvi.

32 Marvell: N. Murray, *Andrew Marvell. World Enough and Time*, Abacus, London, 2000. 'Coy Mistress', 88-92. In *Brief Lives*, MS Aubrey 6, fol. 104; Clark, II, 53-4, 196; Dick, 196.

33 Death of Aubrey's father: Britton, 1845, 14; Powell, 59. The premonition: Aubrey, *Miscellanies*, 90.

CHAPTER TWO

1 Discovery of Avebury: Aubrey, TG, c.24. 23b, 24a; MB, I, 18.

2 Sketch of the Rollright Stones: Aubrey, TG, c.24, 56b; MB, I, 72.

3 Celebrations in 1660: MS Aubrey, 6f, 17; George Monk: MS Aubrey 6, fol. 17; Clark, II, 72-8; Dick, 204-8.

4 Britain's first inhabitants: *Tacitus on Britain and Germany*, trans. H. Mattingly, Penguin, Harmondsworth, 1948, 61; Aubrey and native Britons: J. E. Jackson, 1862, 4-5.

5 The Venerable Bede, *A History of the English Church and People*, 731 AD. Penguin, Harmondsworth, 1968. See Idols: 86, 89, 119, 128, 130, 153, 178, 201-2.

6 Louisfert: G. le Scouëzec, *Guide de la Bretagne Mystérieuse*, Paris, 1979, 382-4; Giot et al, *Préhistoire de la Bretagne*, I, Rennes, 1979, 405.

7 Henry of Huntingdon, *The Chronicle ... c. 1135*, Llanerch, Felinfach, 1991, 77-8.

8 Rollright Stones: T. H. Ravenhill, *The Rollright Stones and the Men Who Erected Them*, Cornish, London, 1932, 2-3, 54.

9 Giants: M. Letts, *Sir John Mandeville. The Man and His Book*, Batchwork, London, 1949, 62, 95, 105, 164.

10 Luckington tomb: Aubrey, TG, c. 25, 60b; MB, II, 811.

11 *Dr Faustus*, lines 321-4 [Greg, 1950]. Cloven hoof: Aubrey, *Remaines of Gentilisme and Judaisme*, see: Buchanan-Brown, 205.

12 Saxons and the Devil: Aubrey, TG, c.24, 29b; MB, I, 31.

13 Stones and the Devil: Grinsell, 1976; Trellech, 255; Devil's Arrows, 172; Pembrokeshire, 251; Devil's Quoits, 145; Avebury, 113; Stonehenge, 121; Innesmill, 213.

14 John Aubrey, witches said the Devil came as a goat: Buchanan-Brown,

Remaines of Gentilisme and Judaisme, see 205, final paragraph.

15 'Bodinus', Jean Bodin: R. E. Guiley, *The Encyclopaedia of Witches and Witchcraft*, Facts on File, London, 1989, 33.

16 Witchcraft in Germany: Aubrey, *Remaines of Gentilisme and Judaisme*, Buchanan-Brown, 136, 228; doorways, *Miscellanies Upon Various Subjects*, 1890, XIII, 'Magick', 89; eggs and witches, *ibid*, XV, 'Magick', 228.

17 Isabel Gowdie: P. G. Maxwell-Stuart, *The Great Scottish Witch-Trials*, Tempus, Chalford, 2007, 214-19; R. E. Guiley, (Note 15) 142-3; P. Hughes, *Witchcraft*, Sutton, Thrupp, 2004, 65, 66, 106; Shakespeare, *Macbeth*, I, 1, 1-12; IV, 1, 1-132 (11-12).

18 The Hurlers: Aubrey, TG, c.24, 66a; MB, I, 104.

19 'Written histories': Dick, *Brief Lives*, cxiii.

20 The long delay: Dick, *Brief Lives*, l.

21 William Harrison's disappearance: Sir George Clark, ed. *The Camden Wonder*, Oxford University Press, Oxford, 1959; H. R. Williamson, *Historical Whodunnits*, Phoenix, London, 1955, 164-80. Anthony à Wood: Powys, 1932, 103-4.

22 Anthony à Wood: his opinion of the Court: Powys, 127.

23 Pepys' wife washing: *Diary*, I, 21 November 1660, 298; at Court, *ibid*, 21 November, 299.

24 Aubrey, *Brief Lives*, [Rochester] MS Aubrey 6, fol.55; Clark, II, 304; Dick, 321.

25 Pepys: *Diary*, VI, 4 April 1665, 110, n. 2.

26 Andrew Marvell: Aubrey, *Brief Lives*, [Rochester] MS Aubrey 6, fol. 55; Clark, II, 304; Dick, 196.

27 Denham, [Mallet] MS Aubrey 8, fol. 6; Clark, I, 219; Dick, 91-3.

CHAPTER THREE

1 Prince Charles at Stonehenge: R. Ollard (1986) *The Escape of Charles II after the Battle of Worcester*, Robinson, London, 116-19; the king told Pepys: Fraser, 1979, 126.

2 Coronation, thunder and lightening: Dick, lxviii.

3 Trefignath: Aubrey, TG, c.24, 55b; MB, I, 41; Wynne, TG, c.25, 55b; MB, II, 780-1. Avebury: Aubrey, TG, c.24, 37b; MB, I, 41. Bagneux: TG, c.25, 48b; MB, II, 801; Burl, 1985, 84. Breton allées-couvertes: Burl, 2002, 169-70.

4 Claude Duval: P. Pringle, *Stand and Deliver. The Story of the Highwaymen*, Museum Press, London, 1951, 98-108; W. Pope, *Memoirs of Du Vall: Containing the History of his Life and Death*, London, 1670. Samuel Pepys: Ollard, 323-4.

5 Momentous years for Aubrey, Powell, 1988, 99, 101-4. Death of Aubrey's grandmother: Powell, 109.

6 Sir H. Lyons, (1944) *The Royal Society, 1660-1940*, Cambridge University Press, Cambridge, 342.

7 Attacks on the Royal Society: Lyons, Note 6; 7; Wood, M. Purver, (1969) *The Royal Society: Concept and Creation*, Routledge & Kegan Paul, London, 72.

8 Charleton: *Chorea Gigantum; OR, The Most Famous Antiquity of GREAT-BRITAIN, Vulgarly called STONE-HENG, standing on Salisbury plain, Restored to the DANES*, Harrington, London, 1663.

9 Danish courtiers on the Stonehenge lintels: Aubrey, MB, II, 862.

10 Aubrey's visit to the royal Court: Aubrey, TG, c.24, 25a; MB, I, 21.

11 Burl, 1982. Pepys: *Diary*, IV, 11 August 1663, 272; Queen's sterility, R. V. Lennard, ed. 'The Watering Places' in *Englishmen at Rest and Play*, *1558-1774*, Clarendon Press, Oxford, 1931, 47; no meeting, Royal Society. *Lib 2*, fol. 193, 211; Pepys: *Diary*, IV, 4 October 1663, 288. To Bath: Pepys, *Diary*, IV, 16 September 1663, 272.

12 Date of meeting: Roy. Soc. Lib 2, fol. 193, 211; Aubrey, TG.c.24, 25a; MB, I, 21.

13 Aubrey and the court: Dick, xxxix.

14 The reality: Falkus, 76-7, 94; Pepys: *Diary*, II, 17 August 1661, 156; brothels, *Diary*, IX, 25 March 1668, 132.

15 John Evelyn, *Diary*, Dobson, 1906: Dining with Mazarin, 6 September 1676, II, 394; at Court, 4 February 1685, III, 144-5.

16 Pepys and the chimney: Pepys, *Diary*, VI, 28 September 1665, 244.

17 Water closets: Harington, Aubrey, D. Eveleigh, 2006, 19-20.

18 Rain: Pepys, *Diary*, IV, 8 July 1663, 220. The plans: Roy. Soc. Lib 2, fol. 168, 197.

19 Avebury and Ariadne's Crown: Aubrey, TG, c.24, 33b; MB, I, 33, 36.

20 Aubrey's social life up to 1663: Britton, 1845, 30-41; Dick, 1949, xliv-lii; Powell 1988, 79-110; Tylden-Wright, 69-138.

21 Fallible memories: Charleton, 1663, 5.

22 Stuart Piggott, 'Introduction', *Inigo Jones, Stone-Heng*; *Walter Charleton, Chorea Gigantum*; *John Webb, A Vindication*; Gregg, Letchworth, 1971, 1, 2.

23 'a gallop': Aubrey, TG, c.24, 26b; MB, I, 25-6.

CHAPTER FOUR

1 Aubrey's survey of Avebury: TG, c.24, 25b; MB, I, 22-3; TG, c.24, 31b; MB, 33.

2 Fourteenth century discoveries at Avebury: I. F. Smith, ed. *Windmill Hill*

and Avebury. Excavations by Alexander Keiller, 1925-1939, Clarendon Press, Oxford, 1965, 177.

3 The name of Avebury: Aubrey, TG, c.24, 37b; MB, I, 40, 41.

4 'Avebury, 1689: Gover, Mawer & Stenton, 211.

5 Stone breaking: Stukeley, 1743, 25.

6 Leland's visit: Leland: T. Hearne, ed. _The Itinerary of John Leland the Antiquary_, 3rd ed., VII, 85, T. Hearne, Oxford, 1749; L. T. Smith, ed. _The Itinerary of John Leland in or about the years 1535–1543_, I-XI, V, Part X, 81, Southern Illinois University Press, Carbondale, 1964.

7 Harington: W. Long, _Abury Illustrated_, Wilts. Arch. Soc., Devizes, 1858, 2.

8 Camden's account of Avebury: 1637, 255. William Lambarde, _Angliae Topographicum & Historiarum_, MS, 1580, published in 1730, 314-15.

9 John Aubrey and Avebury: Gibson's _Britannia_, 1695, 111.

10 Aubrey, _Brief Lives_: Anthony, MS Aubrey 8, fol. 21; Clarke, I, 32; Abbot, MS Wood F, fol. 221; Clarke, I, 24, Barber, 1983, 16; Curtin, MS Aubrey 21, p.11; Clarke, I, 191; Barber, 1983, 83. None is in Dick.

11 Brinsden: Aubrey, TG.c.24, 35b; MB, I, 38; MB, II, 778-9; Mill Barrow, MB, II, 802-3. The cavalier, Symonds: H. C. Brentall, 'Sarsens', _Wiltshire Archaeological Magazine_ 51, 1946, 420.

12 Walter Sloper: Powell, 1988, 87; Abigail Sloper, Dick, cx; Tylden-Wright, 49. Aubrey's reference to Abigail can be found in his _Collectio Geniturarum_ of the 1670s, a collection of horoscopes.

13 The difficulties of the survey: Aubrey, TG c24, 35b, 36b; MB, I, 39-40.

14 Shelving Stones: Aubrey, TG, c.25, 46b; MB, II, 823.

15 The Outer Circle: Aubrey, TG, c.24, 32b; MB, I, 35.

16 P. J. Ucko, M. Hunter, A. J. Clark, A. David, _Avebury Reconsidered. From the 1660s to the 1990s_, I, II, Unwin, Hyman, London, 1991, 226-7.

17 The questionable _allée-couverte_, Aubrey, TG, c.24, 37b; MB, I, 41.

18 Ucko, et al., (Note 16), 18.

19 The Kennet avenue: Aubrey, TG, c.24, 34b; MB, I, 37.

20 Saxon 'historians': Aubrey, TG, c.24, 29b; MB, I, 31.

21 'These Remaynes ...': Aubrey, _Wiltshire. The Topographical Collections of John Aubrey_. [1659-70]. ed. J. E. Jackson, Devizes, 1862, 4.

22 Toope: Aubrey, TG. c.24, 44b; MB, I, 52-3; II, 984-5; Tylden-Wright, 75.

CHAPTER FIVE

1 Two deaths in 1664: Pepys, _Diary_, V, 15 March, 86; Evelyn, Dobson, II, 209; Aubrey's accidents: Clark, I, 47.

2 Aubrey on Lassels: Stephens, 1972, 135.

3 Hobbes' letter of 11 June 1664: Powell, 1978, 111. 'Evelyn and Aubrey's *Antiquities of Surrey* Dick, lxxx; 'An Inquisitive Genius': Hunter, 212.

4 Villon's disappearance: A. Burl, *Danse Macabre. François Villon. Poetry & Murder in Medieval France*, Sutton, Thrupp, 2000, 212-19. Restaurant Villon: *ibid*, xiii.

5 Evelyn and Orléans: Dobson, 1906, I, 105-6.

6 Bagneux and Pierre Folle, 'Pierre-levé': TG, c.25, 56b; MB, II, 801.

7 Aubrey in hospital: Clark, I, 47. Werewolf: Buchan-Brown: Aubrey's *Remaines of Gentilisme and Judaisme*, 226-7.

8 Fairies in the megaliths of Brittany: G. L. Scouëzec, *Guide de la Bretagne Mystérieuse*, Éditions Princesse, Paris, 1979, 154, 210 et al.

9 Giants: Grinsell, 1976, 25-29: 27.

10 Shelving Stones: Aubrey, TG, c.25, 63b ; MB, II, 822-23; Mill Barrow, TG, c,25, 57b. Dean Merewether: R. Castleden, *Neolithic Britain. New Stone Age Sites of England, Scotland and Wales*, Routledge, London, 221.

11 Lugbury: Aubrey, TG, c.25, 58b; MB, II, 809. Burials: Grinsell, 1957, 142.

12 Lanhill [Hubba's Low]: Aubrey, TG, c.25, 58a – 59b; MB, II, 805, 809; MB, I, 326-7;TG, c.24, 173b.

13 *Wiltshire Antiquities (Collections)*, Aubrey and Jackson, 1862, 74.

14 *Anglo-Saxon Chronicle, (A)*, Winchester version, and (E), Peterborough, AD 867, 68-9. Neither mentioned Hubba. Asser: *Alfred the Great. Asser's Life of King Alfred and other contemporary sources*, trans. S. Keynes & M. Lapidge, Penguin, London, 1983; Henry of Huntingdon, *Historia Anglorum*, 152; Roger of Wendover, *Flores Historiarum, c.* 1235: *Roger of Wendover's Flowers of History, I-IV*, trans. G. A. Giles, 1849. Facsimile reprint: Llanerch, Felinfach, 1993, I, 191-202.

15 John Aubrey and Danes-Blood, *Sambucus ebulus, Natural History of Wiltshire*, 1848, 50. The unhistorical battle between Alfred the Danish brothers: Aubrey, TG, c.25, 59b, MB, II, 809; John Milton, *History of Britain, I-VI*, 1670: Aubrey, TG, c.24, 173b, MB, I, 326-7.

16 *Decem Scriptores* and Brompton: J. Thurnam: 'On Lanhill Barrow near Chippenham; and the Battles of Cynuit and Ethandun', *WAM III*, 1858, 82. also J. Thurnam: *WAM III*, 1858, 67-86.

17 'Slaughterford' and the sloe-bush: Gover et al. 111. The ravaged church: Aubrey & Jackson, 110.

18 William Dowsing: *CEDNB, I*, 569; A. Mee, *The King's England, Suffolk*, Hodder & Stoughton, London, 1941, 259.

19 L. V. Grinsell, *The Archaeology of Wessex*, Methuen, London, 1958, 284.

20 *Wodnes dic*: Gover et al. xiv, 17.

21 Wansdyke and Wednesday: Camden, *Britain*, 1637, 241.

22 Edward Leigh: Aubrey, TG, c.25, 88a; MB, II, 887. Clearly, Aubrey had added Leigh's note. He wrote it on the usually blank lefthand, *verso*, side of the page opposite the quotation from Camden.

23 Aubrey's own fieldwork at Wansdyke: TG, c.25, 88b; MB, II, 888-9.

24 Figheldean stone: Aubrey, TG, c.24, 91a; MB, I, 96.

25 Broome standing stone: Aubrey, TG, c.24, 67b; MB, I, 106-7; destruction of the circle: *WAM 23*, 1887, 115-16.

26 The Coate (Day House) circles: *WAM 97*, 2004, 200-4.

27 The prehistoric track passing Stonehenge: Burl, 2006, 92-5.

28 Aubrey, Heel Stone and avenue: TG, c.24, 59a; MB, I, 76; Stonehenge plan: TG, c.24, 65a; MB, I, 80.

29 The Stonehenge avenue: Burl and Mortimer, *Stukeley's "Stonehenge". An Unpublished Manuscript.* 1721 – 1724, Yale University Press, London & New Haven, 2005, 78, manuscript page, 59.

30 Aubrey's regret, 'Umbrages', 'truly nothing': Powell, 74; Aubrey, TG, c.24, 52b, 53b. plan 54b; MB, I, [46, 47], 65-9.

31 Stanton Drew: Aubrey, TG, c.24, 51a; MB, I, 65. [Aubrey later deleted the entry.]

32 The name: K. Lohan, 'The Hautevelle Quoits', *Family Tree Magazine 7(1)*, 1990, 29.

33 'Druids': Aubrey, TG, c.24, 53a; MB, I, 68.

34 The Stanton Drew Cove: W. Johnson, *Byways in British Archaeology*, Cambridge University Press, Cambridge, 1912, 46-7.

35 William Camden, *Britannia*, 1695, 79.

36 William Camden, *Britain*, 1637; 'Somersetshire', 220-40.

37 John Aubrey's description of Stanton Drew: TG, c.24, 53b, 54a, b; MB, I, 65-9.

38 'Utterly confused': C. W. Dymond, *The Ancient Remains of Stanton Drew in the County of Somerset*, Dymond, Bristol, 1896, 3.

39 Aubrey, TG, c.24 53b; MB, I, 67. Plan: TG, c.24 54b; MB, I, 69.

40 Cove: Aubrey, TG, c.24, 52b; MB, I, 66; Not on plan: Dymond [Note 40, above], 2, footnote.

41 South-western ring: Aubrey, TG, c.24, 52b; MB, I, 66.

42 'Hakewell's Coyte': Aubrey, TG, c.24 54a; MB, I, 68.

43 The figure of solid Irish oak: Sir William Cheney: I. L. Durham, *The Church of St. Andrew Chew Magna*, n.d., 8; or John Wych: A. C. Fryer, *Wooden Monumental Effigies in England and Wales*, London, 1924, 29, 60.

Chapter Six

1 Powell, 73; Tyndal-Wright, 149.

2 John Stow, *A Survey of London written in the Year 1598*, Sutton,

Thrupp, 2005, 123.

3 Pepys, 'turds': *Diary*, I, 20 October 1660, 269.

4 Pepys, washing: *Diary*: III, 2 May 1663, 75. A luxurious bath: Fiennes, 106.

5 The crowded city: Leasor, 185; Porter, 212.

6 Scarus, in *Anthony and Cleopatra*, III, 10, 12-13.

7 Charlatans: C. Thompson, 1993, 218-34; Green Dragon Tavern: N. Cawthorne, *The Curious Cures of Old England*, Portrait, London, 2005, 97.

8 Red crosses: Pepys, *Diary*, VI, 7 June 1665, 120.

9 Death-carts: Leasor, 145.

10 Pepys and the London streets: *Diary*, VI, 8 August 1665, 186.

11 Pepys' periwig: *Diary*, VI, 3 September 1665, 210.

12 Evelyn, the empty streets: Dobson, II, 234.

13 Clatford Bottom: Aubrey, TG, c.24. 43b, 44a, plan; MB, I, 50.

14 Legendary dogs near Clatford: K. Jordan, *The Folk-Lore of Wiltshire*, Wiltshire C. C., Trowbridge, 1990, 52-3.

15 Joan Sumner and John Aubrey, Powell, 115-26.

16 Aubrey's opinion of Seend water: Ponting, 1969, 22.

17 Joan Sumner, Gayford and Aubrey: Powell, 120; 125.

18 Maypoles: A. Plowden, 2006, 116-17.

19 Edward Bradby, *Seend, a Wiltshire Village Past and Present*, Sutton, Thrupp, 1981, 14: the 'Festivall', 225; iron ore, 87-88; J. Aubrey: J. Buchanan-Brown, 1972: Sumner's well, 326; iron ore, 326, 361.

20 Aubrey, *Remaines of Gentlisme*: Buchanan-Brown, 137.

21 Wantoness: R. Chambers, ed. *The Book of Days. A Miscellany of Popular Antiquities in Connection with the Calendar*, Chambers, London, 1848, 218-29; Philip Stubbes, *Anatomie of Abuses*, 1583, 149; A. Plowden, *Elizabethan England*, Reader's Digest, 1983, 153-5.

22 The Seend mineral water: Britton, 1845, 16-17.

23 Britton, 1845, 17.

24 'cottleloft': Powys, 174; Wood and his garret: Balme, 16.

25 Aubrey meets Wood for the first time: Balme, 16-17.

26 Pepys' meals: *Diary*, VI, 20 February 1665, 39; 20 June 1665, 132.

27 A. Bryant, *Restoration England*, Collins, London, 1960, 102-110; P. Brears, *Stuart Cookery* English Heritage, London, 2004, 87-90.

28 Fell: *CEDNB*, I, 669.

29 Tom Brown: *CEDNB*, I, 233; Martial, *Epigrammata I*, no. 32: *Martial. Epigrams*, ed., trans. D. R. S. Bailey, Harvard University Press, Cambridge, Mass., 1993, 63; Thomas Forde, *CEDNB*, I, 717.

30 Wood's 'Life' of Selden, *Athenae Oxoniensis*, III, 366-82.

31 Aubrey's account of Selden: MS Aubrey 6, fol. 120; Clark, II, 219-25; Dick, 271-3.

32 R. Gay, *A FOOLS Bolt soon shott at STONAGE*, 26; in R. Legg, *Stonehenge Antiquaries*, Dorset Publishing Co., Milborne Port, 1986, 40.

33 Sanctuary: Aubrey, TG, c.24, 43b; MB, I, 49-56; plans: TG, c.24, 42, 45a.

34 Sanctuary. Evelyn: Dobson, II, 73; Pepys, *Diary, IX*, 15 June 1668, 240-1.

35 Toope: Aubrey, TG, c.24, 44a, 45b; 45b; MB, I, 52-5.

36 Cocherel: Aubrey, TG, c.24, 46b-47b; MB, I, 58-64; *Philosophical Transactions 185*, 1686, 221-6.

37 Excavation at the Sanctuary: M. Cunnington, 'The "Sanctuary" on Overton Hill near Avebury', *WAM 45*, 1931, 300-35.

38 The Cocherel remains: Aubrey, TG, c.24, 50b; MB, I, 64.

CHAPTER SEVEN

1 See Appendix B.

2 Rastell: Chippindale, 2004, 27-8.

3 Stonehenge's 'artificial stones: Camden, 1637, 253.

4 Aubrey's scepticism: Britton, 1847, 97-8.

5 Sarsens, the grievous stones: Britton, 1847, 44; *WAM 51*, 1946, 426.

6 Sarsens: Aubrey, TG, c.24, 88b; MB, I, 91.

7 Lambarde: Chippindale, 2004, 36-7.

8 Camden, 1637, 253; 9.

9 Folkerzheimer and the Roman yoke: Chippindale, 2004, 29-30; Camden and Merlin, 1637, 253.

10 Boudica: Edmund Bolton, *Nero Caesar or Monarchie Depraved*, 1624, 181-2.

11 Buckingham's pit at Stonehenge: Aubrey, TG, c.24, 62b, fig. 2, oval, slightly-off-centre; MB, I, 81.

12 Jones' thuribulum: Aubrey, TG, c.24. 89a; MB, I, 92.

13 Buckingham's bugle: Aubrey, TG, c.24, 93b; MB, I, 100. Mrs Trotman and the owner of Stonehenge: TG, c.24, 89b, 90b; MB, I, 93, 95.

14 Jones, 1655, 1-2. For other details of Jones' work at Stonehenge, see M. Leapman, 197-200, 231.

15 Jones, 1655, 63. plan 6.

16 J. Webb, *A Vindication of Stone-Heng Restored*, 1725, 16: in *Inigo Jones, STONE-HENG; Walter Charleton, CHOREA GIGANTUM; John Webb, A VINDICATION*, Introduction, S. Piggott, Gregg, 1971, Letchworth, 1-228.

17 Jones, 1655, 57, E.

18 Jones, 1655, 69.

19 Jones and the ancient Britons: Jones, 1655, 7.

20 Aubrey and the planets: TG, c.24, 62a, 63b; MB, I, 92.

21 'The seven planets': J. Smith, *Choir Gaur; the Grand Orrery of the Ancient Druids, commonly called Stonehenge, on Salisbury Plain*, Salisbury, 1771, 65.

22 Leapman (Note 14), 199.

23 Aubrey on Jones' book: TG, c.24, 24a, b; MB, I, 19, 20.

24 Burials – Saxons: Jones, 1655, 27; Britons: Aubrey, TG, c.25, 21b; MB, II, 713.

25 Robert Gay, *A Fool's Bolt* …: see R. Legg, *Stonehenge Antiquaries*, Dorset Publishing Co., Milborne Port, 1986, 17-51; Gay's pagination, 3-37, refs: 17, 19, 24. Paschall: Aubrey, TG, c.24, 94a; MB, I, 84.

26 Walter Charleton: *Chorea Gigantum; OR, The Most Famous Antiquity of GREAT-BRITAIN, Vulgarly called STONE-HENG … Restored to the DANES*, Henry Herringman, London, 1663.

27 Colt Hoare: Aubrey, MB, I, 6.

28 Counting the stones at Stonehenge: J. Westwood, *Albion. A Guide to Legendary Britain*, Grafton, London, 1992, 81-2.

29 Prince Charles: R. Ollard, *The Escape of Charles II after the Battle of Worcester*, Robinson, London, 2002, 118-19; Pepys, *Diary, IX*, 11 June 1668, 230.

30 Dimensions: Aubrey, TG, c.24, 58b; MB, I, 75; A. & A. S. Thom, *Megalithic Remains in Britain and Brittany*, Oxford University Press, 1978, 141-4.

31 The Heel Stone and the avenue: Aubrey, TG, c.24, 59b; MB, I, 76.

32 Slaughter Stone: Aubrey, TG, c.24, 65a; MB, I, 80, Plate VII.

33 The Altar Stone: Aubrey, TG, c.24, 58b; MB, I, 75.

34 Aubrey Holes: Hawley, *Antiquaries Journal I*, 1921, 30; Aubrey, TG, c.24, 59b; MB, I, 76.

35 The Devil's Stone: Aubrey, TG, c.24, 90b; MB, I, 95.

36 John Smith, *Choir Gaur; the Grand Orrery of the Ancient Druids, commonly called Stonehenge*, J. Smith, Salisbury, 1771, 51.

37 Local round barrows: Camden, 1637, 253, 255; Aubrey, TG, c.24, 92b; MB, I, 99.

38 Pepys and Stonehenge: *Diary, IX*, 11 June 1688, 229-30.

39 Evelyn at Stonehenge: Dobson, II, 83.

40 'Curse-tablet': Camden, 1637, 254; Aubrey, TG, c.24, 89a; MB, I, 92.

41 Stonehenge superstitions and toads: Aubrey, TG, c.24, 89b; MB, I, 93.

42 Stonehenge and starlings: Aubrey, TG, c.24, 89b; MB, I, 93.

43 Bloodworth: Tinniswood, 44.

44 'God with his great bellows': Tinniswood, 52.

45 Evelyn: Dobson, II, 252-5.

46 'A brick city': Thomas Delaune, *The Present State of London*, 1681.

47 Pepys, *Diary, VII*, Fire: 2-8 September 1666, 267-82; Mrs Bagwell, 12 September 1666, 285.

48 Pepys, *Diary, VIII*, 14 February 1667, 60.

49 'John Aubrey, Kim-kam': Clark, I, 47; Dick, lii.

50 Salisbury Diocesan Registry: Powell, 120, note 1.

CHAPTER EIGHT

1 The Joan Sumner fiasco: Powell, 115-37; Tylden-Wright, 145-9.

2 Aubrey's friends, 1670 and 1671: Clark, I, 41.

3 Evelyn meeting Colonel Blood: Dobson, *Diary, II*, 322.

4 Aubrey to Anthony à Wood: 14 May 1693.

5 Mistress Grace: MS Aubrey 22, folios 29-47; Tylden-Wright, 212-13.

6 Coley's forecast: Powell, 139-40.

7 Aubrey to Wood about Coley: 21 October 1693: Balme, 145.

8 Stawell to Aubrey, MS Aubrey 13, f. 191.

9 Pepys, *Diary, IX*, 31 May 1669, 564-5. His second diary: C. S. Knighton, ed. *Pepys's Later Diaries*, Sutton, Thrupp, 2006, 245-6. Pepys, *Diary, IX*, 31 May 1669, 564-5.

10 Pepys, *Diary, VIII*, 29 March 1667, 136.

11 J. Bedford, *London's Burning*, Abelard-Schumann, London, 1966, 245-6.

12 The rebuilding of St Paul's: Tinniswood, 256-60.

13 M. Cooper, *Robert Hooke and the Rebuilding of London*, Sutton, Thrupp, 2005, 205.

14 Thomas Gale and the Monument: Tinniswood, 271-3.

15 Herrick's death: M. Chute, *Two Gentle Men. The Lives of George Herbert and Robert Herrick*, Secker & Warburg, London, 1960, 267. Milton's death: A. Beer, *Milton. Poet, Pamphleteer and Patriot*, Bloomsbury, London, 2008, 389. Aubrey to Wood: Balme, 68.

16 Aubrey's reminiscences: Clark I, 42.

17 Camden, language, and linguistic scholars: Herendeen, 45.

18 Caesar, *Gallic Wars*, V, 14; Tacitus, *Agricola*, XII.

19 Diodorus Siculus: C. H. Oldfather, *Diodorus of Sicily, II*, Heinemann, London, 1979, 37-41; Burl, 1993, 64-5, 179-80.

20 Aubrey, 'The native Americans': *Topographical Collections*: Jackson, 1862, 4, 5. Hobbes, *Leviathan*, I, ch. 13, published in 1651. see also A. B. Ferguson, *Utter Antiquity. Perceptions of Prehistory in Renaissance England*, Duke University Press, Durham and London,

1993, 114-133.

21 Ussher and Lightfoot: G. Daniel, *The Idea of Prehistory*, Pelican, Harmondsworth, 1964, 19.

22 Bede: Duncan, *Calendar*, 122; Shakespeare, *As You Like It*, IV, 1, 65.

23 'Monuments of Victory: Boscawen-Un: Camden, 1637, 188; Aubrey, TG, c.24, 66b; MB, I, 70, 104-5.

24 Boscawen-Un as a gorsedd: A. H. Allcroft, *The Circle and the Cross. A Study in Continuity, I, II*, Macmillan, London, 1927, I, 'The Circle', 426-7.

25 The Hurlers: A. Thom, A. S. Thom, & A. Burl, *Megalithic Rings*, BAR, Oxford, 1980, 74-5; Burl, 2000, 162-4.

26 John Norden, *Speculi Britanniae. Pars. A Topographical and Historical Description of Cornwall, by the Perambulations View and Declination of John Norden*, Bateman, London, 1728. Reprint, F. Graham, Newcastle upon Tyne, 1966, 23, 65, 66.

27 Richard Carew, *Richard Carew of Antony. The Survey of Cornwall*, Jaggard, London, 1602, reprinted with intro. F. E. Halliday, A. M. Kelley, New York, 1969; 147-50, 323.

28 The Hurlers: Camden, 1637, 192; Aubrey, TG, c.24, 66a; MB, I, 104.

29 Nevison's ride: *Daniel Defoe. A Tour through the Whole Island of Great Britain*, ed. P. Rogers, Penguin, 1971, 121-3; P. Pringle, *Stand and Deliver. The Story of the Highwaymen*, Museum Press, London, 1951, 123-34; Brandon, *Stand and Deliver. A History of Highway Robbery*, Sutton, Thrupp, 2004, 79-82. Turpin's 'ride' on Black Bess: J. Sharpe, *Dick Turpin. The Myth of the English Highwayman*, Profile London, 2004, 153-9.

30 A. Smith, *A Compleat History …*',1719: ed. A. Hayward, Routledge, London, 1926, 25-30; afterthought, 216; Pringle [note 29], 'Who rode to York?', 135-44.

31 Aubrey, Wood and the Rollright Stones: Balme, 65, 66.

32 Exmoor: Camden, 1637, 203.

33 Rollright Stones: Camden, 1637, 374-5. For a general review of the circle in its landscape: G. Lambrick, *The Rollright Stones. Megaliths, Monuments, and Settlement in the Prehistoric Landscape*, English Heritage, London, 1988.

34 '*magni lapides …*': T. H. Ravenhill, *The Rollright Stones and the Men who Erected Them*, Cornish, Birmingham, 2nd ed., 1932, 2-3, 54.

35 Superstitions: A. J. Evans, 'The Rollright Stones and Their Folk-Lore', *Folklore* 6, 1895, 6-50 (18-33); L. V. Grinsell, *The Rollright Stones and Their Folklore*, Toucan Press, St Peter Port, 1977.

36 Rollright Stones: Aubrey, TG, c.24, 66b, 67b; MB, I, 67, 70-3, 226.

37 Death of Andrew Marvell: N. Murray, *Andrew Marvell. World Enough and Time*, Abacus, London, 2000, 238, 294, 300.

38 Aubrey and suspicions: Clark, II, 54. Jesuits: Murray, Note 34 above, 21-3.

39 Mayburgh: Camden, 1637, 776; Aubrey, TG, c.24, plan, 71a, text 71b; MB, I, 113-14.

40 Long Meg & Her Daughters: Camden, 1673, 777.

41 Long Meg & Her Daughters: Aubrey, TG, c.24, 72b; MB, I, 115-16.

42 Ecbert's defeat of the Danes: P. Marron, *Battles of the Dark Ages. British Battlefields AD 410 to 1065*, Pen & Sword, Barnsley, 2006, 104.

43 Hooke and floods before Noah: Hunter, 58, 223; Britton, 1847, 46-7.

CHAPTER NINE

1 Sheldon and Aubrey in London: Powell, 1988, 174.

2 Pembroke: H. R. Williamson, *Historical Whodunits*, Phoenix, London, 1955, 202-10.

3 Wood and Sheldon: Powys, 1932, 164.

4 Wood, accused and exonerated: Powys, 1932, 196-8.

5 Pepys: R. Ollard, *Pepys. A Biography*, Hodder & Stoughton, London, 1974, 247-57.

6 Nell Gwynn: Evelyn, *Diary, III*, 140.

7 The Duke of Monmouth's mother: D. Wilson, *All the King's Women. Love, Sex and Politics in the Life of Charles II*, Smart, St Helens, 2003, 58.

8 Aubrey and Monmouth's rebels; Balme, 108.

9 Aubrey, 1680: Balme, 91-2; Wood and Aubrey's 'Life' of the Duke of Monmouth: Balme, 140.

10 As a suspected Catholic: Aubrey to Wood, 23 October 1688, Balme, 115.

11 Lhwyd to Aubrey, 1693: Powell, 1988, 225. Edward Lhwyd's surname has also been variously spelled as Llwhyd by Britton; as Llwyd by Dick; and Lhuyd by the *Dictionary of National Biography*.

12 Lhwyd and pre-Roman Britain: F. Emery, *Edward Lhwyd, FRS, 1660-1709*, Cardiff, 1971, 55. see also: R. Hatchwell & A. Burl, 'The Commonplace Book of William Stukeley, *Wilts. Arch. So. 91*, 1998, 65-75. Lhwyd: 70-2.

13 Pagan temples: Emery (Note 12 *supra*), 55-7.

14 Mendyk, 1989, 209-10. 'A cold coming ...' T. S. Eliot, 'The Journey of the Magi'.

15 Evan Evans, 1779, in E. Rees & G. Walter, 'The dispersion of the

manuscripts of Edward Lhuyd, *Welsh Historical Review* 7, 1975, 148-78.

16 John Aubrey and Arthur's Stone: TG, c.25, 65b; MB, II, 826-7.

17 Hoskyns' letter: Powell, 102.

18 Bryngwyn Stones: Lhwyd, 'Additions to Anglesey', *Britannia*, 1695, 675.

19 The Druid's Circle: Lhwyd, 'Additions to Caernarvonshire', *Britannia*, 1695, 673-4.

20 'Crom Cruaich' stone circle, plain of Kilnavert, Co. Cavan: Lhwyd, 'Additions to Penbrokeshire [*sic*]', *Britannia*, 1695, 636; Aubrey, TG, c.24, 77a; MB, I, 122; Burl, 2005, 211, 212.

21 Stone circles in Ireland: Aubrey, TG, c.24, 78b; MB, I. 127.

22 Mr Gethyng or Gethin, from Co. Cork: Aubrey, TG, c.24, 76a; MB, I. 127.

23 Gethyng and Merlin's transportation of the Stonehenge sarsens from Ireland: Aubrey, TG, c.24, 78b; MB, I. 127.

24 John Toland: Aubrey, TG, c.24, 78b; MB, I, 127, in the margin.

25 Circles in Scotland: Aubrey, TG, c.24, 78b; MB, I. 129. Robert Moray: TG. c.24, 79a; MB, I. 128.

26 Lhwyd and Garden, *Britannia*, Additions to 'Penbrokeshire' [*sic*], 637.

27 John Aubrey, 'temples of the druids': TG, c.24, 80b; MB, I, 129.

28 Anthony à Wood, *Athenae Oxonienses, I-IV*, ed. P. Bliss, London, 1820. Quotations are from that new edition because it contained additions as Notes by contemporaries such as John Aubrey.

29 Gadbury: Wood, IV, 9. There is a Note from Aubrey; Powell, 221.

30 The sentence and the burning: Powys, 287-90.

31 Clarendon and bribery: Balme, 36.

32 Aubrey to Wood about Clarendon's son: Balme, 141.

33 Aubrey's injuries: Clark, I, 45.

34 Clarendon's exile: D. Ogg, *England in the Reign of Charles II*, Oxford, 1972, 315.

35 Clarendon and Wood: Powys, 314.

36 Wood's pardon: Powys, 312-14; Balme, 154-5.

37 Wood's death: Powys, 312-14; Balme, 154-5.

38 Aubrey's letter to Tanner about Wood's death: Balme, 158.

39 Cost of living: A. Bryant, *Restoration England*, Collins, London, 1960, 'The Means of Life', 127-58; postal service: M. Ashley, *Life in Stuart England*, Batsford, London, 159-60.

40 Garden's nine letters: C. A. Gordon, Garden's letters: 1/ 15 June 1692, 11-16; 2/ 22 January 1693. 17-22; 3/ 6 February 1693. 23-28; 4/ 8 February 1693, 29-30; 5/ 6 March 1693. 31-38; 6/ 2 January 1694. 39-41; 7/ 4 May 1694, 42-50; 8/ 25 March 1695. 51-53; 9/ 16 April 1695. 55-56. Aubrey, Letters 1 to 7 only: TG, c.24, 117b-133b; MB, I, 176-220.

41 Garden and recumbent stone circles: Gordon, 11-15; Aubrey, TG, c.26, 118b, 122b; MB, I, 176-87.

42 Highlanders and the new moon; Gordon, 17: Aubrey, TG, c,24, 114b did not copy the note about the moon, only the comments on bards. There is nothing of Letter 2 in MB, I.

43 A. H. Allcroft, *The Circle and the Cross, I*, Macmillan, London, 1927, 146-7.

44 A. Burl, 'Science or symbolism? Problems of archaeo-astronomy', *Antiquity 54*, 1980, 191-200.

45 Ring of Brodgar and the Stones of Stenness, Orkney: that Danes built them: Gordon, 54-5; Aubrey, TG, c.24, 131b; MB, I, 218-19.

46 Wallace's book about stone circles in Orkney. Reference 45 above.

47 Survival of stone circles: Gordon, 32; Aubrey, TG, c.24, 128a; MB, I, 207.

48 John Dryden and the *Miscellanies*: Aubrey's letter to Wood, 4 April 1693: Balme, 143. Posthumously, the book went into several editions.

49 Transportation: Gordon, 51. In his *Templa Druidum* Aubrey only made copies of Garden's first seven letters. He did include Garden's 'transportation' in his own *Miscellanies* of 1696.

50 Garden's farewell in 1695: Gordon, 56. Aubrey did not include it in his *Templa Druidum*.

51 John Aubrey's quotation: *Templa Druidum*, TG, c.24, 26a, b; MB, I, 25.

Chapter Ten

1 *Britannia*, 1695: Introduction, Stuart Piggott, 5-13. 1695 edition, 9-11 [1971 reprint].

2 Contributors to the *Britannia*: Powell, 262-2.

3 John Evelyn and Surrey: G. Darley, *John Evelyn. Living for Ingenuity*, Yale University Press, London and New Haven, 2006, 288.

4 Pepys's contribution: Ollard 331.

5 Toland and Locke: Hunter, 59.

6 Camden, 1695, 111.

7 Gibson to Tanner: Piggott, in *Britannia*, [1971], 10.

8 Garden to Tanner, April 12, 1694: S. Piggott, in *Britannia*, [1971], 10.

9 Powell, 1988, 271.

10 Stanton Drew: *Britannia*, 1695, 79; additional material, 81-2. Aubrey, TG, c.24, 52b, 53b, 54a, b; MB, I, 65-9.

11 Rollright Stones and 'Kingstolen': *Britannia*, 269.

12 Nine Stones stone circle, Dorset: *Britannia*, 1695, 52.

13 Aubrey's health: Powell, 239-40.

14 The fatal dream: *Miscellanies*, 56.

15 Yew berries: *Culpeper's Colour Herbal*, 1649, ed. D. Potterton, London, 1983, 205.

16 'Force this'. Aubrey, TG, c.24, 226b, 226a; MB, I, 473.

17 'Ghost of the one of those Druids':. Aubrey, TG, c.24, 26b; MB, I: 25-6.

18 Woodroffe and plagiarism: Hunter, 84.

19 Forgotten curiosities: Dick, xcv.

20 Aubrey's death: Britton, 1845, 3-4. Rawlinson: Powell, 244; Tylden-Wright, 252.

21 Aubrey's burial: Powell, 246.

22 The plaque at Oxford: Dick, 1948, ciii-iv.

23 Kington St Michael; A. Mee, *King's England, Wiltshire*, 1929, 202.

24 Gadbury: Powell, 245.

25 Gawen's barrow: Aubrey, TG, c.25, 21a, b; MB, II, 711; Hoare, *Ancient Wiltshire, I*, 245-6.

26 Grinsell, 1957, 162, grid reference, SU 0359 2345.

27 William Aubrey, Powell, 274.

APPENDIX B

1 The fourth stone: Burl, 1991, 5-6, quoting Radclyff, 1621.

2 Thom, Thom and Burl, *Stone Rows and Standing Stones, I. Britain, Ireland and Brittany*, BAR 560 (i), Oxford, 1990, 42-3.

3 Legends: Grinsell, 172; the Devil's grandmother: Pevsner, *Yorkshire. West Riding, I*, 118; anticlockwise circuit: J. Wilcock, *A Guide to Occult Britain*, 1977, 225.

4 Leland, *Itinerary*: Smith, Volume I, 84-5, Boroughbridge.

5 Camden, *Britannia*, 1637: Philemon Holland's English translation, 701.

6 Nameless informant and 'British Deities': Camden, *Britannia* 1637, 734.

7 Aston. Aubrey, TG, c.24, 68a; MB, I, 109. Lister: TG, c.24, 68a; MB, I, 108.

8 Wenceslaus Hollar:. Aubrey, TG, c.24, 68a; MB, I, 108. Collins, *ibid*. Hollar in *Brief Lives*, MS Aubrey 6, fol. 26; Clark, I, 407-8; MS Aubrey 6, fol. 26. see also G. Tindall, 2003.

9 Thomas Gale. Aubrey, TG, c,24, 68a, b; MB, I, 109.

10 Watts. Aubrey, TG, c.24, 68b; MB, I, 109.

11 Aubrey's account of the Devil's Arrows: Aubrey, TG, c.24, 69b, 70a, b; MB, I, 110-12.

12 Alignements du Moulin: Burl, A. *Megalithic Brittany. A Guide to Over*

350 Sites and Ancient Monuments, Thames & Hudson, London, 1985, 91-2.

13 For a recent consideration of the row, see Burl, 'The Devil's Arrows, Boroughbridge, North Yorkshire. The archaeology of a stone row', *Yorkshire Archaeological Journal, 63*, 1991, 1-24.

Appendix C

1 Aubrey and 'old stories': TG, c.24, 29; MB, I, 31.

2 R. Rowley, trans. (2005): Nennius, *Historia Britonum,* 'The History of the Britons, attributed to Nennius', Llanerch, Lampeter: Nennius, Part 46, 47. see also *Nennius. British History and The Welsh Annals*, ed., trans. J. Morris, Phillimore, London and Chichester, 1980. The Saxon uprising: M. Winterbottom, trans., ed., *Gildas, 'The Ruin of Britain, and other documents'*, Phillimore, Chichester, 1978, 26. Gildas, *De Excidio Britaniniae.* 'The Ruin of Britain' Pt 23, 1-4: H. Williams, ed. (1901) Hon. Soc. Cymmrodorion, Bala. Facsimile, Llanerch, Lampeter, 2006, 52-5. For Vortigern and Hengest's treachery, see also M. S. Swanton, *the Anglo-Saxon Chronicles*, Dent, London, 1996: (A) Winchester [Parker]; and (E) Peterborough [Laud] for AD 449, 455.

3 *Anglo-Saxon Chronicle*, AD 449, 455: Swanton, 1996, (A) *Winchester [Parker]*12; (E) *Peterborough [Laud]*, 13.

4 Nennius: the references to the various incidents can be found in sections 37 and 38, 43, and 45-6.

5 Pepys, *Diary, IX*, 24 March 1669, 496-7.

6 Aubrey, TG, c.25, 64b; MB, I, 225; MB, II, 815; and Evelyn, TG, c.24, 135b.

7 The treachery: Nennius, 45-6, 32.

8 L. Sherley-Price, trans. *Bede. A History of the English Church and People*, Penguin, Harmondsworth, 1955, revised 1968: Bk I, Ch. 15, 55; Oeric, Bk II, Ch. 5, 108.

9 Gildas and the folly of Vortigern's Britons: M. J. Hughes, *The English Conquest. Gildas and Britain in the fifth century*, Manchester U. P., Manchester, 1994, 38-42, 155-7 et seq; M. Winterbottom, *Gildas. The Ruin of Britain and other documents*, Phillimore, Chichester, 1978; 32.1, 26; the cry of despair: *ibid.* 23.2-24.4, 26-7.

10 Vortigern in modern histories of post-Roman Britain: H. Marsh, *Dark Age Britain. Sources of History*, Dorset Press, New York, 1970, 74-9 et seq. J. D. Randers-Pehrson, *Barbarians and Romans. The Birth Struggle of Europe, A.D. 400-700*, Croom Helm, London, 1983, 217, 302-4; C. A. Snyder, *An Age of Tyrants. Britain and the Britons A. D. 400 – 600*, Sutton, Thrupp, 1998, 26, 102, 106, 160, 188, 341.

11 L. Thorpe, trans. intro. (1966) Geoffrey of Monmouth, *Historia Regum*

Britanniae, 'The History of the Kings of Britain', (*c.* 1136) Penguin, Harmondsworth, 195. Wessex place-names: Gover et al. xiii-xix.

12 William of Newburgh, (*c.* 1198) *Historia Rerum Anglicarum*, 'The History of the Kings of England', trans. ed. J. Stevenson, 1856, facsimile, Llanerch, Felinfach, 1996. Preface, 399-401; Gerald of Wales: L. Thorpe, trans. (1978) *Itinerarium Cambriae*, 'The Journey through Wales', Book 1, Penguin, Harmondsworth, Ch. 5, 127-8; Ranulf Higden: M. Collins, trans., *CAXTON. The Description of Britain*, Sidgwick & Jackson, London, 1988, 9-27; William Caxton, *ibid*.

13 William Camden, *Britain* ... [in English] trans. Philemon Holland, George Latham, London, 1637, 254; also the Latin *Britannia*, George Bishop, London, 1607, *Fama obtinet Ambrosium ...*, 183-4.

14 *Myrddin* and 'Merlin': M. Dixon-Kennedy, *A Companion to Arthurian and Celtic Myths and Legends*, Sutton, Thrupp, 2004, 295; N. J. Lacy, ed. *The New Arthurian Encyclopedia*, St James Press, London, 1991, 320.

15 T. Forester, trans., ed. (1853) Henry of Huntingdon, *Historia Anglorum*, 'The History of England, from the Invasion of Julius Caesar to the Accession of Henry II', facsimile ed., Llanerch, Felinfach, 1991, 7.

16 Mount Killarus, Ireland: L. Thorpe, (Note 11), VIII, 196.

17 'Killian' and Mr. Gethin. Aubrey, TG. c.24, 78; MB, I, 127.

18 Kildare and St Brigid: the wonderful book: J. J O'Mara, trans. Gerald of Wales, *Topographia Hibernica*, 'The History and Topography of Ireland', Penguin, Harmondsworth, 1982, 81-4, Pts 67-72.

19 The Harroway and standing stones: Burl, 2006, 23.

20 The tall stones around Naas: Craddockstown West, N 911 163; Longstone Rath, N 936 206; Punchestown, N 918 154: E. Evans, *Prehistoric and Early Christian Ireland. A Guide*, Batsford, London, 1966, 136-8.

21 Merlin and heavy stones: Thorpe (Note 11), *Geoffrey of Monmouth*, 198.

22 Sarsen, *sar stan*: Burl, 2006, 170.

23 Sarsens on the Marlborough Downs: *Wiltshire. The Topographical Collections of John Aubrey, FRS*, ed. J. E. Jackson, Devizes, 1862, 314.

24 Sarsens not from Ireland. Aubrey, TG, c.24, 88; MB, I, 91.

25 The weight of the Stonehenge sarsens: The sarsen lintels each weighed over 3 tons, E. H. Stone, *The Stones of Stonehenge*, Robert Scott, London, 1924, 65-6; the sarsen pillars of the outer circle each weighed 23 tons; the heaviest trilithon, Stone 56, was over 40 tons. E. H. Stone, 15-16.

26 Healing powers: L. Thorpe, (Note 3), 196.

27 Culpeper: *Culpeper's Colour Herbal*, 1649, ed. D. Potterton, Foulsham London, 1983: adder's tongue, *ophioglossum vulgatum*, 9; maidenhair, *adiantum capillus veneris*, 118; tansy, *tanacetum vulgare*, 189. See also B. Woolley, *The Herbalist. Nicholas Culpeper and the Fight for Medical Freedom*, HarperCollins, London, 2004.

28 Autolycus, 'a snapper-up': Shakespeare, *The Winter's Tale*, IV, 2, 25.; Holes and starlings: Aubrey, TG, c.24, 89; MB, I, 93.

29 Stone powder, wells and toads: Aubrey, TG, c.24, MB, I, 93.

30 T. Darvill, *Stonehenge. The Story of a Landscape*, Tempus, Brimscombe Port, 2006, 137.

ABBREVIATIONS

BAR	British Archaeological Reports
BCA	Book Club Associates
CEDNB	*Compact Edition of the Dictionary of National Biography* I, II.
CUP	Cambridge University Press
OUP	Oxford University Press
PBA	*Proceedings of the British Academy*
WAM	*Wiltshire Archaeological Magazine*
YUP	Yale University Press

Bibliography

Ashley, M. (1954) *England in the Seventeenth Century 1603-1714*, Penguin, Harmondsworth.

Ashley, M. (1964) *Life in Stuart England*, Batsford, London.

Aubrey, J. (*c.* 1665 - *c.*1693), '*Templa Druidum*', in *Monumenta Britannica: or a Miscellany of British Antiquities, I*, ed. John Fowles, Dorset Publishing Company, Milborne Port, 1980.

Aubrey, J. (2009) *Miscellanies Upon Various Subjects*, Bibliobazaar, Charleston, USA.

Aubrey, J. (1980) *Monumenta Britannica I*, ed. J. Fowles, Dorset Publishing Co., Milborne Port.

Aubrey, J. (1982) *Monumenta Britannica II*, ed. J. Fowles, Dorset Publishing Co., Milborne Port.

See also: Balme; Barber; Britton; Buchanan-Brown; Clark; Dick; Fowles; Hunter; Jackson; Ponting; Powell; Stephens; Strachey; Tylden-Wright; Young.

Baker, T. M. M. (2000) *London. Rebuilding the City after the Great Fire*, Phillimore, Chichester.

Balme, M. (2003) *Two Antiquaries. A Selection from the Correspondence of John Aubrey and Anthony Wood*, Durham Academic Press, Edinburgh, Cambridge, Durham, USA.

Barber, R, ed. (1975) *John Aubrey. Brief Lives. A Selection*, Folio Society, London.

Barber, R., ed. (1982) *John Aubrey. Brief Lives*, BCA, London.

Barber, R., ed. (1988) *The Worlds of John Aubrey*, Folio, London.

Barnatt, J., (1989) *Stone Circles of Britain. Taxonomic and Distributional Analyses and a Catalogue of Sites in England, Scotland and Wales, I, II*, BAR 215 (I, II), Oxford.

Beauclerck, C. (2005) *Nell Gwyn. A Biography*, Macmillan, London.

Bedford, J. (1966) *London's Burning*, Abelard-Schuman, London.

Bédoyère, G. de, ed. (1997) *Particular Friends. The Correspondence of Samuel Pepys and John Evelyn*, Boydell, Woodbridge.

Bédoyère, G. de, ed. (2004) *The Diary of John Evelyn*, Boydell, Woodbridge.

Bosley, K. (1997) *John Aubrey. 1636-1697, 'Shiftless, roving and magotie-headed'*, National Trust, Alexander Keiller Museum, Avebury.

Britton, J. (1845) *Memoir of John Aubrey, FRS, embracing his Auto-Biographical Sketches*, Wiltshire Topographical Society, London.

Britton, J. (1847) *The Natural History of Wiltshire by John Aubrey, FRS*, Wiltshire Topographical Society, London.

Browne, Sir Thomas (1906) *The Religio Medici and Other Writings*, Dent, London.

Bryant, A. (1960) *Restoration England*, Collins, London.

Buchanan-Brown, J., ed. (1972) *John Aubrey. Three Prose Works. Miscellanies; Remaines of Gentilisme and Judaisme; Observations*, Centaur, Fontwell.

Burl, A., (1982) 'John Aubrey's *Monumenta Britannica*. A review', *WAM*, 77, 163-6.

Burl, A. (1985) *Megalithic Brittany. A Guide to over 350 Ancient Sites and Monuments*, Thames & Hudson, London.

Burl, A. (1992) 'Two early plans of Avebury', *WAM 85*, 163-72.

Burl, A. (1993) *From Carnac to Callanish. The Stone Rows and Avenues of Britain, Ireland and Brittany*, YUP, New Haven & London.

Burl, A. (1999) *Great Stone Circles*, YUP, New Haven & London.

Burl, A. (2000) *The Stone Circles of Britain, Ireland Brittany*, YUP, New Haven & London.

Burl, A. (2002) *Prehistoric Avebury*, 2 nd ed., YUP, New Haven & London.

Burl, A. (2005) *A Guide to the Stone Circles of Britain, Ireland and Brittany*, revised ed., YUP, London.

Burl, A. (2006) *A Brief History of Stonehenge*, Robinson, London.

Burl, A. & Hatchwell, R. (1998)'The "Commonplace Book" of William Stukeley', *WAM 91*, 65-75.

Camden, W., (1607) *Britannia*, George Bishop & John Norton, London, 1970, Facsimile reprint, Georg Olms, Hildesheim & New York. *See also*: Nurse, 1993.

(1637) *Britain, or a Chorographicall Description of the Most Flourishing Kingdomes, England, Scotland, and Ireland, and the Islands adjoyning ...*, trans. P. Holland, George Latham, London.

(1695) see: Gibson.

(1974) *Britannia, Translated and Enlarged by the Latest Discoveries by Richard Gough, I-IV*, J. Stockdale, London, 1806. Facsimile reprint, Georg Olms, Hildesheim & New York.

See also: Herendeen.

Clark, A. (1898) *'Brief Lives', Chiefly of Contemporaries, set down by John Aubrey between the Years 1559 & 1696, I, II*, Clarendon Press, Oxford.

Collier, J. (1933) *The Scandal and Credulities of John Aubrey*, Peter Davies, London.

Cooper, M. (2005) *Robert Hooke and the Rebuilding of London*, Sutton, Thrupp.

Daniel, G. (1962) *The Idea of Prehistory*, Penguin, Harmondsworth.

Darley, G. (2006) *John Evelyn. Living for Ingenuity*, YUP, New Haven & London.

Dick, O. L., (1949) *Aubrey's Brief Lives*, Secker & Warburg, London

Dobson, A. (1906) *The Diary of John Evelyn, I-III*, Macmillan, London.

Dotrice, Roy, *see*: Garland.

Edwards, N. (2007) 'Edward Lhuyd and the origins of early medieval Celtic archaeology', *Ant J* 87, 165-96.

Eveleigh, D. J. (2002) *Bogs, Baths and Basins. The Story of Domestic Sanitation*, Sutton, Thrupp.

Evelyn, J., *see*: Bédoyère, 1997; 2004; Darley; Dobson.

Falkus, C. (1972) *The Life and Times of Charles II*, BCA, London.

Ferguson, A. B. (1993) *Utter Antiquity. Perceptions of Prehistory in Renaissance England*, Duke University Press, Durham, North Carolina & London.

Fiennes, C. *The Illustrated Journeys of Celia Fiennes c.1682 – c. 1712*, ed. C. Morris, Webb & Bower, London, 1982.

Fowles, J., *see*: Aubrey, 1980, 1982.

Fraser, A. (1979) *King Charles II*, BCA, London.

Garden J., *see*: Gordon, C. A.

Garland, P. (1967) *Brief Lives by John Aubrey. A Play in Two Acts for One Actor*, Faber & Faber, London, 1947.

Gay, Rev. R. (*c.* 1666) *A Fool's Bolt soon Shott at Stonage*, published 1725. See: Legg.

Gibson, E., ed. (1695) *Camden's BRITANNIA, Newly Translated into English, with Large Additions and Improvements*, E. Gibson, London. [facsimile edition, Introduction, S. Piggott, Times Newspaper Ltd, London, 1971].

Gordon, C. A., 'Professor James Garden's Letters to John Aubrey', *The Miscellany of the Third Spalding Club*, III, 1960, 1-56. (extracts in Aubrey, TG., c.24, 114b-132a; MB, I, 171-220).

Gover, J. E. B., Mawer, A. & Stenton, F. M. (1970) *The Place-Names of Wiltshire*, CUP, Cambridge.

Grinsell, L. V. (1957) *A History of Wiltshire, I*, OUP, London: 'Archaeological Gazetteer. B, List of Wiltshire barrows', 21-226.

Grinsell, L. V. (1976) *Folklore of Prehistoric Sites in Britain*, David & Charles, Newton Abbot.

Gwynne, Nell: *see*, Beauclerk.

Harrison, J. W. J. (1901) 'A Bibliography of the Great Stone Monuments of Wiltshire – Stonehenge and Avebury', *WAM* 32, 1-169.

Hearne, J. T. & Walker, J. eds (1813) *Letters Written by Eminent People*

... *and Lives Of Eminent Men by John Aubrey, I, II*, Longman, Hurst, Rees, Orme and Brown, London.

Hearne, T. (1770) *The Itinerary of John Leland the Antiquary, I-IX*, 3rd ed., Thomas Hearne, Oxford.

Herendeen, W. H. (2007) *William Camden. A Life in Context*, Boydell, Woodbridge.

Hill, C. (1961) *The Century of Revolution, 1603-1714*, Nelson, Edinburgh.

Hooke, Robert, *see*: Cooper; Inwood.

Hughes, P. (2004) *Witchcraft*, Sutton, Thrupp.

Hunter, M. (1975) *John Aubrey and the Realm of Learning*, Duckworth, London.

Inwood, S. (2005) *The Forgotten Genius. The Biography of Robert Hooke 1635-1703*, MacAdam/Cage, San Francisco.

Jackson, J. E., ed. (1862) *Wiltshire. The Topographical Collections of John Aubrey, FRS, 1659-70. Corrected and Enlarged*, Wiltshire Archaeological and Natural History Society, Devizes.

Jones, Inigo, *see*: Leapman.

Knighton, C. S. ed. (2004) *Pepys' Later Diaries*, Sutton, Thrupp.

Lamb, J. (1993) *So Idle a Rogue. The Life and Death of Lord Rochester*, Sutton, Thrupp.

Latham, R., ed. (1978) *The Illustrated Pepys. Extracts from the Diary*, BCA, London.

Latham, R., ed. (2000) *A Pepys Anthology. Passages from the Diary of Samuel Pepys*, HarperCollins, Berkeley & Los Angeles.

Latham, R. & Matthews, W. eds. (1995) *The Diary of Samuel Pepys, Vols I – XI*, HarperCollins, Berkeley, Los Angeles, London [I, Introduction; II-IX, Diary, 1660-1669; X, Subjects: Admiralty – Whitehall; XI, Index].

Leasor, J. (1962) *The Plague and the Fire*, Allen & Unwin, London.

Legg, R. ed, (1986) *Stonehenge Antiquaries*, Dorset Publishing Co., Milborne Port, (*see*: Gay, *Fool's Bolt* ..., 5-37).

Leigh, E. (1659) *England Described*, London.

Leland, J., see: T. Hearne; L. T. Smith.

Long, W. (1876) *Stonehenge and Its Barrows*, W. Long, Devizes.

McClintock, J. (2006) *The Stonehenge Companion*, English Heritage, London.

Mendyk, S. A. E. (1989) *'Speculum Britanniae'. Regional Study, Antiquarianism, and Science in Britain to 1700*, University of Toronto Press, Toronto.

Morse, M. A. (2005) *How the Celts Came to Britain. Druids, Ancient Skulls and the Birth of Archaeology*, Tempus, Brimscombe Port.

Nurse, B. (1993) 'The 1610 edition of Camden's *Britannia*', *Ant J 73*, 158-60.

Ogg, D. (1972) *England in the Reign of Charles II*, OUP, London.

Old House Books (2006) *The Great Fire of London. Map – 1666*, Old House Books, Moretonhampstead.

Ollard, R. (1974) *Pepys. A Biography*, Hodder & Stoughton, London.

Ollard, R. (2002) *The Escape of Charles II. After the Battle of Worcester*, Constable & Robinson, London.

Parry, G. (2007) *The Trophies of Time. English Antiquarians of the Seventeenth Century*, OUP, London & New York.

Partridge, R. B. (1998) *'O Horrible Murder'. The Trial, Execution and Burial of King Charles I*, Rubicon, London.

Pepys, Samuel: *see*, Bédoyère, 1997; Bryant, 1952, 1953; Knighton, 2004; Latham; R.,1978; Latham, R. & L. (2000) Latham, R. & Matthews, W., 1995; Ollard, 1974; Tomalin.

Picard, L. *Restoration London*, Weidenfeld & Nicolson, London (1997).

Piggott, S. (1951) 'William Camden and the *Britannia*', *PBA. 37*, 199-217.

Piggott, S. (1975) *The Druids*, Thames & Hudson, London.

Plowden, A. (2006) *In a Free Republic. Life in Cromwell's England*, Sutton, Thrupp.

Ponting, K. G. (1969) *Aubrey's Natural History of Wiltshire. A Report*, David & Charles, Newton Stewart.

Ponting, K. G. (1975) *Wiltshire Portraits*, Moonraker, Bradford-upon-Avon.

Poole, W. (2010) *John Aubrey and the Advancement of Learning*, Bodleian Library, Oxford.

Porter, S. (2005) *Lord Have Mercy Upon Us. London's Plague Years*, Tempus, Brimscombe Port.

Powell, A., ed. (1949) *Brief Lives and Other Selected Writings by John Aubrey*, Cresset, London.

Powell, A (1988) *John Aubrey and His Friends*, 3rd ed., Hogarth Press, London.

Powys, L. ed. (1932) *The Life and Times of Anthony à Wood*, Wishart, London.

Rochester, John Wilmot, Earl of: *see*: Lamb.

Scott, A. F. (1975) *Every One a Witness. The Stuart Age. Commentaries of an Era*, Crowell, New York.

Smith, L. T. ed. (1964) *'The Itinerary of John Leland in or about the Years 1535-1543*, Books. I-V, Southern Illinois University Press, Carbondale, 1964.

Snyder, C. A. (1998) *An Age of Tyrants. Britain and the Britons A. D. 400-600*, Sutton, Thrupp.

Stephens, J. A., ed. (1972) *Aubrey on Education. A Hitherto Unpublished Manuscript by the Author of Brief Lives*, Routledge & Kegan Paul, London.

Stone, E. H. (1924) *The Stones of Stonehenge*, Robert Scott, London.

Strachey, L (1931) *Portraits in Miniature, and Other Essays*, Chatto & Windus, London.

Stukeley, W. (1743) *Abury, a Temple of the British Druids, with some others, Described*, W. Stukeley, London.

Swanton, M., trans. (1996) *The Anglo-Saxon Chronicle*, Dent, London.

Thompson, C. J. S. (1993) *The Quacks of Old London*, Barnes & Noble, New York.

Tindall, G. (2003) *The Man Who Drew London. Wenceslas Hollar in Reality and Imagination*, Pimlico, London.

Tinniswood, A. (2004) *By Permission of Heaven. The True Story of the Great Fire of London*, Riverhead, New York.

Tomalin, C. (2003) *Samuel Pepys. The Unequalled Self*, Penguin, London.

Tylden-Wright, D. (1991) *John Aubrey. A Life*, HarperCollins, London.

Wilson, D. (2003) *All the King's Women. Love, Sex and Politics in the Life of Charles II*, Hutchinson, London.

Wood, A., à (1969) *Athenae Oxonienses. An Exact History of all the Writers and Bishops who have had their Education in the University of Oxford ... by Anthony à Wood, MA. A new edition with additions and continuation, I-IV*, ed. P. Bliss, Lackington et al. London, 3rd ed. 1820. Facsimile reprint, G. Olms, Hildesheim, 1969. *See also*: Balme; Powys. In the Bodleian Library Aubrey's letters to Wood are contained in MS Aubrey, ff 12, 13, MS Wood, f. 39, and MS Ballard 14. For Wood's letters, *see*: MS Wood, f. 51.

Young, G. M. (1950) *Last Essays*, R. Hart-Davis, London.

Index